THE EXPANSION OF ENGLAND
TWO COURSES OF LECTURES

THE EXPANSION OF ENGLAND

TWO COURSES OF LECTURES

SIR JOHN ROBERT SEELEY

COSIMO CLASSICS

NEW YORK

Cosimo
P.O. Box 416
Old Chelsea Station
New York, NY 10113-0416

or visit our website at:
www.cosimobooks.com

The Expansion of England: Two Courses of Lectures originally published by MacMillian & Co. in 1891.

Library of Congress Cataloging-in-Publication Data
A catalog record for this book is available from the Library of Congress

Cover design by www.wiselephant.com

ISBN: 1-59605-265-1

PREFACE.

In preparing these lectures for the press I have been much indebted to Professor Cowell, who was good enough to take an interest in that part of them which relates to India, and to Mr Cunningham, the author of that most interesting book, *The Growth of English Industry and Commerce.*

CONTENTS.

COURSE I.

COURSE II.

LECTURE I.

TENDENCY IN ENGLISH HISTORY.

It is a favourite maxim of mine that history, while it should be scientific in its method, should pursue a practical object. That is, it should not merely gratify the reader's curiosity about the past, but modify his view of the present and his forecast of the future. Now if this maxim be sound, the history of England ought to end with something that might be called a moral. Some large conclusion ought to arise out of it; it ought to exhibit the general tendency of English affairs in such a way as to set us thinking about the future and divining the destiny which is reserved for us. The more so because the part played by our country in the world certainly does not grow less prominent as history advances. Some countries, such as Holland and Sweden, might pardonably regard their history as in a manner wound up. They were once great, but the conditions of their greatness have passed away, and they now hold a secondary place. Their interest in their own past is therefore either sentimental or purely scientific; the only practical lesson of their history is a lesson of resignation. But England has grown steadily greater and greater, absolutely at least if not always relatively. It is far greater now than it was in the eighteenth century; it was far greater in the eighteenth century than in the seventeenth, far greater in the seventeenth than in the sixteenth. The prodigious greatness to which it has attained makes the question of its future infinitely important and at the same time most anxious, because it is evident that the great colonial extension of our state exposes it to new dangers, from which in its ancient insular insignificance it was free.

The interest of English history ought therefore to deepen steadily to the close, and, since the future grows out of the past, the history of the past of England ought to give rise to a prophecy concerning her future. Yet our popular historians scarcely seem to think so. Does not Aristotle say that a drama ends, but an epic poem only leaves off? English history, as it is popularly related, not only has no distinct end, but leaves off in such a gradual manner, growing feebler and feebler, duller and duller, towards the close, that one might suppose that England, instead of steadily gaining in strength, had been for a century or two dying of mere old age. Can this be right? Ought the stream to be allowed thus to lose itself and evaporate in the midst of a sandy desert? The question brings to mind those lines of Wordsworth:

> It is not to be thought of that the flood
> Of British freedom, which to the open sea
> Of the world's praise, from dark antiquity
> Hath flowed 'with pomp of waters unwithstood',
> Roused though it be full often to a mood
> Which spurns the check of salutary bands,
> That this most famous stream in bogs and sands
> Should perish, and to evil and to good
> Be lost for ever—

Well! this sad fate, which is 'not to be thought of', is just what befals, if not the stream itself of British freedom, yet the reflexion of it in our popular histories.

Now suppose we wish to remedy this evil, how shall we proceed? Here is no bad question for historical students at the opening of an academic year, the opening perhaps to some of their academic course. You are asked to think over English history as a whole and consider if you cannot find some meaning, some method in it, if you cannot state some conclusion to which it leads. Hitherto perhaps you have learned names and dates, lists of kings, lists of battles and wars. The time comes now when you are to ask yourselves, To what end? For what practical purpose are these facts collected and committed to memory? If they lead to no great truths having at the same time scientific generality and momentous practical bearings, then history is but an amusement and will scarcely hold its own in the conflict of studies.

No one can long study history without being haunted by the idea of development, of progress. We move onward, both each of us and all of us together. England is not now what it was under the Stuarts or the Tudors, and in these last centuries at least there is much to favour the view that the movement is progressive, that it is toward something better. But how shall we define this movement, and how shall we measure it? If we are to study history in that rational spirit, with that definite object which I have recommended, we must fix our minds on this question and arrive at some solution of it. We must not be content with those vague flourishes which the old school of historians, who according to my view lost themselves in mere narrative, used to add for form's sake before winding-up.

Those vague flourishes usually consisted in some reference to what was called the advance of civilisation. No definition of civilisation was given; it was spoken of in metaphorical language as a light, a day gradually advancing through its twilight and its dawn towards its noon; it was contrasted with a remote ill-defined period, called the Dark Ages. Whether it would always go on brightening, or whether, like the physical day, it would pass again into afternoon and evening, or whether it would come to an end by a sudden eclipse, as the light of civilisation in the ancient world might appear to have done, all this was left in the obscurity convenient to a theory which was not serious, and which only existed for the purpose of rhetorical ornament.

It is a very fair sample of bad philosophising, this theory of civilisation. You have to explain a large mass of phenomena, about which you do not even know that they are of the same kind—but they happen to come into view at the same time—; what do you do but fling over the whole mass a *word*, which holds them together like a net? You carefully avoid defining this word, but in speaking of it you use metaphors which imply that it denotes a living force of unknown, unlimited properties, so that a mere reference to it is enough to explain the most wonderful, the most dissimilar effects. It was used to explain a number of phenomena which had no further apparent connexion with each other than that they happened often to appear together in history; sometimes the softening of manners, sometimes mechanical inventions, sometimes religious toleration, sometimes the appearance of great poets and artists, sometimes scientific discoveries, sometimes constitutional liberty. It was assumed, though it was never proved, that all these things belonged together and had a hidden cause, which was the working of the spirit of civilisation.

We might no doubt take this theory in hand, and give it a more coherent appearance. We might start with the one principle of freedom of thought, and trace all the consequences that will follow from that. Scientific discoveries and mechanical inventions may flow from it, if certain other conditions are present; such discoveries and inventions coming into general use will change the appearance of human life, give it a complicated, modern aspect; this change then we might call the advance of civilisation. But political liberty has no connexion with all this. There was liberty at Athens before Plato and Aristotle, but afterwards it died out; liberty at Rome when thought was rude and ignorant, but servitude after it became enlightened. And poetical genius has nothing to do with it, for poetry declined at Athens just as philosophy began, and there was a Dante in Italy before the Renaissance, but no Dante after it.

If we analyse this vague sum-total which we call civilisation, we shall find that a large part of it is what might be expected from the name, that is, the result of the union of men in civil communities or states, but that another part is only indirectly connected with this and is more immediately due to other causes. The progress of science, for example, might be held to be the principal factor in civilisation, yet, as I have just pointed out, it by no means varies regularly with civil well-being, though for the most part it requires a certain *modicum* of civil well-being. That part of the human lot 'which laws or kings can cause or cure' is strictly limited. Now history may assume a larger or a narrower function. It may investigate all the causes of human well-being alike; on the other hand it may attach itself to the civil community and to the part of human well-being which depends on that. Now by a kind of unconscious tradition the latter course has more usually been taken. Run over the famous histories that have been written; you will see that the writers have always had in view, more or less consciously, states and governments, their internal development, their mutual dealings. It may be quite true that affairs of this kind are not always the most important of human affairs. In the period recorded by Thucydides the most permanently important events may have been the philosophical career of Socrates and the artistic career of Phidias, yet Thucydides has nothing to say of either, while he enlarges upon wars and intrigues which now seem petty. This is not the effect of any narrowness of view. Thucydides is alive to the unique glory of the city he describes; how else could he have written φιλοκαλοῦμεν μετ᾽ εὐτελείας καὶ φιλοσοφοῦμεν ἄνευ μαλακίας ? nay, so far as that glory was the result of political causes, he is ready to discuss it, as that very passage shows. It is with purpose and deliberation that he restricts himself. The truth is that investigation makes progress by dividing and subdividing the field. If you discuss everything at once, you certainly get the advantage of a splendid variety of topics; but you do not make progress; if you would make progress, you must concentrate your attention upon one set of phenomena at a time. It seems to me advisable to keep history still within the old lines, and to treat separately the important subjects which were omitted in that scheme. I consider therefore that history has to do with the State, that it investigates the growth and changes of a certain corporate society, which acts through certain functionaries and certain assemblies. By the nature of the State every person who lives in a certain territory is usually a member of it, but history is not concerned with individuals except in their capacity of members of a State. That a man in England makes a scientific discovery or paints a picture, is not in itself an event in the history of England. Individuals are important in history in proportion, not to their intrinsic merit, but to their relation to the State. Socrates was a much greater man than Cleon, but Cleon has a much greater space in Thucydides. Newton was a greater man than Harley, yet it is Harley, not Newton, who fixes the attention of the historian of the reign of Queen Anne.

After this explanation you will see that the question I raised, What is the general drift or goal of English history? is much more definite than it might at first sight appear. I am not thinking of any general progress that the human race everywhere alike, and therefore also in England, may chance to be making, nor even necessarily of any progress peculiar to England. By England I mean solely the state or political community which has its seat in England. Thus strictly limited, the question may seem to you perhaps a good deal less interesting; however that may be, it certainly becomes much more manageable.

The English State then, in what direction and towards what goal has that been advancing? The words which jump to our lips in answer are Liberty, Democracy! They are words which want a great deal of defining. Liberty has of course been a leading characteristic of England as compared with continental countries, but in the main liberty is not so much an end to which we have been tending as a possession which we have long enjoyed. The struggles of the seventeenth century secured it—even if they did not first acquire it—for us. In later times there has been a movement towards something which is often called liberty, but not so correctly. We may, if we like, call it democracy; and I suppose the current opinion is that if any large tendency is discernible in the more recent part of English history, it is this tendency, by which first the middle class and then gradually the lower classes have been admitted to a share of influence in public affairs.

Discernible enough no doubt this tendency is, at least in the nineteenth century, for in the eighteenth century only the first beginnings of it can be traced. It strikes our attention most, because it has made for a long time past the staple of political talk and controversy. But history ought to look at things from a greater distance and more comprehensively. If we stand aloof a little and follow with our eyes the progress of the English State, the great governed society of English people, in recent centuries, we shall be much more struck by another change, which is not only far greater but even more conspicuous, though it has always been less discussed, partly because it proceeded more gradually, partly because it excited less opposition. I mean the simple obvious fact of the extension of the English name into other countries of the globe, the foundation of Greater Britain.

There is something very characteristic in the indifference which we show towards this mighty phenomenon of the diffusion of our race and the expansion of our state. We seem, as it were, to have conquered and peopled half the world in a fit of absence of mind. While we were doing it, that is in the eighteenth century, we did not allow it to affect our imaginations or in any degree to change our ways of thinking; nor have we even now ceased to think of ourselves as simply a race inhabiting an island off the northern coast of the Continent of Europe. We constantly

betray by our modes of speech that we do not reckon our
colonies as really belonging to us; thus if we are asked
what the English population is, it does not occur to us to
reckon-in the population of Canada and Australia. This
fixed way of thinking has influenced our historians. It
causes them, I think, to miss the true point of view
in describing the eighteenth century. They make too much
of the mere parliamentary wrangle and the agitations about
liberty, in all which matters the eighteenth century of
England was but a pale reflexion of the seventeenth. They
do not perceive that in that century the history of England
is not in England but in America and Asia. In like
manner I believe that when we look at the present state
of affairs, and still more at the future, we ought to
beware of putting England alone in the foreground and
suffering what we call the English possessions to escape
our view in the back-ground of the picture.

Let me describe with some exactness the change that
has taken place. In the last years of Queen Elizabeth
England had absolutely no possessions outside Europe, for
all schemes of settlement, from that of Hore in Henry
VIII's reign to those of Gilbert and Raleigh, had failed
alike. Great Britain did not yet exist; Scotland was a
separate kingdom, and in Ireland the English were but a
colony in the midst of an alien population still in the tribal
stage. With the accession of the Stuart family commenced
at the same time two processes, one of which was brought
to completion under the last Stuart, Queen Anne, while the
other has continued without interruption ever since. Of
these the first is the internal union of the three kingdoms,
which, though technically it was not completed till much
later, may be said to be substantially the work of the
seventeenth century and the Stuart dynasty. The second

was the creation of a still larger Britain comprehending
vast possessions beyond the sea. This process began with
the first Charter given to Virginia in 1606. It made a
great advance in the seventeenth century; but not till the
eighteenth did Greater Britain in its gigantic dimensions
and with its vast politics first stand clearly before the
world. Let us consider what this Greater Britain at the
present day precisely is.

Excluding certain small possessions, which are chiefly
of the nature of naval or military stations, it consists
besides the United Kingdom of four great groups of
territory, inhabited either chiefly or to a large extent by
Englishmen and subject to the Crown, and a fifth great
territory also subject to the Crown and ruled by English
officials, but inhabited by a completely foreign race. The
first four are the Dominion of Canada, the West Indian
Islands, among which I include some territories on the
continent of Central and Southern America, the mass of
South African possessions of which Cape Colony is the
most considerable, and fourthly the Australian group, to
which, simply for convenience, I must here add New
Zealand. The dependency is India.

Now what is the extent and value of these possessions?
First let us look at their population, which, the territory
being as yet newly settled, is in many cases thin. The
Dominion of Canada with Newfoundland had in 1881 a
population of rather more than four millions and a half,
that is, about equal to the population of Sweden; the West
Indian group rather more than a million and a half, about
equal to the population at the same time of Greece; the
South African group about a million and three quarters,
but of these much less than a half are of European blood;
the Australian group about three millions, rather more

than the population of Switzerland. This makes a total of ten millions and three quarters, or about ten millions of English subjects of European and mainly English blood outside the British Islands.

The population of the great dependency India was nearly a hundred and ninety-eight millions, and the native states in India which look·up to England as the paramount Power had about fifty-seven millions in addition. The total makes a population roughly equal to that of all Europe excluding Russia.

But of course it strikes us at once that this enormous Indian population does not make part of Greater Britain in the same sense as those ten millions of Englishmen who live outside of the British Islands. The latter are of our own blood, and are therefore united with us by the strongest tie. The former are of alien race and religion, and are bound to us only by the tie of conquest. It may be fairly questioned whether the possession of India does or ever can increase our power or our security, while there is no doubt that it vastly increases our dangers and responsibilities. Our colonial Empire stands on quite a different footing; it has some of the fundamental conditions of stability. There are in general three ties by which states are held together, community of race, community of religion, community of interest. By the first two our colonies are evidently bound to us, and this fact by itself makes the connexion strong. It will grow indissolubly firm if we come to recognise also that interest bids us maintain the connexion, and this conviction seems to gain ground. When we inquire then into the Greater Britain of the future we ought to think much more of our Colonial than of our Indian Empire.

This is an important consideration when we come to

estimate the Empire not by population but by territorial
area. Ten millions of Englishmen beyond the sea,—this
is something; but it is absolutely nothing compared with
what will ultimately, nay with what will speedily, be seen.
For those millions are scattered over an enormous area,
which fills up with a rapidity quite unlike the increase of
population in England. That you may measure the importance of this consideration, I give you one fact. The
density of population in Great Britain is two hundred and
ninety-one to the square mile, in Canada it is not much
more than one to the square mile. Suppose for a moment
the Dominion of Canada peopled as fully as Great Britain,
its population would actually be more than a thousand
millions. That state of things is no doubt very remote,
but an immense increase is not remote. In not much more
than half a century the Englishmen beyond the sea—
supposing the Empire to hold together— will be equal in
number to the Englishmen at home, and the total will
be much more than a hundred millions.

These figures may perhaps strike you as rather overwhelming than interesting. You may make it a question
whether we ought to be glad of this vast increase of our
race, whether it would not be better for us to advance
morally and intellectually than in mere population and
possessions, whether the great things have not for the
most part been done by the small nations, and so on. But
I do not quote these figures in order to gratify our national
pride. I leave it an open question whether our increase is
matter for exultation or for regret. It is not yet time to
consider that. What is clear in the mean time is the
immense importance of this increase. Good or bad, it is
evidently the great fact of modern English history. And it
would be the greatest mistake to imagine that it is a merely

material fact, or that it carries no moral and intellectual consequences. People cannot change their abodes, pass from an island to a continent, from the 50th degree of north latitude to the tropics or the Southern Hemisphere, from an ancient community to a new colony, from vast manufacturing cities to sugar plantations, or to lonely sheep-walks in countries where aboriginal savage tribes still wander, without changing their ideas and habits and ways of thinking, nay without somewhat modifying in the course of a few generations their physical type. We know already that the Canadian and the Victorian are not quite like the Englishman ; do we suppose then that in the next century, if the colonial population has become as numerous as that of the mother country, assuming that the connexion has been maintained and has become closer, England itself will not be very much modified and transformed? Whether good or bad then, the growth of Greater Britain is an event of enormous magnitude.

Evidently as regards the future it is the greatest event. But an event may be very great, and yet be so simple that there is not much to be said about it, that it has scarcely any history. It is thus that the great English Exodus is commonly regarded, as if it had happened in the most simple, inevitable manner, as if it were merely the unopposed occupation of empty countries by the nation which happened to have the greatest surplus population and the greatest maritime power. I shall show this to be a great mistake. I shall show that this Exodus makes a most ample and a most full and interesting chapter in English history. I shall venture to assert that during the eighteenth century it determines the whole course of affairs, that the main struggle of England from the time of Louis XIV. to the time of Napoleon was for the possession of the New

World, and that it is for want of perceiving this that most of us find that century of English history uninteresting.

The great central fact in this chapter of history is that we have had at different times two such Empires. So decided is the drift of our destiny towards the occupation of the New World that after we had created one Empire and lost it, a second grew up almost in our own despite. The figures I gave you refer exclusively to our second Empire, to that which we still possess. When I spoke of the ten millions of English subjects who live beyond the sea, I did not pause to mention that a hundred years ago we had another set of colonies which had already a population of three millions, that these colonies broke off from us and formed a federal state, of which the population has in a century multiplied more than sixteenfold, and is now equal to that of the mother country and its colonies taken together. It is an event of prodigious magnitude, not only that this Empire should have been lost to us, but that a new state, English in race and character, should have sprung up, and that this state should have grown in a century to be greater in population than every European state except Russia. But the loss we suffered in the secession of the American colonies has left in the English mind a doubt, a misgiving, which affects our whole forecast of the future of England.

For if this English Exodus has been the greatest English event of the eighteenth and nineteenth centuries, the greatest English question of the future must be, what is to become of our second Empire, and whether or no it may be expected to go the way of the first. In the solution of this question lies that moral which I said ought to result from the study of English history.

It is an old saying, to which Turgot gave utterance a quarter of a century before the Declaration of Independence, 'Colonies are like fruits which cling to the tree only till they ripen.' He added, 'As soon as America can take care of herself, she will do what Carthage did.' What wonder that when this prediction was so signally fulfilled, the proposition from which it had been deduced rose, especially in the minds of the English, to the rank of a demonstrated principle! This no doubt is the reason why we have regarded the growth of a second Empire with very little interest or satisfaction. 'What matters,' we have said, 'its vastness or its rapid growth? It does not grow for us.' And to the notion that we cannot keep it we have added the notion that we need not wish to keep it, because, with that curious kind of optimistic fatalism to which historians are liable, the historians of our American war have generally felt bound to make out that the loss of our colonies was not only inevitable, but was even a fortunate thing for us.

Whether these views are sound, I do not inquire now. I merely point out that two alternatives are before us, and that the question, incomparably the greatest question which we can discuss, refers to the choice between them. The four groups of colonies may become four independent states, and in that case two of them, the Dominion of Canada and the West Indian group, will have to consider the question whether admission into the United States will not be better for them than independence. In any case the English name and English institutions will have a vast predominance in the New World, and the separation may be so managed that the mother-country may continue always to be regarded with friendly feelings. Such a separation would leave England on the same level as the states nearest to us on the Continent, populous, but less so than Germany and scarcely equal to France. But two states, Russia and the United States would be on an altogether higher scale of magnitude, Russia having at once, and the United States perhaps before very long, twice our population. Our trade too would be exposed to wholly new risks.

The other alternative is, that England may prove able to do what the United States does so easily, that is, hold together in a federal union countries very remote from each other. In that case England will take rank with Russia and the United States in the first rank of state, measured by population and area, and in a higher rank than the states of the Continent. We ought by no means to take for granted that this is desirable. Bigness is not necessarily greatness; if by remaining in the second rank of magnitude we can hold the first rank morally and intellectually, let us sacrifice mere material magnitude. But though we must not prejudge the question whether we ought to retain our Empire, we may fairly assume that it is desirable after due consideration to judge it.

With a view to forming such a judgment, I propose in these lectures to examine historically the tendency to expansion which England has so long displayed. We shall learn to think of it more seriously if we discover it to be profound, persistent, necessary to the national life, and more hopefully if we can satisfy ourselves that the secession of our first colonies was not a mere normal result of expansion, like the bursting of a bubble, but the result of temporary conditions, removable and which have been removed.

LECTURE II.

ENGLAND IN THE EIGHTEENTH CENTURY.

IT was in the eighteenth century that the expansion of England advanced most rapidly. If therefore we would understand the nature of that expansion, and measure how much it absorbed of the energy and vitality of the nation, we cannot do better than consult the records of the eighteenth century. Those records too, if I mistake not, will acquire new interest from being regarded from this point of view.

I constantly remark, both in our popular histories and in occasional allusions to the eighteenth century, what a faint and confused impression that period has left upon the national memory. In a great part of it we see nothing but stagnation. The wars seem to lead to nothing, and we do not perceive the working of any new political ideas. That time seems to have created little, so that we can only think of it as prosperous, but not as memorable. Those dim figures George I. and George II., the long tame administrations of Walpole and Pelham, the commercial war with Spain, the battles of Dettingen and Fontenoy, the foolish Prime Minister Newcastle, the dull brawls of the Wilkes period, the miserable American war; everywhere alike we seem to remark a want of greatness, a distressing commonness and flatness in men and in affairs. But what we chiefly miss is unity. In France the corresponding period has just as little greatness, but it has unity; it is intelligible; we can describe it in one word as the age of the approach of the Revolution. But what is the English eighteenth century, and what has come of it? What was approaching then?

But do we take the right way to discover the unity of a historical period?

We have an unfortunate habit of distributing historical affairs under reigns. We do this mechanically, as it were, even in periods where we recognise, nay, where we exaggerate, the insignificance of the monarch. The first Georges were, in my opinion, by no means so insignificant as is often supposed, but even the most influential sovereign has seldom a right to give his name to an age. Much misconception, for example, has arisen out of the expression, Age of Louis XIV. The first step then in arranging and dividing any period of English history is to get rid of such useless headings as Reign of Queen Anne, Reign of George I., Reign of George II. In place of these we must study to put divisions founded upon some real stage of progress in the national life. We must look onward not from king to king, but from great event to great event. And in order to do this we must estimate events, measure their greatness; a thing which cannot be done without considering them and analysing them closely. When with respect to any event we have satisfied ourselves that it deserves to rank among the leading events of the national history, the next step is to trace the causes by which it was produced. In this way each event takes the character of a development, and each development of this kind furnishes a chapter to the national history, a chapter which will get its name from the event.

For a plain example of the principle take the reign of George III. What can be more absurd than to treat this long period of sixty years as if it had any historical unity, simply because one man was king during the whole of it? What then are we to substitute for the king as a principle of division? Evidently great events. One part of the reign will make a chapter by itself as the period of the loss of America, another as that of the struggle with the French Revolution.

But in a national history there are large as well as smaller divisions. Besides chapters there are, as it were, books or parts. This is because the great events, when examined closely, are seen to be connected with each other; those which are chronologically nearest to each other are seen to be similar; they fall into groups, each of which may be regarded as a single complex event, and the complex events give their names to the parts, as the simpler events give their names to the separate chapters, of the history.

In some periods of history this process is so easy that we perform it almost unconsciously. The events bear their significance written on their face, and the connexion of events is also obvious. When you read the reign of Louis XV. of France, you feel without waiting to reason that you are reading of the fall of the French Monarchy. But in other parts of history the clue is less easy to find, and it is here that we feel that embarrassment and want of interest which, as I have said, Englishmen are conscious of when they look back upon their eighteenth century. In most cases of this kind the fault is in the reader; he would be interested in the period if he had the clue to it, and he would find the clue if he sought it deliberately.

We are to look then at the great events of the eighteenth century, examine each to see its precise significance, and compare them together with a view to discovering any general tendency there may be. I speak roughly of course when I say the eighteenth century. More precisely I mean the period which begins with the Revolution of 1688 and ends with the peace of 1815. Now what are the great events during this period? There are no revolutions. In the way of internal disturbance all that we find is two abortive Jacobite insurrections in 1715 and 1745. There is a change of dynasty, and one of an unusual kind, but it is accomplished peacefully by Act of Parliament. The great events are all of one sort, they are foreign wars.

These wars are on a much larger scale than any which England had waged before, since the Hundred Years' War of the fourteenth and fifteenth centuries. They are also of a more formal business-like kind than earlier wars. For England has now for the first time a standing army and navy. The great English navy first took definite shape in the wars of the Commonwealth, and the English Army, founded on the Mutiny Bill, dates from the reign of William III. Between the Revolution and the Battle of Waterloo it may be reckoned that we waged seven great wars, of which the shortest lasted seven years and the longest about twelve. Out of a hundred and twenty-six years, sixty-four years, or more than half, were spent in war.

That these wars were on a greater scale than any which had preceded, may be estimated by the burden which they laid upon the country. Before this period

England had of course often been at war; still at the commencement of it England had no considerable debt—her debt was less than a million—but at the end of this period, in 1817, her debt amounted to eight hundred and forty millions. And you are to beware of taking even this large amount as measuring the expensiveness of the wars. Eight hundred and forty millions was not the cost of the wars; it was only that part of the cost which the nation could not meet at once; but an enormous amount had been paid at once. And yet this debt alone, contracted in a period of a hundred and twenty years, is equivalent to seven millions a year spent on war during the whole time, while for a good part of the eighteenth century the whole annual cost of government did not exceed seven millions.

This series of great wars is evidently the characteristic feature of the period, for not only does it begin with this period, but also appears to end with it. Since 1815 we have had local wars in India and some of our colonies, but of struggles against great European Powers, such as this period saw seven times, we have only seen one in a period more than half as long, and it lasted but two years.

Let us pass these wars in review. There was first the European war in which England was involved by the Revolution of 1688. It is pretty well remembered, since the story of it has been told by Macaulay. It lasted eight years, from 1689 to 1697. There was then the great war called from the Spanish Succession, which we shall always remember, because it was the war of Marlborough's victories. It lasted eleven years, from 1702 to 1713. The next great war has now passed almost entirely out of memory, not having brought to light any very great commander, nor achieved any definite result. But we have all heard speak of the fable of Jenkins' ears, and we have heard of the battles of Dettingen and Fontenoy, though perhaps few of us could give a rational account either of the reason for fighting them or of the result that came of them. And yet this war too lasted nine years, from 1739 to 1748. Next comes the Seven Years' War, in which we have not forgotten the victories of Frederick. In the English part of it we all remember one grand incident, the battle of the Heights of Abraham, the death of Wolfe, and the conquest of Canada. And yet in the case of this war also it may be observed how much the eighteenth century has faded out of our imaginations. We have quite forgotten that that victory was one of a long series, which to contemporaries seemed fabulous, so that the nation came out of the struggle intoxicated with glory, and England stood upon a pinnacle of greatness which she had never reached before. We have forgotten how, through all that remained of the eighteenth century, the nation looked back upon those two or three splendid years[1] as upon a happiness that could never return, and how long it continued to be the unique boast of the Englishman

> That Chatham's language was his mother-tongue
> And Wolfe's great heart compatriot with his own.

This is the fourth war. It is in sharp contrast with the fifth, which we have tacitly agreed to mention as seldom as we can. What we call the American war, which from the first outbreak of hostilities to the Peace of Paris lasted

[1] Mark how the unenthusiastic Walpole writes of them : 'Intrigues of the Cabinet or of Parliament scarcely existed at that period. All men were, or seemed to be, transported with the success of their country, and content with an Administration which outwent their warmest wishes or made their jealousy ashamed to show itself. One episode indeed there was, in which less heroic affections were concerned...it will diversify the story, and by the intermixture of human passions serve to convince posterity that such a display of immortal actions as illustrate the following pages is not the exhibition of a fabulous age.'

eight years, from 1775 to 1783, was indeed ignominious enough in America, but in its latter part it spread into a grand naval war, in which England stood at bay against almost all the world, and in this, through the victories of Rodney, we came off with some credit. The sixth and seventh are the two great wars with Revolutionary France, which we are not likely to forget, though we ought to keep them more separate in our minds than we do. The first lasted nine years from 1793 to 1802, the second twelve, from 1803 to 1815.

Now probably it has occurred to few of us to connect these wars together, or to look for any unity of plan or purpose pervading them. If such a thought did occur, we should probably find ourselves hopelessly baffled in our first attempts. In one war the question appears to be of the method of succession to the Crown of Spain, in another war of the Austrian succession and of the succession to the Empire. But if there seems so far some resemblance, what have these succession questions to do with the right of search claimed by the Spaniards along the Spanish Main, or the limits of Acadie, or the principles of the French Revolution? And as the grounds of quarrel seem quite accidental, so we are bewildered by the straggling haphazard character of the wars themselves. Hostilities may break out in the Low Countries or in the heart of Germany, but the war is waged, so it seems, anywhere or everywhere, at Madras, or at the mouth of the St Lawrence, or on the banks of the Ohio. Thus Macaulay says in speaking of Frederick's invasion of Silesia, 'In order that he might rob a neighbour whom he had promised to defend, black men fought on the coast of Coromandel and red men scalped each other by the Great Lakes of North America.' On a first survey such is the confused appearance which these wars present.

But look a little closer, and after all you will discover some uniformities. For example, out of these seven wars of England five are wars with France from the beginning, and both the other two, though the belligerent at the outset was in the first Spain and in the second our own colonies, yet became in a short time and ended as wars with France.

Now here is one of those general facts which we are in search of. The full magnitude of it is not usually perceived, because the whole middle part of the eighteenth century has passed too much into oblivion. We have not forgotten that there were two great wars with France just about the junction of the eighteenth and nineteenth centuries, and two other great wars with France about the junction of the seventeenth and eighteenth, but we have half forgotten that near the middle of the eighteenth century there was another great war of England and France, and that, as prelude and afterpiece to this war, there was a war with Spain which turned into a war with France, and a war with America which turned into a war with France. The truth is, these wars group themselves very symmetrically, and the whole period stands out as an age of gigantic rivalry between England and France, a kind of second Hundred Years' War. In fact in those times and down to our own memory the eternal discord of England and France appeared so much a law of nature that it was seldom spoken of. The wars of their own times, blending with a vague recollection of Crécy, Poictiers and Agincourt, created an impression in the minds of those generations, that England and France always had been at war and always would be. But this was a pure illusion. In the sixteenth and seventeenth centuries England and France had not been these persistent enemies. The two states had often been in alliance against Spain. In the seventeenth century an Anglo-French Alliance had been almost the rule. Elizabeth and Henri IV. are allies, Charles I. has a French queen, Cromwell acts in concert with Mazarin, Charles II. and James II. make themselves dependent upon Louis XIV.

But may not this frequent recurrence of war with France have been a mere accident, arising from the nearness of France and the necessary frequency of collisions with her? On examination you will find that it is not merely accidental, but that these wars are connected together in internal causation as well as in time. It is rather the occasional cessation of war that is accidental; the recurrence is natural and inevitable. There is indeed one long truce of twenty-seven years after the Peace of Utrecht; this was the natural effect of the exhaustion in which all Europe was left by the war of the Spanish Succession, a war almost as great in comparison with the then magnitude of the European states as the great struggle with Napoleon. But when this truce was over we may almost regard all the wars which followed as constituting one war interrupted by occasional pauses. At any rate the three wars between 1740 and 1783, those commonly called the War of the Austrian Succession, the Seven Years' War and the American War, are, so far as they are wars of England and France, intimately connected together, and form as it were a trilogy of wars. I call your attention particularly to this, because this group of wars, considered as one great event with a single great object and result, supplies just the grand feature which that time seems so sadly to want. It is only our own blindness and perversity which leads us to overlook the grandeur of that phase in our history, while we fix our eyes upon petty domestic occurrences, parliamentary quarrels, party intrigue, and court-gossip. It so happens that the accession of George III. falls in the middle of this period, and seems to us, in consequence of our childish mode of arranging history, to create a division, where there is no real division, but rather unusually manifest continuity. And as in parliamentary and party politics the accession of George III. really did make a considerable epoch, and the temptation of our historians is always to write the history rather of the Parliament than of the State and nation, a false scent misleads us here, and we remain quite blind to one of the grandest and most memorable turning-points in our history. I say these wars make one grand and decisive struggle between England and France. For look at the facts. Nominally the first of these three wars was ended by the Treaty of Aix-la-Chapelle in 1748. Nominally there followed eight years of peace between England and France. But really it was not so at all. Whatever virtue the treaty of Aix-la-Chapelle may have had towards settling the quarrels of the other European Powers concerned in the war, it scarcely interrupted for a moment the conflict between England and France. It scarcely even appeared to do so, for the great question of the boundary of the English and French settlements in America, of the limits of Acadie and Canada, was disputed with just as much heat after the Treaty as before it. And not in words only but by arms, just as much as if war were still going on. Moreover what I remark of the American frontier is equally true of another frontier, along which at that time the English and French met each other, namely in India. It is a remarkable, little-noticed fact that some of the most memorable encounters between the English and the French which have ever taken place in the course of their long rivalry, some of the classic occurrences of our military history, took place in these eight years when nominally England and France were at peace. We have all heard how the French built Fort Duquesne on the Ohio River, how our colony of Virginia sent a body of 400 men under the command of George Washington, then a very young man and a British subject, to attack it, and how Washington was surrounded and forced to capitulate. We have heard too of the defeat and death of General Braddock in the same parts. Still better do we remember the struggle between Dupleix and Clive in India, the defence of Arcot and the deeds which led to the founding of our Indian Empire. All these events were part of a desperate struggle for supremacy between England and France, but you will find that most of them took place after the Treaty of Aix-la-Chapelle in 1748 and before the commencement of the second war in 1756.

We have then one great conflict lasting from 1744 or a little earlier to the Peace of Paris in 1763 through a period of about twenty years. It ended in the most disastrous defeat that has ever, in modern times, been suffered by France except in 1870, a defeat which in fact sealed the fate of the House of Bourbon. But fifteen years later, and just within the lifetime of the great states- man who had guided us to victory, England and France were at war again. France entered into relations with our insurgent colonies, acknowledged their independence, and assisted them with troops. Once more for five years there was war by land and sea between England and France. But are we to suppose that this was a wholly new war, and not rather a sort of afterswell of the great disturbance that had so recently been stilled? It was not for a moment dissembled that France now in our hour of distress took vengeance for what she had suffered from us. This was her revenge for the loss of Canada, namely, to create the United States. In the words which on a later occasion became so celebrated, she 'called a new world into existence to redress the balance of the old.'

Thus these three great wars are more clearly connected together than they might appear to be. But how closely connected they are we shall not see until we ask ourselves what the ground of quarrel was, and whether the same ground of quarrel runs under all of them. At first sight it appears to be otherwise. For the war of England and France does not at any time stand out distinct and isolated, but is mixed up with other wars which are going on at the same time. Such immense complex medleys are characteristic of the eighteenth century. What, for instance, can the capture of Quebec have to do with the struggle of Frederick and Maria Theresa for Silesia? In such medleys there is great room for historical mistakes, for premature generalisation. What is really at issue may be misunderstood; as for instance, when we remark that in the Seven Years' War all the Protestant Powers of Europe were ranged on one side, we should go very far astray if we tried to make out that it was Protestantism that prevailed in India or in Canada over the spirit of Catholicism.

I said that the expansion of England in the New World and in Asia is the formula which sums up for England the history of the eighteenth century. I point out now that the great triple war of the middle of that century is neither more nor less than the great decisive duel between England and France for the possession of the New World. It was perhaps scarcely perceived at the time, as it has been seldom remarked since; but the explanation of that second Hundred Years' War between England and France which fills the eighteenth century is this, that they were rival candidates for the possession of the New World, and the triple war which fills the middle of the century is, as it were, the decisive campaign in that great world-struggle.

We did not take possession of North America simply because we found it empty and had more ships than other nations by which we might carry colonists into it. Not indeed that we conquered it from another Power which already had possession of it. But we had a competitor in the work of settlement, a competitor who in some respects had got the start of us, namely France.

The simple fact about North America is this, that about the same time that James I. was giving charters to Virginia and New England the French were founding further North the two settlements of Acadie and Canada, and again, about the time that William Penn got his Charter for Pennsylvania from Charles II., the Frenchman La Salle, by one of the greatest feats of discovery, made his way from the great lakes to the sources of the Mississippi, and putting his boats upon the stream descended the whole vast river to the Gulf of Mexico, laying open a great territory, which immediately afterwards became the French colony of Louisiana. Such was the relation of France and England in North America, at the time when the Revolution of 1688 opened what I have called the Second Hundred Years' War of England and France. England had a row of thriving colonies lying from North to South along the Eastern coast, but France had the two great rivers, the St Lawrence and the Mississippi. A political prophet comparing the prospects of the two colonising Powers at the time of the Revolution, and indeed much later, might have been led by observing what an advantage the two rivers gave to France to think that in the future North America would belong to her rather than to England.

But now it is most important to observe further that not only in America, but in Asia also, France and England in that age advanced side by side. The conquest of India by English merchants seems a unique and abnormal phenomenon, but we should be mistaken if we supposed that there was anything peculiarly English, either in the originality which conceived the idea or in the energy which carried it into execution. So far as an idea of conquering India was deliberately conceived, it was conceived by Frenchmen; Frenchmen first perceived that it was feasible and saw the manner in which it could be done; Frenchmen first set about it and advanced some way towards accomplishing it. In India indeed they had the start of us much more decidedly than in North America; in India we had at the outset a sense of inferiority in comparison with them, and fought in a spirit of hopeless self-defence. And I find, when I study the English conquest of India, that we were actuated neither by ambition nor yet by mere desire to advance our trade, but that from first to last, that is, from the first efforts of Clive to the time when Lord Wellesley, Lord Minto and Lord Hastings established our authority over the whole vast peninsula, we were actuated by fear of the French. Behind every movement of the native Powers we saw French intrigue, French gold, French ambition, and never, until we were masters of the whole country, got rid of that feeling that the French were driving us out of it, which had descended from the days of Dupleix and Labourdonnais.

This fact then that, both in America and in Asia, France and England stood in direct competition for a prize of absolutely incalculable value, explains the fact that France and England fought a second Hundred Years' War. This is the ultimate explanation, but the true ground of discord was not always equally apparent even to the belligerents themselves, and still less to the rest of the world. For as in other ages so in this, occasional causes of difference frequently arose between such near neighbours, causes often sufficient by themselves to produce a war; and it was only in those three wars of the middle of the eighteenth century that they fought quite visibly and apparently on the question of the New World. In the earlier wars of William III. and of Anne other causes are more, or certainly not less, operative, for the New World quarrel is not yet at its height. And again in the later wars, that is the two that followed the French Revolution, the question of the New World is again falling into the background, because France has fairly lost her hold both upon America and India, and can now do no more than make despairing efforts to regain it. But in those three wars between 1740 and 1783 the struggle, as between England and France, is entirely for the New World. In the first of them the issue is fairly joined; in the second France suffers her fatal fall; in the third she takes her signal revenge. This is the grand chapter in the history of Greater Britain, for it is the first great struggle in which the Empire fights as a whole, the colonies and settlements outside Europe being here not merely dragged in the wake of the mother-country, but actually taking the lead. We ought to register this event with a very broad mark in our Calendar of the eighteenth century. The principal and most decisive incidents of it belong to the latter half of the reign of George II.

But in our wars with Louis XIV. before and in our wars with the French Revolution afterwards, it will be found on examination that, much more than might be supposed, the real bone of contention between England and France is the New World. The colonial question had indeed been growing in magnitude throughout the seventeenth century, while the other burning question of that age, the quarrel of the two Churches, had been falling somewhat into the background. Thus when Cromwell made war on Spain, it is a question whether he attacked her as the great Catholic Power or as the great monopolist of the New World. In the same age the two great Protestant Powers, England and Holland, who ought in the interest of religion to have stood side by side, are found waging furious war upon each other as rival colonial Powers. Now it was by the great discovery and settlement of Louisiana in 1683 that France was brought into the forefront of colonial Powers, and within six years of that event the Hundred Years' War of England and France began.

In the first war of the series however, though it stands marked in histories of North America as the ' first intercolonial war,' the colonial question is not very prominent. But it is prominent in the second, which has been called the War of the Spanish Succession. We must not be misled by this name. Much has been said of the wicked waste of blood and treasure of which we were guilty, when we interfered in a Spanish question with which we had no concern, or terrified ourselves with a phantom of French Ascendency which had no reality. How much better, it has been said, to devote ourselves to the civilising pursuits of trade ! But read in Ranke[1]

---

[1] Better still in *Europäische Geschichte im* 18*ten Jahrhunderte*, by C. v. Noorden, in which book that great European transition is for the first time adequately treated.

how the war broke out. You will find that it was precisely trade that led us into it. The Spanish Succession touched us because France threatened, by establishing her influence in Spain, to enter into the Spanish monopoly of the New World and to shut us irrevocably out of it. Accordingly the great practical results of this war to England were colonial, namely, the conquest of Acadie and the Asiento contract, which for the first time made England on the great scale a slave-trading Power.

Not less true is it of our wars with the French Revolution and with Napoleon, that the possession of the New World was among the grounds of quarrel. As in the American war France avenges on England her expulsion from the New World, so under Napoleon she makes Titanic efforts to recover her lost place there. This indeed is Napoleon's fixed view with regard to England. He sees in England never the island, the European State, but always the World-Empire, the network of dependencies and colonies and islands covering every sea, among which he was himself destined to find at last his prison and his grave. Thus when in 1798 he was put in charge for the first time of the war with England, he begins by examining the British Channel, and no doubt glances at Ireland. But what he sees does not tempt him, although a few months afterward Ireland broke out in a terrible rebellion, during which if the conqueror of Italy had suddenly landed at the head of a French army, undoubtedly he would have struck a heavier blow at England than any she has yet suffered. His mind is preoccupied with other thoughts. He remembers how France once seemed on the point of conquering India, until England[1] checked her progress;

[1] In his Corsican period he had actually dreamed of entering the Anglo-Indian service and coming back a rich nabob. See Jung, *Lucien Bonaparte et ses Mémoires* I. p. 74.

accordingly he decides and convinces the Directory that
the best way to carry on the contest with England is by
occupying Egypt, and at the same time by stirring up
Tippoo Sultan to war with the Calcutta Government.
And he actually carries out this plan, so that the whole
struggle is transferred from the British Channel into the
boundless spaces of Greater Britain, and when the Irish
shortly afterwards rise, they find to their bitter disap-
pointment that France cannot spare them Bonaparte, but
only General Humbert with eleven hundred men.

When this war was brought to an end by the treaty of
Amiens in 1802, the results of it were such as to make
a great epoch in the history of Greater Britain. In the
first place Egypt is finally evacuated by France, that is
to say, Bonaparte's grand scheme of attack against our
Indian Empire has failed, his ally Tippoo—*Citoyen Tipou*,
as he was called—had been defeated and slain some time
before, and General Baird had moved with an English
force up the Red Sea to take part with General Hutchinson
in the expulsion of the French from Egypt. In the colonial
world at the same time England remained mistress of
Ceylon and Trinidad.

But the last war, that which lasted from 1803 to 1815,
was this in any sense a war for the New World? It does
not seem to be so; and naturally, because England from
the beginning had such a naval superiority, that Napoleon
could never again succeed in making his way back into
the New World. Nevertheless I believe that it was
intended by Napoleon to be so. In the first place look
at the origin and cause of it. It was at the outset a war
for Malta. By the treaty of Amiens, England had engaged
within a given time to evacuate Malta, and this for certain
reasons, which need not here be discussed, she after-

wards refused to do. Now why did Napoleon want her
to leave Malta, and why did she refuse to do so? It was
because Malta was the key of Egypt, and she had good
reason to believe that he would in a moment reoccupy
Egypt, and that the struggle for India would begin again.
Thus the war was ultimately for India, though it was
diverted into Germany by the Third Coalition. Moreover,
though by the retention of Malta we did effectually and
once for all ward off this attack, yet we did not ourselves
know how successful we had been. We still believed India
to be full of French intrigue; we believed the Mahratta
and Afghan princes and the Persian Shah to be puppets
worked by the French, as indeed they had many French
officers in their service. Probably the great Mahratta War
of 1803 seemed to Lord Wellesley to be a part of the
war with France, and probably Arthur Wellesley believed
that at Assaye and Argaum he struck at the same enemy
as afterwards at Salamanca and Waterloo. The fact is
that Napoleon's intention in this war is obscured to us by
the grand failure of the maritime enterprise which he has
planned, and the grand success of the German campaign
which he has not planned. He drifts in a direction he
does not intend, yet the Continental System and the
violent seizure of Spain and Portugal (great New World
Powers) show that he does not forget his original object.
Moreover, Colonel Malleson shows in his *Later Struggles
of France in the East*, what a destructive privateering war
the French were able to keep up in the Indian Ocean from
their island of Mauritius long after their naval power
had been destroyed at Trafalgar. It was by the conquest
of this island and its retention at the Peace by England
that the Hundred Years' War of England and France for
the New World came to an end.

This general view of the wars of the eighteenth century will show you that more is meant than might at first appear by the statement that expansion is the chief character of English history in the eighteenth century. At first it seems merely to mean that the conquest of Canada, India and South Africa are greater events in intrinsic importance than such European or domestic events as Marlborough's war, or the succession of the House of Brunswick, or the Jacobite rebellion, or even the war with the French Revolution. It means in fact, as you will now see, that these other great events which seem to have nothing to do with the growth of Greater Britain, were really closely connected with it, and were indeed only successive moments in the great process. At first it may seem to mean that the European policy of England in that century is of less importance than its colonial policy. It really means that the European policy and the colonial policy are but different aspects of the same great national development. And this, nay even more than this, is what I desire to show. This single conception brings together not only the European with the colonial affairs, but also the military struggles with the whole peaceful expansion of the country, with that industrial and commercial growth, which during the same century exceeded in England all previous example. But in order to understand this it will be necessary for us to examine the peculiar nature of the English colonisation of the New World.

LECTURE III.

THE EMPIRE.

THE expression 'Colonial Empire' is familiar to us, and yet there is something strange in the juxtaposition of words. The word Empire seems too military and despotic to suit the relation of a mother-country to colonies.

There are two very different kinds of colonisation. First there is a kind which may be called *natural,* in the sense that it has manifest analogies in the natural world. 'Colonies are like fruits which only cling till they ripen,' said Turgot. Colonisation, say others, is like the swarming of bees; or it is like the marriage and migration to another house of the grown-up son. And no doubt history furnishes us with real examples of such easy and natural colonisation. The primitive migrations may often have been of this kind. In the first chapters of European history, in the earliest traditions of Greece and Italy, which show us the Greco-Italian branch of the Aryan family in the act of occupying the territory which was afterwards to be the scene of its greatness, we see this easy process going on under the influence of primitive ideas. We read of the institution called *ver sacrum,* by which all the children born in one spring would be dedicated to some deity, who was supposed to accept emigration in lieu of sacrifice[1]; the votaries accordingly, when they grew up, were driven across the frontier, and sometimes they settled and founded a city on the spot where an animal accidentally overtaken on the journey, in whom they saw a guide sent by the god, had chanced to stop. From such a sacred animal we are told that some cities, e.g. Bovianum and Picenum, received their name.

This may be called perhaps natural colonisation, but out of such a system there could grow no colonial empire. Accordingly the Greek ἀποικία, though the word is translated colony, was essentially different in fact from the modern colony. By a colony we understand a community which is not merely derivative, but which remains politically connected in a relation of dependence with the parent community. Now the Greek ἀποικία was not such a dependent community. Technically it was entirely independent of the mother-state, though the sense of kindred commonly held it in a condition of permanent alliance. The dependency indeed was by no means unknown to the Greeks. Subordinate governments were often among them established by a State in a community outside itself. But among the Greeks the dependency was not a colony, as the colony was not a dependency.

The Latin *colonia* was no doubt dependent enough, but it was an institution so peculiar, being a sort of contrivance for the purpose of garrisoning conquered territory without the expense of maintaining an army in it, that we need not discuss it further here.

It is a remarkable and fundamental fact that the old

[1] Thus Paulus: Magnis periculis adducti vovebant Itali quaecunque proximo vere nata essent apud se animalia immolaturos. Sed quom crudele videretur pueros ac puellas innocentes interficere, perductos in adultam aetatem velabant atque ita extra fines suos exigebant.

primitive system of the Greeks has not been revived in modern times. The colonisation which began with the discovery of Columbus, or more strictly with the conquest of the Canaries by Bethencourt in 1404, has been on a vast scale; it has peopled a territory more extensive a hundredfold than the few Mediterranean islands and peninsulas which those primitive Greek adventurers occupied, yet nowhere, I think, did the mother-state willingly allow its emigrants to form independent communities. Whatever license might be allowed to the first adventurers, to a Cortez or Pizarro, whatever formidable powers of levying armies and making war or peace might be granted, for example, to our East India Company, the State nevertheless retained invariably the supreme control in its hands, except where a successful rebellion forced it out of them. Though it seems not to have occurred to Corinth that it could possibly carry on government at the distance of Sicily, on the other hand it seems just as little to have occurred to the Spanish or Portuguese or Dutch or French or English Governments that their emigrants could pretend to independence on the ground that they were hidden away in the Pampas of South America or in the Archipelagos of the Pacific Ocean.

The modern system may be less natural if by 'natural' we mean 'instinctive,' but if we mean by it 'reasonable,' which is surely different, we must not call it unnatural simply because it is not the system of bees or of plants. At any rate let us not take up at once the scolding strain, and say; 'See the contrast between the humane wisdom of the ancient world and the tyranny of the Gothic Middle Ages! The Goth never relaxes for any distance his barbarous system of constraint; the mild intelligent Greek, guided by nature, perceives that the grown-up child has a right to be independent, and so he blesses him and bids him farewell.'

Perhaps if we examine the circumstances of the modern colonisation we shall see that it grew as inevitably out of them as the instinctive system grew out of the conditions of the ancient world.

The appropriation by a settled community of lands on the other side of an ocean is wholly different from the gradual diffusion of a race over a continuous territory or across narrow seas. Slight motives calling into operation moderate forces may suffice for the latter, but the former demands a prodigious leverage. In the life of Columbus it may be remarked that he needs the help of the State at every turn. It is the State which has equipped him and paid the expense of the discovery. Moreover when the discovery is made, it is observable that no irresistible impulse prompts the Europeans to take advantage of it. When the floodgates are thrown open, there is no stream ready to flow, for in Europe at that time there was no superfluous population seeking an outlet, only individual adventurers ready to go in search of gold. Columbus can make no progress but by proving to the Sovereigns that the territory he discovers will yield revenue to *them*. In these circumstances the State, as its help was always needed, had the less difficulty in maintaining its authority.

We may observe also that the modern State almost necessarily colonises in a different way, because its nature is different from that of the Greek State. The Greek mind identifies the State and City so completely that the language, as you know, has but one word for both. Aristotle, though he knew of country-states such as Macedonia and Persia, yet in his Politics seems almost to omit them from consideration. Frequently he lays down principles from which it appears that he could not bring himself to regard them as states in the proper sense of the word, because they were not cities. The modern idea on the other hand—few of us know how modern it is, or how gradually it has been formed—is that the people of one nation, speaking one language, ought in general to have one government.

Now it is evident that these different ideas of the State involve of necessity different ideas of the effect of emigration. If the State is the City, it follows that he who goes out of the City goes out of the State. Hence the Greek view of the colony was natural to the Greeks, for those Greeks who undertook to form a new city (πόλις) did *ipso facto* and inevitably undertake to form a new state. But if the State is the Nation (not the Country, observe, but the Nation), then we see a sufficient ground for the universal usage of modern states, which has been to regard their emigrants not as going out of the State but as carrying the State with them. The notion was, Where Englishmen are there is England, where Frenchmen are there is France, and so the possessions of France in North America were called New France, and one group at least of the English possessions New England.

It is involved in this, but it is so important that it must be stated separately, that the organization of the modern State admits of unbounded territorial extension, while that of the ancient State did not. The Greek πόλις, as it actually was a city, could not be modified so as to become anything else. I must never be tired of quoting that passage of the Politics which is so infinitely important to the student of political science, where Aristotle lays it down that the State must be of moderate population, because 'who could command it in war, if the population were excessive, or what herald short of a Stentor could speak to them? (τίς δὲ κήρυξ μὴ Στεντόρειος;).' The modern State, being already as large as a country, would bear to become larger. Either it had no national assemblies, as was practically the case with France and Spain, or its national assembly, as in the case of England, was representative, that is to say, was expressly contrived to overcome the difficulty of bringing together the whole body of the citizens.

I have indulged in these general reflexions upon the nature of modern colonisation in order that we may understand what our Empire is, and how it necessarily came into existence. There might easily have been a great emigration from England which would not in any way have enlarged the English State. For by Greater Britain we mean an enlargement of the English State, and not simply of the English nationality. It is not simply that a population of English blood is now found in Canada and in Australia, as in old time a Greek population was spread over Sicily, South Italy and the Western Coast of Asia Minor. That was an extension of the Nationality but not of the State, an extension which gave no new strength, and did not in any way help the Greek name when it was attacked and conquered from Macedonia. In like manner at present we see a constant stream of emigration from Germany to America, but no Greater Germany comes into existence, because these emigrants, though they carry with them and may perhaps not altogether lose their language and their ideas, do not carry with them their State. This is the case with Germany because its emigration has happened too late, when the New World is already carved into States, into which its emigrants are compelled to enter, as with Greece it was the result of a theory of the

State, which identified it with the City. But Greater
Britain is a real enlargement of the English State; it
carries across the seas not merely the English race, but the
authority of the English Government. We call it for
want of a better word an Empire. And it does resemble
the great Empires of history in this respect, that it is an
aggregate of provinces, each of which has a government
sent out to it from the political head-quarters, which
is a kind of delegation from the supreme government.
But yet it is wholly unlike the great Empires of the
Old World, Persian or Macedonian or Roman or Turkish,
because it is not in the main founded on conquest, and
because in the main the inhabitants of the distant provinces are of the same nation as those of the dominant
country. It resembles them in its vast extent, but it
does not resemble them in that violent military character
which has made most Empires short-lived and liable to
speedy decay.

We may see now out of what conditions it arose. It is
the only considerable survivor of a family of great
Empires, which arose out of the contact of the Western
States of Europe with the New World so suddenly laid
open by Vasco da Gama and Columbus. What England
did, was done equally by Spain, Portugal, France and
Holland. There was once a Greater Spain, a Greater
Portugal, a Greater France and a Greater Holland, as well
as a Greater Britain, but from various causes those four
Empires have either perished or have become insignificant.
Greater Spain disappeared and Greater Portugal lost its
largest province Brazil half a century ago in wars of
independence similar to that which tore from us our
American colonies. Greater France and a large part of
Greater Holland were lost in war and became merged

in Greater Britain. Greater Britain itself after suffering
one severe shock has survived to the present day, and
remains the single monument of a state of the world
which has almost passed away. At the same time it differs
in a very essential point from some of those Empires.

The countries which were suddenly thrown open to
Europe at the end of the fifteenth century fall into three
classes. Vasco da Gama threw open countries in which for
the most part ancient and extensive states existed, such as
the adventurers did not for a long time think of subverting.
Columbus on the other hand discovered a Continent in
which only two such states appeared to exist, and even
these were soon proved to have no solidity. The contact
which Columbus established, being the most strange and
violent which ever took place between two parts of the
human family, led to a fierce struggle and furnished one of
the most terrible pages to the annals of the world. But in
this struggle there was no sort of equality. The American
race had no more power of resisting the European than
the sheep has of resisting the wolf. Even where it was
numerous and had a settled polity, as in Peru, it
could make no resistance; its states were crushed, the
ruling families extinguished, and the population itself reduced to a form of slavery. Everywhere therefore the
country fell into the hands of the immigrating race, and was
disposed of at its pleasure as so much plunder. The immigrants did not merely, as in India, gradually show a great
military superiority to the native race, so as in the end to
subdue them, but overwhelmed them at once like a party of
hunters suddenly assailing a herd of antelopes. This was
the case everywhere, but yet the countries of America also
fall into two classes. There was a great difference between
the regions of Central and Southern America, which fell

principally to the Spanish and Portuguese, and the North American territories which fell to England. In Mexico, Peru and some other parts of South America the native population, though feeble compared to the Europeans, was not insignificant in numbers; it was counted by millions, had reached the agricultural stage of civilisation, and had cities. But the tribes of Indians which wandered over the territories of North America, which now belong to the United States and the Dominion of Canada, were much more insignificant. It has been estimated that 'the total Indian population within the territory of the United States east of the Rocky Mountains, did not at any time subsequent to the discovery of America exceed, if indeed it even reached, three hundred thousand individuals.' Accordingly whereas in New Spain the European, though supreme, yet lived in the midst of a population of native Indians, the European in North America supplanted the native race entirely, pushed it ever further back as he advanced, and did not blend with it at all.

It was ultimately the fortune of England to acquire the most important share both of what Vasco da Gama and of what Columbus laid open. On one side has grown up her Indian, and mainly on the other her Colonial Empire. But of the latter group of countries, the countries wanting in strong states, England occupied those which were comparatively empty, and the Australian territory which has since fallen to her is in the same condition. This fact has an all-important consequence.

I remarked before that Greater Britain is an extension of the English State and not merely of the English nationality. But it is an equally striking characteristic of Greater Britain that nevertheless it *is* an extension of the English nationality. When a nationality is extended with-

out any extension of the State, as in the case of the Greek
colonies, there may be an increase of moral and intellectual influence, but there is no increase of political power.
On the other hand when the State advances beyond the
limits of the nationality, its power becomes precarious and
artificial. This is the condition of most empires; it is the
condition for example of our own empire in India. The
English State is powerful there, but the English nation is
but an imperceptible drop in the ocean of an Asiatic
population. And when a nation extends itself into other
territories the chances are that it will there meet with
other nationalities which it cannot destroy or completely
drive out, even if it succeeds in conquering them.
When this happens, it has a great and permanent difficulty
to contend with. The subject or rival nationalities cannot
be perfectly assimilated, and remain as a permanent cause
of weakness and danger. It has been the fortune of
England in extending itself to evade on the whole this
danger. For it has occupied parts of the globe which were
so empty that they offered an unbounded scope for new
settlement. There was land for every emigrant who chose
to come, and the native races were not in a condition
sufficiently advanced to withstand even the peaceful competition, much less the power, of the immigrants.

This statement is true on the whole. The English
Empire is on the whole free from that weakness which has
brought down most empires, the weakness of being a mere
mechanical forced union of alien nationalities. It is sometimes described as an essentially feeble union which could
not bear the slightest shock, with what reason I may
examine later, but it has the fundamental strength which
most empires and some commonwealths want. Austria for
instance is divided by the nationality-rivalry of German,

Slav, and Magyar; the Swiss Confederation unites three languages, but the English Empire in the main and broadly may be said to be English throughout.

Of course however considerable abatements are to be made. It is only in one of the four great groups, namely, in the Australian colonies, that the statement is true almost without qualification. The native Australian race is so low in the ethnological scale that it can never give the least trouble, but even here, since we reckon New Zealand in this group, we are to bear in mind that the Maori tribes occupy the Northern island in some force, much as in the last century the Highland Clans gave us trouble in the northern part of our own island, and the Maori is by no means a contemptible type of man. Nevertheless the whole number of Maories is not supposed to exceed forty thousand, and it is rapidly diminishing. When we turn to another group, the North American colonies, included principally in the Dominion of Canada, we find that the nucleus of it was acquired originally, not by English settlement, but by the conquest of French settlements. At the outset therefore the nationality-difficulty, instead of being absent here, was present in the gravest form. The original Canada of the French was afterwards known as Lower Canada, and since the establishment of the Dominion it has borne the name of the Province of Quebec. It has a population of nearly a million and a half, while the whole Dominion does not contain four millions and a half. These are Frenchmen and Catholics in the midst of a population mainly English and Protestant. It is not so long since the inconvenience of this alien population was felt in Canada by discords essentially similar to those which the nationality-question has created in Austria and Russia. The Canadian Rebellion

which marked the first years of the reign of Queen
Victoria, was in fact a war of nationality in the British
Empire, though it wore the disguise of a war of liberty, as
Lord Durham expressly remarks in the opening of his
famous Report on Canada: 'I expected to find a contest
between a government and a people; I found two nations
warring in the bosom of a single state; I found a struggle
not of principles but of races.' It is however to be
remarked on the other side that here too the alien element
dwindles and is likely ultimately to be lost in the English
immigration, and also that its animosity has been much.
pacified by the introduction of federal institutions.

In the third or West Indian group also the differences
of nationality are considerable. Here almost alone in our
Empire are to be traced the effects of the peculiar
phenomenon of the history of the New World, negro
slavery. Here it first appeared on a considerable scale, as
the immediate result of the discovery of Columbus. So
long as it lasted, it did not call into existence the
nationality-difficulty, for a thoroughly enslaved nation is a
nation no longer, and a servile insurrection is wholly
different from the insurrection of an oppressed nationality.
But when slavery is abolished, while the slaves themselves
remain, stamped so visibly in colour and physical type
with the badge of their different nationality, yet now
free and laying claim to citizenship, then it is that the
nationality-difficulty begins to threaten. But in the
West-Indian group such difficulties for the present do not
take a serious form, because the colonies are in the main
dispersed in small islands and have no community of
feeling.

It is in the fourth or South African group that the
nationality-difficulty is most serious. It is here a double

difficulty. There have been two conquests, the one super-induced upon the other. The Dutch first settled themselves among the native races, and then the Dutch colony was conquered by England. So far the case may seem to resemble that of Canada, where the French settled among the Indians and were then conquered by the English. But there are two differences. In the first place the native tribes of South Africa, instead of disappearing and dwindling before the whites, greatly outnumber them, and show a power of combination and progress such as the Red Indian never showed. Thus in the census of 1875 I find that the Cape Colony had a total population of nearly three quarters of a million, but two out of the three quarters were native and only one European. And behind this native population dwelling among the settlers there is an indefinite native population extending without limit into the interior of the vast continent. But secondly the other difficulty, which arises from the fact that the settlers themselves were at the outset not English but Dutch, does not diminish or tend to disappear, as it has done in Canada. In Canada there took place a rapid immigration of English, who, showing themselves in a marked degree more energetic than the French and increasing much faster, gradually gave the whole community a predominantly English character, so that in fact the rising of the French in 1838 was the convulsion of despair of a sinking nationality. Nothing similar has happened in South Africa, no rapid English immigration has come to give a new character to the community.

These are the abatements which must be made to the general proposition that Greater Britain is homogeneous in nationality. They need not prevent us from laying down this general proposition as true. If in these islands we feel ourselves for all purposes one nation, though in Wales, in Scotland and in Ireland there is Celtic blood and Celtic languages utterly unintelligible to us are still spoken, so in the Empire a good many French and Dutch and a good many Caffres and Maories may be admitted without marring the ethnological unity of the whole.

This ethnological unity is of great importance when we would form an opinion about the stability and chance of duration of the Empire. The chief forces which hold a community together and cause it to constitute one State are three, common nationality, common religion, and common interest. These may act in various degrees of intensity, and they may also act singly or in combination. Now when it is argued that Greater Britain is a union which will not last long and will soon fall to pieces, the ground taken is that it wants the third of these binding forces, that it is not held together by community of interest. 'What,' it is said, 'can the inhabitants of Australia and New Zealand, living on the other side of the Tropic of Capricorn, have in common with ourselves who live beyond the 50th degree of north latitude? Who does not see that two communities so remote from each other cannot long continue parts of one political whole?' Now this is a very important consideration, especially as it is backed by the impressive fact that our American Colonies did in the last century find their union with us intolerable. But, allowing its importance, we may remark that, even if this bond is wanting, the other two bonds which hold states together are not wanting. Many empires in which hostile nationalities and religions have been but artificially united have nevertheless lasted several centuries, but Greater Britain is not a mere empire, though we often call it so. Its union is of the more vital kind. It is united by blood and religion, and though circumstances may be imagined in which these ties might snap, yet they are strong ties, and will only give way before some violent dissolving force.

I have enlarged in this lecture upon the essential nature of our colonial Empire, because there is much ambiguity both about the word 'colonial' and about the word 'Empire.' Our colonies do not resemble the colonies which classical students meet with in Greek and Roman history, and our Empire is not an Empire at all in the ordinary sense of the word. It does not consist of a congeries of nations held together by force, but in the main of one nation, as much as if it were no Empire but an ordinary state. This fact is fundamental when we look to the future and inquire whether it is calculated for duration.

But I have also enlarged upon the whole class of Empires which sprang out of the discovery of the New World, to which class our own Empire belongs, in order that we may understand the past. England in the eighteenth century is regarded, I said, too much as a European insular State and too little as an American and Asiatic Empire; in short, we think of Great Britain too much and of Greater Britain too little. But the misconception spreads further, for in that century there is also a Greater France, a Greater Holland, a Greater Portugal and a Greater Spain, and all these we overlook as we overlook Greater Britain.

Here is a fundamental characteristic of the European States during the eighteenth and seventeenth centuries, which is seldom borne in mind, namely that each of the five Western States has an Empire in the New World attached to it. Before the seventeenth century this condition

4—2

of things was but beginning, and since the eighteenth it has ceased again to exist. The vast immeasurable results of the discovery of Columbus were developed with extreme slowness, so that the whole sixteenth century passed away before most of these nations bestirred themselves to claim a share in the New World. There existed no independent Holland till near the end of that century, so that *a fortiori* there could be no Greater Holland, nor did either England or France in that century become possessors of colonies. France did indeed plan a settlement in North America, as the name Carolina, derived from Charles IX. of France, still remains to prove, but the neighbouring Spaniards of Florida interfered to destroy it. A little later Sir Walter Raleigh's colony in the same neighbourhood disappeared altogether, leaving no trace behind it. Accordingly during almost the whole of that century the New World remained in the possession of the two States which had done most to lay it open, viz., Spain and Portugal, Spain looking chiefly towards America and Portugal towards Asia, until in 1580 the two States coalesced in a union which lasted sixty years. The Dutch made their grand entrance into the competition for empire in the seven years from 1595 to 1602, and they were followed by France and England in the early years of the seventeenth century, that is, in the reign of our King James I.

Again in the nineteenth century the competition of these five states in the New World ceased. It ceased from two causes, wars of independence, in which Transatlantic colonies severed themselves from the mother-country, and the colonial conquests of England. I have described already the Hundred Years' War in which Greater France was swallowed up in Greater Britain; Greater Holland in like manner suffered serious diminution, losing the Cape

of Good Hope and Demerara to England, though even now
a Greater Holland may be said to exist in the magnificent
dependency of Java with a population of not less than
nineteen millions. The fall of Greater Spain and Greater
Portugal has happened in the present century within the
life-time of many who are still among us. If we estimated
occurrences less by the excitement they cause at the
moment and more by the consequences which are certain to
follow them, we should call this one of the most stupendous
events in the history of the globe, for it is the beginning of
the independent life of almost the whole of Southern and
Central America. It took place mainly in the twenties of
this century, and was the result of a series of rebellions
which, when we inquire into their origin, we find to have
arisen out of the shock given to Spain and Portugal by
Napoleon's invasion of them, so that in fact one of the
chief, if not the chief, result of Napoleon's career has been
the fall of Greater Spain and Greater Portugal, and the
independence of South America.

The result of all these mighty revolutions—of which
however I fancy that few of you know anything—is that
the Western States of Europe, with the exception of
England, have been in the main severed again from the
New World. This of course is only roughly true. Spain
still possesses Cuba and Porto Rico, Portugal still has
large African possessions, France has begun to found a new
Empire in North Africa. Nevertheless these four states
have materially altered their position in the world. They
have become in the main purely European States again, as
they were before Columbus crossed the Atlantic. It is
easy to show you the immense magnitude of this change.
Spain has lately passed through a disturbed time. She expelled a Bourbon sovereign and tried for a time the experi-

ment of a Republic. This change was doubtless very serious in the peninsula, but it produced wonderfully little excitement in the world at large. Now if anything similar had happened in the eighteenth or in the seventeenth century, the shock of it would have been felt over a great part of the planet. From Mexico to Buenos Ayres, from above the Tropic of Cancer to below the Tropic of Capricorn, every territory probably would have been convulsed with rebellion and civil war. In like manner the recent calamities in France would in the eighteenth century have shaken the St Lawrence, the Great Lakes of North America and the Mississippi, and have influenced the policy of princes in the Deccan and the valley of the Ganges, nay perhaps have altered the balance of Hindostan. As it was, those calamities were nearly confined to France itself; elsewhere sympathies were excited, but interests were not touched.

Thus then we see in the seventeenth and still more the eighteenth century a period when the New World was attached in a peculiar way to the five Western States of the European system. This attachment modifies and determines all the wars and negociations, all the international relations of Europe, during that period. In the last lecture I pointed out that the struggle between England and France in those centuries cannot be understood so long as we look at Europe alone, and that the belligerents are really the World-Powers, Greater Britain and Greater France. Now I remark that in like manner during the same period we must always read for Holland, Portugal and Spain, Greater Holland, Greater Portugal and Greater Spain. I remark also that this state of things has now passed away, that the Spanish Empire, and in the main also the Portuguese and Dutch Empires, have gone

the same way as the Empire of France. But Greater
Britain still remains. And thus we perceive the historical
origin and character of this Empire. It is the sole survivor of a whole family of Empires, which arose out of the
action of the discovery of the New World upon the peculiar
condition and political ideas of Europe. All these Empires
were beset by certain dangers, which Greater Britain
alone has hitherto escaped, though she too has felt the
shock of them and is still exposed to them, and the
great question now is whether she can modify her de-
fective constitution in such a way as to escape them for
the future.

I REMARKED that ancient Greek colonisation, compared with the modern system, might be called in a certain sense the natural system. And yet the modern system might be represented as natural also. The Greeks regard the State as essentially small, and infer that a surplus population can only be accommodated by founding another State. But is there anything necessarily unnatural in the other view, that the State is capable of indefinite growth and expansion? The ripe fruit dropping from the tree and giving rise to another tree may be natural, but so is the acorn spreading into the huge oak, that has hundreds of branches and thousands of leaves. If Miletus among its daughter-cities may remind us of the one, England expanding into Greater Britain resembles the other.

And yet surely there must be something unnatural in the system against which our own colonists revolted a hundred years ago and the colonists of Spain and Portugal a few years later.

The truth is that the simple idea of expansion has seldom been conceived or realised clearly.

Let us work out a little in our minds the conception of a Greater Britain, of the English State extended indefinitely without being altered. The question is often asked, What is the good of colonies ? but no such question could possibly be raised, if colonies really were such a simple extension of the mother-state. Whether this extension is practicable may be questioned, but it cannot be questioned that if it were practicable it would be desirable.

We must begin by recognising that the unoccupied territory of the globe is to those who take possession of it so much wealth in the most absolute sense of the word. The epitaph which said that to Leon and Aragon Columbus *gave* a new world was almost literally true. He conferred upon certain persons a large landed estate, and if, as the result, many poor people did not become rich and many unfortunate people prosperous, the fault must have lain in the distribution or administration of the wealth which he conferred. By his discovery the nations of Europe came in for a landed estate so enormously large that it might easily have converted every poor man in Europe into a landed proprietor.

But one thing was necessary before all this wealth could be reduced into possession and enjoyment. Property can exist only under the guardianship of the State. In order therefore that the lands of the New World might become secure enjoyable property, States must be set up in the New World. Without the State the settler would run the risk of being murdered by Indians, or attacked by rival settlers of some hostile nationality. On the other hand suppose the reign of law and government established in the New World, as in Europe, so that property is equally secure; then the poor man in Europe who finds life painful and the acquisition of land in these crowded countries utterly beyond his power, has only to transfer himself to the New World, where land is cheaper, and he is at once enriched as much as if he had received a legacy.

Thus there can be no dispute about the value of
organised States in the less crowded parts of the globe.
But why should these be our own colonies? There is
nothing to prevent the emigrant from settling in a colony
belonging to some different European State or in an
independent State. Why need we trouble ourselves therefore to keep up colonies of our own?

This is a strange question, which would never be asked
in England but for an exceptional circumstance. Most
people like to live among their own countrymen, under
the laws, religion and institutions they are accustomed to.
They place themselves moreover most really and practically
at a disadvantage by going to live among people who
speak a different language. As a matter of fact, we do
not find that, the course of emigration being free, any
large number of Englishmen yearly settle in those New
World States which are really foreign, that is, in the South
American Republics or in Brazil or in Mexico. There
would be no question at all about the value of colonies, and
we should all as a matter of course consider that only by
means of colonies was it possible to bring the wealth of the
New World within the reach of our population, if it were
not for the existence of the United States. But the United
States are to us almost as good as a colony; our people
can emigrate thither without sacrificing their language or
chief institutions or habits. And the Union is so large
and prosperous and fills our view so much, that we forget
how very exceptional its relation to us is, and also that if it
is to us almost as good as a colony, this is only because it
was constructed out of English colonies. In estimating the
value of colonies in the abstract, we shall only confuse ourselves by recollecting this unique case; we ought to put the
United States entirely out of view.

Considered in the abstract then, colonies are neither more nor less than a great augmentation of the national estate. They are lands for the landless, prosperity and wealth for those in straitened circumstances. This is a very simple view, and yet it is much overlooked, as if somehow it were too simple to be understood. History offers many examples of nations cramped for want of room; it records in many cases how they swarmed irresistibly across their frontiers and spread like a deluge over neighbouring countries, where sometimes they found lands and wealth. Now we may be very sure that never any nation was half so much cramped for want of room in the olden time as our own nation is now. Populations so dense as that of modern England are a phenomenon quite new at least in Europe. We continually speak of our country as crowded, and, since the rate of increase of population is tolerably constant, we sometimes ask with alarm what will be its condition half a century hence. 'The territory,' we say, 'is a fixed quantity; we have but 120,000 square miles; it is crowded already and yet the population doubles in some seventy years. What will become of us?' Now here is a curious example of our habit of leaving our colonial possessions out of account. What! our country is small; a poor, 120,000 square miles? I find the fact to be very different. I find that the territory governed by the Queen is of almost boundless extent. Let us deduct from the vast total India, as not much open to settlement; still the territory subject to the Queen is much greater than that of the United States, though that is uniformly cited as the example of a country *not* crowded and in which there is boundless room for expansion. It may be true that the mother-country of this great Empire is crowded, but in order to relieve the pressure it is not necessary for us, as if we were Goths or Turcomans, to seize upon the territory of our neighbours, it is not necessary even to incur great risks or undergo great hardships; it is only necessary to take possession of boundless territories in Canada, South Africa and Australia, where already our language is spoken, our religion professed, and our laws established.   If there is pauperism in Wiltshire and Dorsetshire, this is but complementary to unowned wealth in Australia; on the one side there are men without property, on the other there is property waiting for men. And yet we do not allow these two facts to come together in our minds, but brood anxiously and almost despairingly over the problem of pauperism, and when colonies are mentioned we ask, What is the good of colonies?

Partly no doubt this is due simply to a want of system in our way of thinking on subjects of this kind, but partly also it is evident that colonies have never been regarded in England as a simple extension of the English state and nation over new territory.   They have been thought of no doubt as belonging to England, though precariously, but at the same time as outside of England, so that what goes out of England to them is in a manner lost to England. This appears clearly from the argument which is often urged against emigration on any large scale, viz., that it might be good for the emigrants, but that it would be ruinous to England, which would be deprived of all the best and hardiest part of its population—*deprived*, for it is not imagined that such emigrants could remain Englishmen, or be still serviceable to the English commonwealth. Compare this view of emigration with that taken in the United States, where the constant movement of the population westward, the constant settlement of new Territories, which in due time rise to be States, is not regarded as either a symptom or a cause of weakness, not at all as a draining-out of vitality, but on the contrary as the greatest evidence of vigour and the best means of increasing it.

We have not really then as yet a Greater Britain. When I speak of the creation of Greater Britain during the eighteenth century, I in a certain sense exaggerate. In our colonial Empire was laid the foundation of a Greater Britain, and a Greater Britain may in the end arise out of it, but nothing of the kind was originally intended, nor later was the true significance of what had taken place perceived. A colony was not really thought of as an extension of the mother-state, but as something different. What then was the precise conception formed of a colony? We find ourselves forced to ask this question again.

I have pointed out already that in the sixteenth century there was no natural overflow of population from Europe into the New World. Europe was not over-peopled; there was no imperious demand for more room. Why then should the conception, so natural to us in these days, of a territorial extension of the State occur to those who lived at the time of the discoveries? We see on the contrary that contemporary statesmen were puzzled to decide what use could be made, and even doubted whether any use could be made, of the new lands. Sebastian Cabot is encouraged by Henry VII., until it is found that he does not bring back spices; then he is neglected, and abandons England for the Spanish service[1]. Thus the same cause which made it necessary to call in the help of the State led to a peculiarly materialistic view of the work of settlement. What the State wanted was revenue; hence it became necessary to regard the new countries rather as so much

[1] Schanz, *Englische Handelspolitik*. Read the whole chapter entitled, *Die Stellung der beiden ersten Tudors zu den Entdeckungen.*

wealth to be transported into Europe than as a new seat
for European civilisation.

I spoke before of natural colonisation, intending such
colonisation as results from the spread of a race over an
unbounded territory at a time when political institutions
are in their infancy. The colonisation of the sixteenth
century is curiously different. It arises from the discovery
of remote regions of unknown wealth by nations accustomed to a limited space and to a rigorous government.
As in the former kind the State scarcely appears, but individuals or rather tribes accomplish the work, and in making
a new settlement make a new state, in the latter kind the
State takes the lead, superintends the settlement, recruits
for it, holds it in subjection when it is made, and, as a consequence, looks to make a profit out of it. At first sight
this latter system might seem less materialistic than the
other, for it conceives the State as resting not upon mere
locality but upon kindred, but it becomes more materialistic in practice because it looks at the colony purely with
the eyes of the Government, and therefore from a purely
fiscal point of view. Hence in the first settlement of
America the conception of a Spanish colony as an extension of Spain was mixed up with a different conception
of it as a possession belonging to Spain. And whereas the
first conception, though it was formed instinctively, yet
answered to nothing in experience,—for who had ever
heard of two parts of the same State separated by the
whole breadth of the Atlantic Ocean?—the second conception was less embarrassing in practice because it was
by no means new. There had been examples in the
Middle Ages of States possessing dependencies separated from them by the sea, and I dare say it might be
possible to show that the Spanish Council of the Indies

was guided at times by the precedents afforded by Venice
in its dealings with Candia and with its dependencies
in the Adriatic. The Venetian conception of a dependency was purely selfish and commercial. So far from
thinking of it as forming part of the Republic, they
regarded it as so much live stock forming part of the
wealth of the Republic. Thus it was by confounding
together two theories radically inconsistent with each
other that the modern colonial system, first formed by
Spain and adopted with more or less modification by the
other powers of Europe, came into existence.

Now we have this conception more or less distinctly in
our minds whenever we ask the question, What is the
good of colonies? That question implies that we think
of a colony, not as part of our State, but as a possession
belonging to it. For we should think it absurd to raise
such a question about a recognised part of the body
politic. Who ever thought of inquiring whether Cornwall
or Kent rendered any sufficient return for the money
which we lay out upon them, whether those counties were
worth keeping? The tie that holds together the parts of
a nation-state is of another kind; it is not composed of
considerations of profit and loss, but is analogous to the
family bond. The same tie would hold a nation to its
colonies, if colonies were regarded as simply an extension
of the nation. If Greater Britain in the full sense of the
phrase really existed, Canada and Australia would be to us
as Kent and Cornwall. But if once we cease to regard a
colony in this way, if we consider that the emigrants, who
have gone forth from us, have ceased to belong to our
community, then we must form some other conception of
their relation to us. And this must either be the old
Greek conception which treats them as grown-up children

who have married and settled at a distance, so that the
family bond has dissolved away by the mere necessity of
circumstances, or if the connexion is maintained, as the
modern States insisted on maintaining it, it must change
its character. It must rest on interest. The question
must be asked, What is the good of the colony? and it
must be answered by some proof that the colony considered
as a piece of property, or as an investment of public money,
pays.

Now this may be a very good basis for the union of
two countries, provided the benefit received from the union
is mutual. In this case it constitutes a federation, and there
are many instances in which, without any tie of kindred,
countries have been held together in such a union simply
by the sense of a common interest. Among these instances
are Austria and Hungary, the German, French and Italian
cantons of the Swiss Confederation. Such would be the
case of our own Empire, if not only we ourselves felt that
our colonies paid, that is, that we reaped some advantage
from them which we should cease to reap if they became
independent, but also the colonies felt that the mother-
country paid, and that they gained something by the
connexion with it. And in the present day it is quite
easy to imagine such a sense of common interest existing
between us and even the remotest of our colonies, because
in the present day distance has been almost abolished by
steam and electricity. But in the first ages after the
discovery of the New World such a common interest was
less possible. The Atlantic Ocean was then for practical
purposes a far deeper and wider gulf, across which any
reciprocal exchange of services could not easily take place.
And so the old colonial system in general had not the
character of an equal federation.

It is the custom to describe the old colonies as sacrificed to the mother-country. We must be careful not to admit that statement without qualification. It is supposed for instance that the revolt of our own American colonies was provoked by the selfish treatment of the mother-country, which shackled their trade without rendering them any benefit in return for these restraints. This is far from being true. Between England and the American colonies there was a real interchange of services. England gave defence in return for trade-privileges. In the middle of the last century, at the time when the American quarrel began, it was perhaps rather the colonies than the mother-country that had fallen into arrear. We had been involved in two great wars mainly by our colonies, and the final breach was provoked not so much by the pressure of England upon the colonies as by that of the colonies upon England. If we imposed taxes upon them, it was to meet the debt which we had incurred in their behalf, and we saw with not unnatural bitterness that we had ourselves enabled our colonies to do without us, by destroying for their interest the French power in North America.

Still it was true of the old colonial system in general that it placed the colony in the position, not so much of a state in federation, as of a conquered state. Some theory of the kind is evidently implied in the language which is commonly used. We speak of the colonial *possessions* of England or of Spain. Now in what sense can one population be spoken of as the possession of another population ? The expression almost seems to imply slavery, and at any rate it is utterly inappropriate, if it merely means that the one population is subject to the same Government as the other. At the bottom of it certainly was the idea that the colony was an estate which was to be worked for the benefit of the mother-country.

S. L.   5

The relation of Spain to its colonies had become a type which other states kept before their eyes. A native population reduced to serfdom, in some parts driven to compulsory labour by caciques turned into state-officials, in other parts exterminated by overwork and then replaced by negroes; an imperious mother-country drawing from the colony a steady revenue, and ruling it through an artful mechanism of division, by which the settlers were held in check by the priesthood and by a serf-population treated paternally that it might be available for that purpose; such was the typical colonial system. It was wholly unfit to be a model to such a colony as New England, which paid no revenue, where there were neither subject Indians nor mines of gold and silver. Nevertheless governments could not afford to forget the precedent of profitable colonies, and I find Charles II. appealing to it in 1663. It became an established principle that a colony was a possession.

Now it is essentially barbaric that one community should be treated as the property of another and the fruits of its industry confiscated, not in return for benefits conferred, but by some absolute right whether of conquest or otherwise. Even where such a relation rests avowedly upon conquest, it is too immoral to last long, except in a barbarous state of manners. Thus for example we may have acquired India by conquest, but we cannot and do not hold it for our own pecuniary advantage. We draw no tribute from it; it is not to us a profitable investment; we should be ashamed to acknowledge that in governing it we in any way sacrificed its interest to our own. *A fortiori* then it is barbaric to apply such a theory to colonies, for it is to treat one's own countrymen, those with whom we have no concern at all except on the ground of kindred, as if they were conquered enemies, or rather in a way in which a civilised nation cannot treat even conquered enemies. And probably even in the old colonial system such a theory was not consciously and deliberately adopted. But since in the sixteenth century there was no scruple in applying it to conquered dependencies, and since the colonies of Spain were in a certain sense conquered dependencies, we can understand that unconsciously, unintentionally the barbaric principle crept into her colonial system, and that it lurked there and poisoned it in later times. We can understand too how the example of Spain and the precedents set by her influenced the other European States, Holland, France and England, which entered upon the career of colonisation a century later.

In the case of some of these States, for example France, the result of this theory was that the mother-country exercised an iron authority over her colonies. In Canada the French settlers were subject to a multitude of rigid regulations, from which they would have been free if they had remained in France. Nothing of the kind certainly can be said of the English colonies. They were subject to certain fixed restrictions in the matter of trade but apart from these they were absolutely free. Carrying their nationality with them, they claimed everywhere the rights of Englishmen. It has been observed by Mr Merivale that the old colonial system admitted no such thing as the modern Crown Colony, in which Englishmen are governed administratively without representative assemblies. In the old system assemblies were not formally instituted, but grew up of themselves, because it was the nature of Englishmen to assemble. Thus the old historian of the colonies, Hutchinson, writes under the year 1619, 'This year a House of Burgesses *broke out* in Virginia.' And assuredly the Home Government in those times did

not sin by too much interference. So completely were
the colonies left to themselves, that some of them, especially those of New England, were from the very beginning
for most practical purposes independent States. As early
as 1665, only forty years after the first settlement and a
hundred years before the Declaration of Independence, I
find that Massachusetts did not regard itself as practically
subject to England. 'They say,' writes a Commissioner [1],
'that so long as they pay the fifth of all gold and silver,
according to the terms of the Charter, they are not
obliged to the King but by civility.'

Thus our old colonial system was not practically at all
tyrannous, and when the breach came the grievances of
which the Americans complained, though perfectly real,
were smaller than ever before or since led to such mighty
consequences. The misfortune of that system was not
that it interfered too much, but that such interference as it
admitted was of an invidious kind. It claimed very little,
but what it did claim was unjust. It gave unbounded
liberty except in one department, namely trade, and in
that department it interfered to fine the colonists for the
benefit of the home traders. Now this was to put the
mother-country in a false position. It put her forward as
claiming to treat the colonies as a possession, as an estate
to be worked for the benefit of those Englishmen who
remained at home. No claim could be more invidious.
If it was not quite the claim that a master makes upon a

[1] *Calendar of State Papers; Colonial*, December, 1665. He adds : They
say they can easily spin out seven years by writing, and before that time a
change may come: nay, some have dared to say, Who knows what the
event of this Dutch war may be? They furnished Cromwell with many
instruments out of their corporation and college, and solicited him by one
Mr Winsloe to be declared a Free State, and now style and believe themselves to be so.

slave, it was at least similar to that which an absentee landlord makes upon tenants in whom he takes no further interest, and yet even the absentee landlord, if he gives nothing else, does at least give the use of land which was really his own. But what—a Massachusetts colonist might say—has England given to us that she should have this perpetual mortgage on our industry? The Charter of James I. allowed us the use of lands which James I. never saw and which did not belong to him, lands too which, without any Charter, we might perhaps have occupied for ourselves without opposition.

Thus this old system was an irrational jumble of two opposite conceptions. It claimed to rule the colonists because they were Englishmen and brothers, and yet it ruled them as if they were conquered Indians. And again while it treated them as conquered people, it gave them so much liberty that they could easily rebel.

I have shown how this strange hybrid conception of colonies may have originally sprung up. It is not very difficult perhaps to understand how the English, after once adopting, may have retained it, and may have never seen their way to a better conception. In the then condition of the world, if the English had thought of reforming their colonial system, their most natural course would have been to cast off the colonies altogether. For the analogy of grown-up sons and daughters applies very properly to the case of colonies, when they are so remote from the mother-country that they have come to have wholly different interests. All practical union, and therefore all authority on the part of the mother-country, fall into abeyance in these circumstances, and the Greek system is then most appropriate, which gives complete independence to the colony, but binds it in perpetual alliance. Now in the seventeenth century our colonies were, at least in ordinary times, practically too remote for union. This is so true that the difficulty is rather to understand how the secession of New England can have been delayed so long; but I imagine the retarding cause was the growth of the French Power in North America towards the end of the seventeenth century. After the great colonial struggle of France and England had fairly begun, the colonies were drawn somewhat nearer to us than before, and we can imagine that if Canada had not been conquered from the French in 1759, and if the struggle with France instead of coming to an end had grown more intense, the colonies would have issued no Declaration of Independence, and our connexion with them might have been put on a better footing instead of being dissolved. As it was, the need of union was at first not felt, it was then felt strongly for a time, and then by a sudden deliverance all pressure was removed, so that the thought of a reformed colonial system gave way at once to the dream of independence.

In these circumstances the old colonial system would naturally be retained as long as possible by the mother-country, because it was dangerous to touch it, because the least alteration would snap the tie that held the colonies altogether. The invidious rights were doggedly maintained simply because they existed, and because no alteration for the better was thought possible.

Probably also no healthier relation could then be even clearly conceived. I have described colonies as the natural outlet for superfluous population, the resource by which those who find themselves crowded out of the mother-country may live at ease, without sacrificing what ought to be felt as most valuable, their nationality. But how

could such a view occur to Englishmen a century ago?
England in those days was not overpeopled. The whole
of Great Britain had perhaps not more than twelve million
inhabitants at the time of the American War. And if
even then there was more diffused prosperity in the colonies
than at home, on the other hand the love of native soil, the
dominion of habit, the dread and dislike of migration, were
infinitely greater. We are not to suppose that the steady
stream of emigration to the New World, which we witness,
has been flowing ever since there was a New World, or
even ever since we had prosperous colonies. This movement did not begin till after the peace of 1815. Under
the old colonial system circumstances were quite different,
and may be illustrated by what we know of the history
of the New England colonies. Of these we learn that from
their commencement in 1620 for twenty years, until the
meeting of the Long Parliament, immigration did indeed
flow in a steady stream, but for a quite special reason, viz.,
because the Anglican Church was then harsh, and New
England afforded a refuge for Puritanism and Brownism or
Independency. Accordingly we are told that as soon as
the Long Parliament met this stream ceased to flow, and
that afterwards for a hundred years there was so little
immigration into New England from Old England that it
was believed not to balance the counter-movement of
colonists quitting the colony[1].

[1] 'The accessions which New England henceforward (i.e. after 1640)
received from abroad were more than counterbalanced by perpetual
emigrations, which in the course of two centuries have scattered her sons
over every part of North America and indeed of the globe. The immigrants of the preceding period had not exceeded twenty-five thousand,
a primitive stock, from which has been derived not less perhaps than a
fourth part of the present population of the United States.' Hildreth,
Hist. of U. S. ɪ. p. 267.

These were circumstances in which, though there might be colonies, there could be no Greater Britain. The material basis of a Greater Britain might indeed be laid, that is, vast territories might be occupied, and rival nations might be expelled from them. In this material sense Greater Britain was created in the seventeenth and eighteenth centuries. But the idea that could shape the material mass was still wanting. Towards this only one step was taken, namely, in laying down the principle that colonies did in some way belong together with the mother-country, that England did in some sense go with them across the sea, and that they could not cease to be English but through a war.

And what is true of the English colonies in the eighteenth century is equally true of the colonies of other States. Greater Spain, Greater Portugal, Greater Holland, and Greater France, were all, as much as Greater Britain, artificial fabrics, wanting organic unity and life.

Consequently they were all short-lived, and Greater Britain itself appeared likely to be short-lived. It seemed indeed likely to be more short-lived than many of its rivals. The Spanish colonies in America, which had been founded a hundred years before the English, did not break off so soon. The Declaration of Independence of 1776 was not only the most striking, but also the first act of rebellion on the part of colonies against mother-countries.

Nor did Greater Britain ultimately escape this danger by any wisdom in its rulers. When the utter weakness of the old colonial system had been exposed, we did not abandon it and take up a better. A new Empire gradually grew up out of the same causes which had called into existence the old, and it grew up under much the same system. We had not learnt from experience wisdom, but only despair.

We saw that under that system we could not permanently keep our colonies, but, instead of inferring that the system must be changed, we only inferred that sooner or later the colonies must be lost.

Then came, in the forties of this century, the victory of free-trade. Among other restraints upon trade it condemned *in toto* the old colonial system. This system was abolished, but at the same time the opinion grew up that our colonies were useless, and that the sooner they were emancipated the better. And this doctrine would have been obviously sound, if the general conditions of the world had remained the same in the nineteenth century as they were in the eighteenth and seventeenth. Our forefathers had found that they could make no use of colonies except by extracting trade-advantages from them. What then could remain to the mother-country, when her monopoly was resigned?

There followed a quiet period, in which the very slender tie which held the Empire together suffered no strain. In these favourable circumstances the natural bond was strong enough to prevent a catastrophe. Englishmen in all parts of the world still remembered that they were of one blood and one religion, that they had one history and one language and literature. This was enough, so long as neither colonies nor mother-country were called upon to make very heavy sacrifices each for the other. Such a quiet time favours the growth of a wholly different view of the Empire. This view is founded upon the consideration that distance has now no longer the important influence that it had on political relations.

In the last century there could be no Greater Britain in the true sense of the word, because of the distance between the mother-country and its colonies and between the colonies themselves. This impediment exists no longer. Science has given to the political organism a new circulation, which is steam, and a new nervous system, which is electricity. These new conditions make it necessary to reconsider the whole colonial problem. They make it in the first place possible actually to realise the old utopia of a Greater Britain, and at the same time they make it almost necessary to do so. First they make it possible. In the old time such large political organisms were only stable when they were of low type. Thus Greater Spain was longer-lived than Greater Britain, precisely because it was despotically governed. Greater Britain ran on the rock of parliamentary liberties, which were then impossible on so great a scale, while despotism was possible enough. Had it then been thought possible to give parliamentary representation to our colonists, the whole quarrel might easily have been avoided. But it was not thought possible; and why? Burke gives you the answer in the well-known passage, in which he throws ridicule upon the notion of summoning representatives from so vast a distance. This notion has now ceased at any rate to be ridiculous, however great the difficulties of detail may still be. Those very colonies, which then broke off from us, have since given the example of a federal organisation, in which vast territories, some of them thinly peopled and newly settled, are held easily in union with older communities, and the whole enjoys in the fullest degree parliamentary freedom. The United States have solved a problem substantially similar to that which our old colonial system could not solve, by showing how a State may throw off a constant stream of emigration, how from a fringe of settlement on the Atlantic a whole Continent as

far as the Pacific may be peopled, and yet the doubt never
arise whether those remote settlements will not soon claim
their independence, or whether they will bear to be taxed
for the benefit of the whole.

And lastly what is thus shown to be possible appears
now to be much more urgently important than in the last
century. For the same inventions which make vast
political unions possible, tend to make states which are on
the old scale of magnitude unsafe, insignificant, second-
rate. If the United States and Russia hold together for
another half century, they will at the end of that time
completely dwarf such old European States as France and
Germany, and depress them into a second class. They will
do the same to England, if at the end of that time England
still thinks of herself as simply a European State, as the
old United Kingdom of Great Britain and Ireland, such as
Pitt left her. It would indeed be a poor remedy, if we
should try to face these vast states of the new type by an
artificial union of settlements and islands scattered over
the whole globe, inhabited by different nationalities, and
connected by no tie except the accident that they happen
all alike to acknowledge the Queen's authority. But I
have pointed out that what we call our Empire is no such
artificial fabric, that it is not properly, if we exclude India
from consideration, an Empire at all, that it is a vast
English nation, only a nation so widely dispersed that
before the age of steam and electricity its strong natural
bonds of race and religion seemed practically dissolved by
distance. As soon then as distance is abolished by science,
as soon as it is proved by the examples of the United
States and Russia that political union over vast areas has
begun to be possible, so soon Greater Britain starts up, not
only a reality, but a robust reality. It will belong to the

stronger class of political unions.   If it will not be stronger
than the United States, we may say with confidence that
it will be far stronger than the great conglomeration of
Slavs, Germans, Turcomans and Armenians, of Greek Christians, Catholics, Protestants, Mussulmans and Buddhists,
which we call Russia.

LECTURE V.

IN a former lecture I pointed out how much unity is given to the history of England in the eighteenth century, how all the great wars of that time are shown to belong together and fall into a connected series, if you remark the single fact that Greater Britain during that period was establishing itself in opposition to Greater France. And I have since proceeded further in the same train of reflexion, by remarking that during the eighteenth and seventeenth centuries it is not England and France only that have great colonies, but Spain, Portugal and Holland also. You will, I think, find it very helpful in studying the history of those two centuries, always to bear in mind that throughout most of that period the five states of Western Europe all alike are not properly European states but world-states, and that they debate continually among themselves a mighty question, which is not European at all and which the student with his eye fixed on Europe is too apt to disregard, namely the question of the possession of the New World.

This obvious fact, sufficiently borne in mind, gives much unity to the political history of those nations, and reduces

to a simple formula most of their wars and alliances.
But I now proceed to show, especially with respect to
England, that the European States were greatly modified,
not only in their mutual dealings with each other, but
internally in the nature of each community, by their connexion with the New World. It will be found that the
modern character of England, as it has come to be since
the Middle Ages, may also be most briefly described on the
whole by saying that England has been expanding into
Greater Britain.

Two great events happened within thirty years of each
other, the discovery of the New World and the Reformation. These two events closely involved with two
others, viz., the consolidation of the great European States
and the closing of the East by the Turkish Conquest,
caused the vast change which we know as the close of the
Middle Ages and the opening of the modern period. But
of the two leading events the one was of far more rapid
operation than the other. The Reformation produced its
effect at once and in the very front of the stage of history.
For more than half a century the historical student finds
himself mainly concerned with the struggle between the
Habsburg House and the Reformation, first in Germany,
where it is assisted by France, then in the Low Countries
where it is helped, sometimes by France, sometimes by
England. Meanwhile the occupation of the New World is
going on in the background, and does not force itself upon
the attention of the student who is contemplating Europe.
The achievements of Cortez and Pizarro do not seem to
have any reaction upon the European struggle. And perhaps it is not till near the end of the sixteenth century,
when the raids of Francis Drake and his fellows upon the
Spanish settlements in Central America mainly contributed

to decide Spain to her great enterprise against England, perhaps it is not till the time of the Spanish Armada, that the New World begins in any perceptible degree to react upon the Old.

But from this time forward European affairs begin to be controlled by two great causes at once, viz., the Reformation and the New World, and of these the Reformation acts with diminishing force, and the New World has more and more influence. It is characteristic of the seventeenth century that these two causes act throughout it in combination. This is illustrated, as I mentioned above, by Cromwell's policy of war against Spain, which is double-faced and, while it seems to be a blow of Protestantism against Catholicism, is really a stroke for territory in the New World, so that it results in the conquest of Jamaica. It is illustrated too by the alliance of France and England against Holland in 1672, when one Protestant Power assails another with the pointed approbation of the Cromwellian statesman Shaftesbury, because they have rival interests in the New World. But by the end of that century the Reformation as a force in politics has declined, and in the eighteenth century the ruling influence is throughout the New World. This is what gives to that century the prosaic commercial character which distinguishes it. The religious question with all its grandeur has sunk to rest, and the colonial question, made up of worldly and material considerations, has taken its place.

Now the New World, considered as a boundless territory open to settlement, would act in two ways upon the nations of Europe. In the first place it would have a purely political effect, that is, it would act upon their Governments. For so much debatable territory would be a standing cause of war. It is this action of the New

World that we have been considering hitherto, while we
have observed how mainly the wars of the eighteenth
century, and particularly the great wars of England and
France, were kindled by this cause. But the New World
would also act upon the European communities themselves,
modifying their occupations and ways of life, altering their
industrial and economical character. Thus the expansion
of England involves its transformation.

England is now preeminently a maritime, colonising and
industrial country. It seems to be the prevalent opinion
that England always was so, and from the nature of her
people can never be otherwise. In Rückert's poem the
deity that visited the same spot of earth at intervals of
five hundred years, and found there now a forest, now a
city, now a sea, whenever he asked after the origin of what
he saw, received for answer, 'It has always been so, and
always will be.' This unhistorical way of thinking, this
disposition to ascribe an inherent necessity to whatever we
are accustomed to, betrays itself in much that is said about
the genius of the Anglo-Saxon race. That we might have
been other than we are, nay that we once were other, is to
us so inconceivable that we try to explain *why* we were
always the same, before ascertaining by any inquiry whether
the fact is so. It seems to us clear that we are the great
wandering, working, colonising race, descended from sea-
rovers and Vikings. The sea, we think, is ours by nature's
decree, and on this highway we travel to subdue the earth
and to people it.

And yet in fact it was only in the Elizabethan age that
England began to discover her vocation to trade and to the
dominion of the sea.

Our insular position and the fact that our island
towards the West and North looks right out upon the

Atlantic Ocean, may lead us to fancy that the nation must always have been maritime by the necessity of the case. We entered the island in ships and afterwards we were conquered by a nation of sea-rovers. But after all England is not a Norway; it is not a country which has only narrow strips of cultivable land, and therefore forces its population to look to the sea for their subsistence. England in the time of the Plantagenets was no mistress of the seas; in fact she was scarcely a maritime state at all. Occasionally in war-time we find medieval England in possession of a considerable navy. But as soon as peace arrives the navy dwindles away again. The constant complaints of piracy in the Channel show how little control England was able to exercise even over her own seas. It has been justly remarked that, as the Middle Ages know of no standing army, so, excepting the case of some Italian city-states, they know of no standing fleet. Over and over again in those times this decay of the navy recurs. Then when a new war broke out, the Government would issue a general licence to all merchant-ships to act as privateers, and the merchant-ships would respond to it by becoming not merely privateers but pirates. In fact, though under the Plantagenets the English nation was more warlike in spirit than it has been since, yet it is observable that in those days its ambition was directed much more to fighting by land than by sea. The glories of the English army of those days greatly eclipse those of the English navy; we remember the victories of Crécy and Poitiers, but we have forgotten that of Sluys.

The truth is that the maritime greatness of England is of much more modern growth than most of us imagine. It dates from the civil wars of the seventeenth century and from the career of Robert Blake. Blake's pursuit of Prince Rupert through the Straits of Gibraltar up the eastern coast of Spain is said to have been the first appearance of an English fleet in the Mediterranean after the time of the Crusades. There are no doubt naval heroes older than Blake. There is Francis Drake, and Richard Grenville, and John Hawkins. But the navy of Elizabeth was only the English navy in infancy, and the heroes themselves are not far removed from buccaneers. Before the Tudor period we find only the embryo of a navy. In the fifteenth century English naval history, except during the short reign of Henry V., shows only feebleness; before that too feebleness is the rule and efficiency the exception, until we arrive at the reign of Edward I., who was the first to conceive even the idea of a standing navy.

And not in maritime war only but in maritime discovery, in maritime activity of all kinds, the greatness of England is modern. In the great unrivalled explorations of the fifteenth and sixteenth centuries we did no doubt something, but we had no pretension whatever to take the lead. It is true that we made a promising commencement. A ship from Bristol was absolutely the first to touch the American Continent, so that there were English sailors who saw America proper a year or so before Columbus himself. At that moment we seemed likely to rival Spain, for if the commander Cabot[1] was no Englishman, neither was Columbus a Spaniard. But we fell behind again; Henry VII. was unwisely parsimonious, Henry VIII. was caught in the vortex of the Reformation. In the first

---

[1] John Cabot was an Italian, by citizenship a Venetian, but if his son Sebastian was born after the father settled in Bristol, and if the son not the father commanded the ship, the whole achievement might be made out to be English. The evidence however points the other way. See the discussion in Hellwald, *Sebastian Cabot,*

generation of great discoverers there is no English name. Frobisher, Chancellor and Francis Drake did not appear on the Ocean till Columbus had lain for half a century in his grave. Among nations of maritime renown whether in war, discovery or colonisation, before the time of the Spanish Armada England could not pretend to take any high rank. Spain had carried off the prize, less by merit than by the good fortune which sent her Columbus, but the nation which had really deserved it was beyond dispute Portugal, which indeed had almost reason to complain of the glorious intrusion of Columbus. Even against him she might urge that, if the object was to find the Indies, she took the right way and found them, while he took the wrong way and missed them[1]. After these nations, and in quite a lower class, might be placed England and France, and I do not know that England would have a right to stand before France. This is somewhat disguised in our histories owing to the natural desire of the historians to make the most of our actual achievements. In later times, after our maritime supremacy had once begun, we should be surprised at any nation competing with us for the first place, whereas we are content to appear as spirited aspirants venturing to contest the preeminence of Spain after she has enjoyed it for the best part of a century. And even at the end of the sixteenth century, when a large part of the American Continent has been carved out in Spanish vice-royalties, and Portugal has sent out governors to rule in the Indian Ocean, when Spanish missionaries

[1] Even if it were answered in his behalf that it is better to be wrong and find America than to be right and find India, Portugal might answer that she did both, since in the second voyage made from Lisbon to India she discovered Brazil, only eight years after the first voyage of Columbus, and would undoubtedly have discovered it, if Columbus had never been born.

have visited Japan, when the great poet of Portugal has led a literary career for sixteen years and written an epic poem in regions which to former poets had seemed fabulous, even as late as this the English are quite beginners in the maritime career, and have as yet no settlements.

But from naval affairs let us turn to manufactures and commerce. Here again we shall find that it is not a natural vocation, founded upon inherent aptitudes, that has given us our success in these pursuits. In manufactures our success depends upon our peculiar relation to the great producing countries of the globe. The vast harvests of the world are reaped in countries where land is wide and population generally thin. But those countries cannot manufacture their own raw materials, because all hands are engaged in producing and there is no surplus population to be employed in manufacture. The cotton of America and wool of Australia therefore come to England, where not only such a surplus population exists, but where also the great standing instrument of manufacture, coal, is found in abundance and near the coast. Now all this is modern, most of it very modern. The reign of coal began with machinery, that is, in the latter half of the eighteenth century. The vast tracts of production were not heard of till the New World had been laid open, and could not be used freely till two centuries and a half later, when railways were introduced. Evidently therefore the basis of our manufacturing greatness could not be laid till very recent times. The England of the Plantagenets occupied a wholly different economical position. Manufactures were not indeed wanting, but the nation was as yet so far from being remarked for its restless industry and practical talent, that a description written in the fifteenth century says that the English, ' being seldom fatigued with hard labour, lead a life more *spiritual* and *refined*[1].' In the main England at that time subsisted upon its lucrative intercourse (*magnus intercursus*) with Flanders. She produced the wool which was manufactured there; she was to Flanders what Australia is now to the West Riding. London was as Sydney, Ghent and Bruges were as Leeds and Bradford.

This continued in the main to be the case till the Elizabethan age. But then, about the time that the maritime greatness of England was beginning, she began also to be a great manufacturing country. For the manufactures of Flanders perished in the great catastrophe of the religious war of the Low Countries with Spain. Flemish manufacturers swarmed over into England, and gave a new life to the industry which had long had its centre at Norwich. There began what may be called the Norwich period of our manufacturing history, which lasted through the whole seventeenth century. The peculiarity of it was that in this period England manufactured her own product, wool. Instead of being mainly a producing country as before, or mainly a manufacturing country as now, she was a country manufacturing what she herself produced.

So much for manufactures. But the present industrial greatness of England is composed only in part of her greatness in manufacture. She has also the carrying trade of the world, and is therefore its exchange and business-centre. Now this carrying trade has come to her as the great maritime country; it is therefore superfluous to remark that she had it not in the Middle Ages, when she

---

[1] Fortescue, quoted by Mr Cunningham, *Growth of English Industry and Commerce*, p. 217. Besides being indolent and contemplative, the Englishman of the fifteenth century was preeminent in urbanity and totally devoid of domestic affection! See Gairdner's *Paston Letters*, vol. III. Intr. p. lxiii.

had not yet become a maritime country. Indeed in those times a carrying trade can hardly be spoken of. It implies a great sea-traffic, and a great sea-traffic did not begin till the New World was thrown open. Before that event business had its centre in the central countries of Europe, in Italy and the Imperial Cities of Germany. The great business men of the fifteenth century were the Medici of Florence, the Fuggers of Augsburg, the founders of the Bank of St George at Genoa.

In the Middle Ages England was, from the point of view of business, not an advanced, but on the whole a backward country. She must have been despised in the chief commercial countries; as now she herself looks upon the business-system and the banking of countries like Germany and even France as old-fashioned compared to her own, so in the Middle Ages the Italians must have looked upon England. With their city-life, wide business-connexions and acuteness in affairs they must have classed England, along with France, among the old-world, agricultural, and feudal countries, which lay outside the main-current of the ideas of the time.

Nor when the great change took place, which left Italy and Germany in their turn stranded, and turned the whole course of business into another channel, are we to suppose that England stepped at once into their place. Their successor was Holland. Through a great part of the seventeenth century the carrying trade of the world was in the hands of the Dutch, and Amsterdam was the exchange of the world. It is against this Dutch monopoly that England struggles in Cromwell's time and in the earlier part of the reign of Charles II. Not till late in that century does Holland begin to show signs of defeat. Not till then does England decidedly take the lead in commerce.

And thus, if we put together all the items, we arrive at the conclusion that the England we know, the supreme maritime commercial and industrial Power, is quite of modern growth, that it did not clearly exhibit its principal features till the eighteenth century, and that the seventeenth century is the period when it was gradually assuming this form. If we ask when it began to do so, the answer is particularly easy and distinct. It was in the Elizabethan Age.

Now this was the time when the New World began to exert its influence, and thus the most obvious facts suggest that England owes its modern character and its peculiar greatness from the outset to the New World. It is not the blood of the Vikings that makes us rulers of the sea, nor the industrial genius of the Anglo-Saxon that makes us great in manufactures and commerce, but a much more special circumstance, which did not arise till for many centuries we had been agricultural or pastoral, warlike, and indifferent to the sea.

In the school of Carl Ritter much has been said[1] of three stages of civilisation determined by geographical conditions, the *potamic* which clings to rivers, the *thalassic*, which grows up around inland seas, and lastly the *oceanic*. This theory looks as if it had been suggested by the change which followed the discovery of the New World, when indeed European civilisation passed from the thalassic to the oceanic stage. Till then trade had clung to the Mediterranean Sea. Till then the Ocean had been a limit, a boundary, not a pathway. There had been indeed a certain amount of intercourse across the narrow seas of the North, which had nourished the trade of the Hanseatic League. But in the main the Mediterranean continued to

[1] See Peschel, *Abhandlungen zur Erd-und Völkerkunde*, p. 398.

be the head-quarters of industry as of civilisation, and
the Middle Age moved so far in the groove of the ancient
world that Italy in both seemed to have a natural superiority over the countries on this side of the Alps.   France
and England had no doubt advanced greatly, but to the
Italian in the fifteenth century they still seemed comparatively barbarous, intellectually provincial and second-
rate.   The reason of this was that for practical purposes
they were inland, while Italy reaped the benefit of
the civilising sea.   The greatness of Florence rested
upon woollen manufactures, that of Venice, Pisa and
Genoa upon foreign trade and dependencies, and all this
at a time when France and England comparatively were
given up to feudalism and rusticity.   By the side of
the Italian republics, France and England showed like
Thessaly and Macedonia in comparison with Athens and
Corinth.

Now Columbus and the Portuguese altered all this by
substituting the Atlantic Ocean for the Mediterranean Sea
as the highway of commerce.   From that moment the reign
of Italy is over.   The relation of cause and effect is here in
some degree concealed by the misfortunes which happened to
Italy at the same time.   The political fall of Italy happened
accidentally just at the same moment.   The foreigner crossed
the Alps; Italy became a battle field in the great struggle
of France and Spain; she was conquered, partitioned,
enslaved; and her glory never revived afterwards.   Such a
catastrophe and its obvious cause, foreign invasion, blinds
us to all minor influences, which might have been working
to produce the same effect at the same time.   But assuredly,
had no foreign invasion taken place, Italy would just then
have entered on a period of decline.   The hidden source
which fed her energy and glory was dried up by the dis-

covery of the New World. She might be compared to one of those seaports on the coast of Kent from which the sea has receded. Where there had once been life and movement, silence and vacancy must have set in throughout the great city republics of Italy, even if no stranger had crossed the Alps. The Mediterranean Sea had not indeed receded, but it had lost once for all the character which it had had almost from the days of the Odyssey. It had ceased to be the central sea of human intercourse and civilisation, the chief, nay, almost the one sea of history. It so happened that, soon after commerce began to cover the Atlantic, it was swept out of the Mediterranean by the besom of the Turkish sea-power. Thus Ranke remarks that the trade of Barcelona seemed to be little affected by the new discoveries, but that it sank rapidly from about 1529, in consequence of the maritime predominance of the Turks caused by the successes of Barbarossa, the league of France with Solyman, and the foundation of the Barbary States. So clearly had the providential edict gone forth that European civilization should cease to be thalassic and should become oceanic.

The great result was that the centre of movement and intelligence began to pass from the centre of Europe to its Western Coast. Civilisation moves away from Italy and Germany; where it will settle is not yet clear, but certainly further west. See how strikingly this change stands out from the history of the sixteenth century. At the beginning of that century all the genius in the world seems to live in Italy or Germany. The golden age of modern art is passing in the first country, but if there are any rivals to the Italian painters they are German, and Michael Angelo is obliged at least to reason with those who prefer the *maniera tedesca.* Meanwhile the Reformation belongs to Germany. For France and England in those days it seems sufficient glory to have given a welcome to the Renaissance and to the Reformation. But gradually in the latter part of the sixteenth century we become aware that civilisation is shifting its head-quarters. Italy and Germany are first rivalled and then eclipsed; gradually we grow accustomed to the thought that great things are rather to be looked for in other countries. In the seventeenth century almost all genius and greatness is to be found in the western or maritime states of Europe.

Now these are the states which were engaged in the struggle for the New World. Spain, Portugal, France, Holland and England have the same sort of position with respect to the Atlantic Ocean that Greece and Italy had in antiquity with respect to the Mediterranean. And they begin to show a similar superiority in intelligence. Vast problems of conquest, colonisation and commerce occupy their minds, which before had vegetated in a rustic monotony. I have already shown you at length what an effect this change had upon the English nation. The effect produced upon the Dutch was quite as striking and much more rapid. The Golden Age of Holland is the first half of the seventeenth century. Let us examine for a moment the causes which produced its prosperity.

The Low Countries which revolted against Philip II. of Spain were, as you know, not merely the seven provinces which afterwards made the Dutch Republic and now make the Dutch Monarchy, but those other provinces which now make the kingdom of Belgium. It was the latter group which at the time of the rebellion were most prosperous. They were the great manufacturing region, the Lancashire or West Riding of the Middle

Ages. The former group, the Dutch provinces, were then of much less importance. They were maritime and chiefly occupied in the herring fishery. Now the result of the Rebellion was that Spain was able to retain possession of the Belgian group, which from this time is known as the Spanish Low Countries, but she was not able to hold the Dutch group, which, after a war which seemed interminable, she was forced to leave to their independence. Now during the struggle the prosperity of the Belgian Provinces, as I have pointed out, was ruined. The Flemish manufacturers emigrated and founded the woollen manufacture of England. But the maritime provinces, poorer at the outset, instead of being ruined grew rich during the war, and had become, before it was ended, the wonder and the great commercial state of the world. How was this? It was because they were maritime, and because their sea was the highway which led to the New World. As they had devoted themselves earlier to the sea, they had the start of the English, and their war with the Spaniards proved actually an advantage to them, because it threw open to their attack all the thinly-peopled ill-defended American Empire of Spain. The world was astonished to see a petty state with a barren soil and insignificant population, not only hold its own against the great Spanish Empire, but in the midst of this unequal contest found a great colonial Empire for itself in both hemispheres. Meanwhile the intellectual stimulus, which the sea had begun to give to these Western States, was nowhere more manifest than in Holland. This same small population took the lead in scholarship as in commerce, welcomed Lipsius, Scaliger and Descartes, and produced Grotius at the same time as Piet Hein and Van Tromp.

This is the most startling single instance of the action
of the New World. The effects produced in Holland
were nothing like so momentous as those which I have
traced in England, for the greatness of Holland, wanting
a basis sufficiently broad, was short-lived, but they were
more sudden and more evidently referable to this single
cause.

Such then was the effect of the New World on the Old.
It is visible not merely in the wars and alliances of the
time, but also in the economic growth and transformation
of the Western States of Europe. Civilisation has often
been powerfully promoted by some great enterprise
in which several generations continuously take part.
Such was the war of Europe and Asia to the ancient
Greeks; such the Crusades in the Middle Ages. Such
then for the Western States of Europe in recent centuries
has been the struggle for the New World. It is
this more than anything else which has placed these
nations, where they never were before, in the van of
intellectual progress, and especially it is by her success
in this field that our own country has acquired her
peculiar greatness.

I will conclude this lecture with some remarks on the
large causes which, in the struggle of five states, left the
final victory in the hands of England. Among these five
we have seen that Spain and Portugal had the start by a
whole century, and that Holland was in the field before
England. Afterwards for about a century France and
England contended for the New World on tolerably equal
terms. Yet now of all these states England alone remains
in possession of a great and commanding colonial power.
Why is this?

We may observe that Holland and Portugal laboured

under the disadvantage of too small a basis. The decline of Holland had obvious causes, which have often been pointed out. For her sufferings in a war of eighty years with Spain she found the compensations I have just described. But when this was followed, first by naval wars with England, and then by a struggle with France which lasted half a century, and she had now England for a rival on the seas, she succumbed. At the beginning of the eighteenth century she shows symptoms of decay, and at the Treaty of Utrecht she lays down her arms, victorious indeed, but fatally disabled.

The Portuguese met with a different misfortune. From the outset they had recognised the insufficiency of their resources, regretting that they had not been content with a less ambitious course of acquisition on the northern coast of Africa. In 1580 they suffered a blow such as has not fallen on any other of the still existing European states. Portugal with all her world-wide dependencies and commercial stations fell under the yoke of Spain, and underwent a sixty years' captivity. In this period her colonial Empire, which by becoming Spanish was laid open to the attacks of the Dutch, suffered greatly; Portuguese writers accuse Spain of having witnessed their losses with pleasure, and of having made a scapegoat of Portugal; certain it is that the discontent which led to the insurrection of 1640, and founded a new Portugal under the House of Bragança, was mainly caused by these colonial losses. Yet the insurrection itself cost her something more in foreign possessions; she paid the Island of Bombay for the help of England. Nor could the second Portugal ever rival the first, that nurse of Prince Henry, Bartholomew Diaz, Vasco da Gama, Magelhaens and Camoens, which has quite a peculiar glory in the history of Europe.

Be it remarked in passing that this passage also of the history of the seventeenth century shows us the New World reacting on the Old. As the rise of Holland, the great occurrence of its first years, so the Revolution of Portugal, which occupies the middle of it, is caused by the influence of the colonies.

As to the ill-success of Spain and France, it would no doubt be idle to suppose that any one cause will fully explain it. But perhaps one large cause may be named which in both cases contributed most to produce the result.

Spain lost her colonial Empire only, as it were, the other day. Having founded it a century earlier, she retained it nearly half a century later, than England retained her first empire. Compared to England, she has been inferior only in not having continued to found new colonies. And this was the effect of that strange decay of vitality which overtook Spain in the latter half of the sixteenth century. The decline of population and the ruin of finance dried up in her every power, that of colonisation included.

No similar decline is observable in France. France lost her colonies in a series of unsuccessful wars, and perhaps you may think that it is not necessary to inquire further, and that the fortune of war explains everything. But I think I discern that both States were guilty of the same error of policy, which in the end mainly contributed to their failure. It may be said of both that they 'had too many irons in the fire.'

There was this fundamental difference between Spain and France on the one side and England on the other, that Spain and France were deeply involved in the struggles of Europe, from which England has always been able to hold herself aloof. In fact, as an island, England is distinctly nearer for practical purposes to the New World, and almost belongs to it, or at least has the choice of belonging at her pleasure to the New World or to the Old. Spain might perhaps have had the same choice, but for her conquests in Italy and for the fatal marriage which, as it were, wedded her to Germany. In that same sixteenth century in which she was colonising the New World, Spain was merged at home in the complex Spanish Empire, which was doomed beforehand to decline, because it could never raise a revenue proportioned to its responsibilities. It was almost bankrupt when Charles V. abdicated, though it could then draw upon the splendid prosperity of the Netherlands; when, soon after, it alienated this province, lost the poorer half of it and ruined the richer, when it engaged in chronic war with France, when after eighty years of war with the Dutch it entered upon a quarter of a century of war with Portugal, it could not but sink, as it did, into bankruptcy and political decrepitude. These overwhelming burdens, coupled with a want of industrial aptitude in the Spanish people, whose temperament had been formed in a permanent war of religion, produced the result that the nation to which a new world had been given could never rightly use or profit by the gift.

As to France, it is still more manifest that she lost the New World because she was always divided between a policy of colonial extension and a policy of European conquest. If we compare together those seven great wars between 1688 and 1815, we shall be struck with the fact that most of them are double wars, that they have one aspect as between England and France and another as between France and Germany. It is the double policy of France that causes this, and it is France that suffers by it. England has for the most part a single object and wages a single war, but France wages two wars at once for two distinct objects. When Chatham said he would conquer America in Germany, he indicated that he saw the mistake which France committed by dividing her forces, and that he saw how, by subsidising Frederick, to make France exhaust herself in Germany, while her possessions in America passed defenceless into our hands. Napoleon in like manner is distracted between the New World and the Old. He would humble England; he would repair the colonial and Indian losses of his country. But he finds himself conquering Germany and at last invading Russia. His comfort is that through Germany he can strike at English trade, and through Russia perhaps make his way to India.

England has not been thus distracted between two objects. Connected but slightly with the European system since she evacuated France in the fifteenth century, she has not since then lived in chronic war with her neighbours. She has not hankered after the Imperial Crown or guaranteed the Treaty of Westphalia. When Napoleon by his Continental System shut her out from Europe, she showed that she could do without Europe. Hence her hands have always been free, while trade of itself inevitably drew her thoughts in the direction of the New World. In the long run this advantage has been decisive. She has not had to maintain a European Ascendency, as Spain and France have had; on the other hand she has not had to withstand such an Ascendency by mortal conflict within her own territory, as Holland and Portugal, and Spain also, have been forced to do. Hence nothing has interrupted her or interfered with her, to draw her off from the quiet progress of her colonial settlements. In one word, out of the five states which competed for the New World success has fallen to that one—not which showed at the outset the strongest vocation for colonisation, not which surpassed the others in daring or invention or energy—but to that one which was least hampered by the Old World.

LECTURE VI.

COMPETITION for the New World between the five western maritime States of Europe; this is a formula which sums up a great part of the history of the seventeenth and eighteenth centuries. It is one of those generalisations which escape us so long as we study history only in single states.

Much would be gained if the student of history would look at modern Europe as he has already the habit of looking at ancient Greece. Here he has constantly before him three or four different states at once, Athens, Sparta, Thebes, Argos, not to mention Macedonia and Persia, and is led to make most instructive comparisons and most useful reflexions upon large general tendencies. This is entirely owing to the accident that Greece was not a State but a complex of States, which fact our historians do not perceive clearly enough to conclude, as in consistency they ought, that they ought not to write a history of Greece at all, but separate histories of Athens, Sparta &c.

Let me ask those of you who know Grecian history to apply
to these Western States the mode of conceiving to which
you have accustomed yourselves. You have been in the
habit of thinking of a cluster of States gathered round
a common sea, which is studded with islands, and which
has on the other side of it large territories imperfectly
known and inhabited by strange races. You have thought
of all these States together, and not merely of each by
itself, you have traced the general results produced upon
the Hellenic world as a whole by all the intricate play
of interests between the several Hellenic city-states. Now
the five States we have in view, Spain, Portugal, France,
Holland and England were ranged in like manner on the
North Eastern shore of the Atlantic Ocean, and had
in like manner a common interest in what that Ocean
contained or hid. If the States seem to you so large,
the Ocean so boundless, and the settlements so scattered that you cannot bring them into one view, make
an effort, bring them into the same map, and draw the
map on a small scale. But your great effort must be
to raise your head above the current of mere chronological
narrative, to apply a fixed principle to the selection of
facts, grouping them not by nearness in time, nor by their
personal biographical connexion, but by the internal affinity
of causation. This great struggle of five States for the
New World differs from the struggles of those old Greek
States in this, that it is not isolated. It was superinduced
by the discovery of Columbus upon other struggles, themselves sufficiently complicated, which were going on within
the European States; in particular it is entangled with
the great religious struggle of the Reformation. Altogether what a tangled web! Now in a case like this
what shall science do? Surely the first thing will be to

7—2

separate and arrange together all the effects which can
be traced to any one cause. In order to do this it must
evidently neglect chronological order; it must break the
fetters of narrative. Following this method, it will see in
the sixteenth, seventeenth and eighteenth centuries, as
I have pointed out, two grand causes, each followed by its
multitude of effects, viz. the Reformation and the attraction
of the New World; these two grand causes it will study
separately, tracing each through the long series of effects
produced by it, and then perhaps, but not till then,
it will consider the mutual action of the two causes
upon each other. It is our business at present to consider
separately the effects produced on the five Western States
by the attraction of the New World.

Now why should the New World have produced any
further effect upon those States than simply to rouse them
to a new commercial activity, and perhaps more gradually
to enlarge their ideas by enlarging their knowledge? That
it did produce this latter effect I explained in the last
lecture by pointing out how in the course of the sixteenth
century the centre of civilisation moves from the Mediterranean to the neighbourhood of the Atlantic, so that,
whereas in the earlier years of it the eye turns always
to Italy or Germany, where the Raphaels and Michael
Angelos, the Ariostos and Macchiavelli's, the Dürers and
Hüttens and Luthers live, at the end of it and in the
seventeenth century the eye turns just as naturally Westward and Northward. We see Cervantes and Calderon in
Spain, Shakspeare and Spenser and Bacon in England;
Scaliger and Lipsius, then Grotius arise in Holland,
Montaigne and Casaubon in France, the destinies of the
world are in the hands of Henry IV., Queen Elizabeth, the
Prince of Orange, and, as time goes on, we grow more and

more accustomed to expect everything great in this
quarter, and to regard Italy and the Mediterranean as
out of date. So much was natural. The contact of the
New World might have been expected to produce this
effect, for, as we have always been accustomed to trace
ancient civilisation to the influence of the Mediterranean,
we are prepared to find that the Atlantic, when once
it becomes a Mediterranean, that is, when once lands are
laid open on the further side of it, should produce similar
effects on a grander scale. But it does not at once appear
why any further effects should be produced. To understand this we must consider the peculiar nature of the
contact between the New World and the Old, and, now
that we have looked a little into modern colonisation, we
are in a condition to do so.

Let us think how the New World might have acted
on the Old quite otherwise than as it did. What if
America had been found to be full of powerful and
consolidated States like those of Europe? Then our
relations with it would have been similar to our present
relations with China or Japan. Our advances might have
been met with a certain prudery, as by China; in that
case the result would either have been non-intercourse,
or some attempt, successful or otherwise, to force intercourse upon them. Or the American States might have
proved open-minded and liberal like the Japanese; then
there might have followed intercourse, exchange of ideas,
and mutual benefit. But in either case it does not appear
that important political consequences would have followed,
for in those days, while communication was so difficult,
it is not likely that any fusion of the European political
system with the American system, any alliances of European
with American States, would have taken place. The two

worlds would have remained aware of each other, yet
almost closed to each other, in a relation less like that
we now see between England and China or Japan than
that of England with the same countries or with India and
Persia during the seventeenth century.

Well! there were no such consolidated States in
America except in Mexico and Peru, where they were
overwhelmed in a moment by the Spanish adventurers.
Hence the New World had not the power it would
otherwise have had of keeping the Old at arm's length.
And the consequence was that there began between the
Old World and the New an emigration.

Now this by itself is a great fact. It implies that the
Atlantic had become, not merely a Mediterranean, but
something more. To the Greeks the Mediterranean gave
trade, intercourse with foreigners, movement and change
of ideas, but it did not, unless perhaps at a certain time,
afford a means of unbounded emigration. Emigration
there was, but on a scale not only inferior but inferior
in proportion. Political Powers, some of them exclusive,
guarded the opposite shore. But even this fact is rather
social than political. Emigration is in itself only a private
affair; it does not, as such, concern Governments, and
though it may produce a great effect upon them, as for
example the Puritan emigration to New England produced
no doubt a perceptible effect in our civil troubles, yet this
effect is only indirect.

Governments might have shut their eyes to all the
affairs of the New World. In that case the great adventurers would perhaps have set up kingdoms for themselves, and the reaction of the New World upon the Old
would have been confined within narrow limits. The
Continent of America was so roomy, so thinly peopled,

that the action of such adventurers, whatever it might have been, would have had no remote consequences, and the Governments of Europe might have looked on without anxiety. The New World would then have exerted as little influence upon the Old as, for example, the South American States now exert upon Europe. Revolutionary violence may rage there, but it rages unheeded, and its effects evaporate in the boundless territory peopled by so few inhabitants.

By considering thus what might have been we are brought to discern the critical point in the course which was actually pursued. The New World could not but exert a strong influence, but it need not have exerted, directly at least, any properly political influence upon the Old. It was made into a political force of the most tremendous magnitude by the interference of the European Governments, by their assuming the control of all the States set up by their subjects in it. The necessary effect of this policy was to transform entirely the politics of Europe, by materially altering the interest and position of five great European States. I bring this fact into strong relief because I think it has been too much overlooked, and it is the fundamental fact upon which this course of lectures is founded. In one word, the New World in the seventeenth and eighteenth centuries does not lie outside Europe, but exists inside it as a principle of unlimited political change. Instead of being an isolated region in which history is not yet interested, it is a present influence of the utmost importance to which the historian must be continually alive, an influence which for a long time rivalled the Reformation, and from the beginning of the eighteenth century surpassed the Reformation, in its effect upon the politics of the European States.

Historians of those centuries have kept in view mainly two or perhaps three great movements, first, the Reformation and its consequences, secondly, the constitutional movement in each country leading to liberty in England and to revolution through despotism in France. They have also considered the great Ascendancies which from time to time have arisen in Europe, that of the House of Austria, that of the House of Bourbon, and again that of Napoleon. These great movements have been, as it were, the framework in which they have fitted all particular incidents. The framework is insufficient and too exclusively European. It furnishes no place for a multitude of most important occurrences, and the movement which it overlooks is perhaps greater and certainly more continuous and durable than any of those which it recognises. Each view of Europe separately is true. Europe is a great Church and Empire breaking up into distinct kingdoms and national or voluntary Churches, as those say who fix their eyes on the Reformation; it is a group of monarchies in which popular freedom has been gradually developing itself, as the constitutional lawyer says; it is a group of states which balance themselves uneasily against each other, liable therefore to be thrown off its equilibrium by the preponderance of one of them, as the international lawyer says. But all these accounts are incomplete and leave almost half the facts unexplained. We must add, 'It is a group of States, of which the five westernmost have been acted upon by a steadfast gravitation towards the New World, and have dragged in their train great New World Empires.'

I have already applied this observation to the eighteenth century, and shown you how it explains the perpetual struggles which that century witnessed between England

and France. These struggles, I am persuaded, are treated by historians of the Balance of Power from a point of view much too exclusively European. This strikes me particularly in the picture they give of the career of Napoleon. They see in him simply a ruler who had the ambition to undertake the conquest of all Europe, and who had the genius almost to succeed in this enterprise. Now the main peculiarity of his career is that, though he did this, he did not intend it, but something different. He intended to make great conquests, and he made great conquests, but the conquests he made were not those he intended to make. Napoleon did not care about Europe. '*Cette vieille Europe m'ennuie,*' he said frankly. His ambition was all directed towards the New World. He is the Titan whose dream it is to restore that Greater France which had fallen in the struggles of the eighteenth century, and to overthrow that Greater Britain which had been established on its ruins. He makes no secret of this ambition, nor does he ever renounce it. His conquests in Europe are made, as it were, accidentally, and he treats them always as a starting-point for a new attack on England. He conquers Germany, but why? Because Austria and Russia, subsidised by England, march against him while he is brooding at Boulogne over the conquest of England. When Germany is conquered, what is his first thought? That now he has a new weapon against England, since he can impose the Continental System upon all Europe. Does he occupy Spain and Portugal? It is because they are maritime countries with fleets and colonies that may be used against England. Lastly, when you study such an enterprise as the Russian expedition, you are forced to admit, either that it had no object, or that it was directed against England. But this view escapes most historians, because from the outset they have underestimated the magnitude of that great historical cause, the attraction of the New World upon the Old. To them colonies have seemed unimportant, because they were distant and thinly peopled, as it were, inert, almost lifeless appendages to the parent-states. And true it is that the colonies received very little direct attention in the head-quarters of politics. In London or Paris no doubt few people troubled themselves with the affairs of Virginia and Louisiana; there no doubt domestic topics absorbed attention, and politics seemed centered in the last par-liamentary division or the last court intrigue. But the eye is caught by what is on the surface of things, not by what is at the bottom of them; and the hidden cause which made Ministers rise and fall, which convulsed Europe and led it into war and revolution, was, far more than might be sup-posed, the standing rivalry of interests in the New World.

But if this is so, it ought to be applicable to the seven-teenth century as well as to the eighteenth. In the history of the relation of the New World to the Old the three centuries, the sixteenth, seventeenth, and eighteenth, have each their marked character. The sixteenth century may be called the Spain-and-Portugal period. As yet the New World is monopolised by the two nations which discovered it, by the country of Vasco da Gama and the adopted country of Columbus, until late in the century Spain and Portugal become one State in the hands of Philip II. In the seventeenth century the other three states, France, Holland and England, enter the colonial field. The Dutch take the lead. In the course of their war with Spain they get possession of most of the Portuguese possessions, which have now become Spanish, in the East Indies; they even succeed for a time in annexing Brazil. France and England soon after establish their colonies in

North America. From this time then, or almost from this time, we may expect to trace that transformation in the politics of Europe, which I showed to be the necessary consequence of the new position assumed by these five states. During the course of this century a certain change takes place in the relative colonial importance of the five States. Portugal declines; so later does Holland. Spain remains in a condition of immobility; her vast possessions are not lost, but additions are no longer made to them, and they remain secluded, like China itself, from intercourse with the rest of the world. England and France have both decidedly advanced; Colbert has placed France in the first rank of commercial countries, and she has explored the Mississippi. But the English colonies have decidedly the advantage in population. And thus it is that the eighteenth century witnesses the great duel of France and England for the New World.

I exhibited that great duel early in this course, in order to show you at once by a conspicuous instance that the expansion of England has been neither a tranquil process nor yet belonging purely to the most recent times: that throughout the eighteenth century that expansion was an active principle of disturbance, a cause of wars unparalleled both in magnitude and number. I could not at that stage go further, but now that we have analysed the attraction of the New World upon the Old in general and upon England in particular, now that we have considered the nature and intensity of that attraction, we are in a condition to trace further back and even to its beginning the expansion of England into Greater Britain.

It was in the Elizabethan age, as I showed, that England first assumed its modern character, and this means, as I showed at the same time, that then first it began to find itself in the main current of commerce, and then first to direct its energies to the sea and to the New World. At this point then we mark the beginning of the expansion, the first symptom of the rise of Greater Britain. The great event which announces to the world England's new character and the new place which she is assuming in the world, is the naval invasion by the Spanish Armada. Here, we may say decidedly, begins the modern history of England. Compare this event with anything that preceded it in English history; you will see at once how new it is. And if you inquire in what precisely the novelty consists, you will arrive at this answer that the event is throughout *oceanic*. Of course we had always been an island; of course our foreign wars had always begun at least on the sea. But by the sea in earlier times had always been meant the strait, the channel, or at most the narrow seas. Now for the first time it is different. The whole struggle begins, proceeds and ends upon the sea, and it is but the last act of a drama which has been played, not in the English seas at all, but in the Atlantic, the Pacific, and the Gulf of Mexico. The invader is the master of the New World, the inheritor of the legacies of Columbus and Vasco da Gama; his main complaint is that his monopoly of that New World has been infringed; and by whom is the invasion met? Not by the Hotspurs of medieval chivalry, nor by the archers who won Crécy for us, but by a new race of men, such as medieval England had not known, by the hero-buccaneers, the Drakes and Hawkins, whose lives had been passed in tossing upon that Ocean which to their fathers had been an unexplored, unprofitable desert. Now for the first time might it be said of England—what the popular song assumes to have been always true of her—that 'her march is on the Ocean wave.'

But there is no Greater Britain as yet; only the impulse has been felt to found one, and the path has been explored, which leads to the transatlantic seats where the Englishmen of Greater Britain may one day live. While Drake and Hawkins have set the example of the rough heroism and love of roaming which might find the way into the Promised Land, Humphrey Gilbert and Walter Raleigh display the genius which settles, founds and colonises. In the next reign Greater Britain is founded, though neither Gilbert nor Raleigh are allowed to enter into it. In 1606 James I. signs the Charter of Virginia, and in 1620 that of New England. And now very speedily the new life with which England is animated, her new objects and her new resources, are exhibited so as to attract the attention of all Europe. It is in the war of King and Parliament, and afterwards in the Protectorate, that the new English policy is first exhibited on a great scale. Under Cromwell England appears, but prematurely and on the unsound basis of imperialism, such as she definitely became under William III. and continued to be throughout the eighteenth century, and this is England steadily expanding into Greater Britain.

It seems to me to be the principal characteristic of this phase of England that she is at once commercial and warlike. A commonplace is current about the natural connexion between commerce and peace, and hence it has been inferred that the wars of modern England are attributable to the influence of a feudal aristocracy. Aristocracies, it is said, naturally love war, being in their own origin military; whereas the trader just as naturally desires peace, that he may practise his trade without interruption. A good specimen of the *a priori* method of reasoning in politics! Why! how came we to conquer

India ? Was it not a direct consequence of trading with India ? And that is only the most conspicuous illustration of a law which prevails throughout English history in the seventeenth and eighteenth centuries, the law, namely, of the intimate interdependence of war and trade, so that throughout that period trade leads naturally to war and war fosters trade. I have pointed out already that the wars of the eighteenth century were incomparably greater and more burdensome than those of the Middle Ages. In a less degree those of the seventeenth century were also great. These are precisely the centuries in which England grew more and more a commercial country. England indeed grew ever more warlike at that time as she grew more commercial. And it is not difficult to show that a cause was at work to make war and commerce increase together. This cause is the old colonial system.

Commerce in itself may favour peace, but when commerce is artificially shut out by a decree of Government from some promising territory, then commerce just as naturally favours war. We know this by our own recent experience with China. The New World might have favoured trade without at the same time favouring war, if it had consisted of a number of liberal-minded States open to intercourse with foreigners, or if it had been occupied by European colonies which pursued an equally liberal system. But we now know what the old colonial system was. We know that it carved out the New World into territories, which were regarded as estates, to be enjoyed in each case by the colonising nation. The hope of obtaining such splendid estates and enjoying the profits that were reaped from them, constituted the greatest stimulus to commerce that had ever been known, and it was a stimulus which acted without intermission for centuries. This vast historic cause had gradually the effect of bringing to an end the old medieval structure of society and introducing the industrial ages. But inseparable from the commercial stimulus was the stimulus of international rivalry. The object of each nation was now to increase its trade, not by waiting upon the wants of mankind, but by a wholly different method, namely, by getting exclusive possession of some rich tract in the New World. Now whatever may be the natural opposition between the spirit of trade and the spirit of war, trade pursued in this method is almost identical with war, and can hardly fail to lead to war. What is conquest but appropriation of territory? Now appropriation of territory under the old colonial system became the first national object. The five nations of the West were launched into an eager competition for territory, that is, they were put into a relation to each other in which the pursuit of wealth naturally led to quarrels, a relation in which, as I said, commerce and war were inseparably entangled together, so that commerce led to war and war fostered commerce. The character of the new period which was thus opened showed itself very early. Consider the nature of that long desultory war of England with Spain, of which the expedition of the Armada was the most striking incident. I have said that the English sea-captains were very like buccaneers, and indeed to England the war is throughout an industry, a way to wealth, the most thriving business, the most profitable investment, of the time. That Spanish war is in fact the infancy of English foreign trade. The first generation of Englishmen that invested capital, put it into that war. As now we put our money into railways or what not? so then the keen man of business took shares in the new ship which John Oxenham or Francis Drake was fitting out at

Plymouth, and which was intended to lie in wait for the
treasure galleons, or make raids upon the Spanish towns in
the Gulf of Mexico. And yet the two countries were formally not even at war with each other. It was thus that
the system of monopoly in the New World made trade and
war indistinguishable from each other. The prosperity of
Holland was the next and a still more startling illustration
of the same law. What more ruinous, you say, than a long
war, especially to a small state? And yet Holland made
her fortune in the world by a war of some eighty years with
Spain. How was this? It was because war threw open
to her attack the whole boundless possessions of her anta-
gonist in the New World, which would have been closed to
her in peace. By conquest she made for herself an Empire,
and this Empire made her rich.

These are the new views which begin to determine
English policy under the Protectorate. From the point
from which we here regard English history, the great occurrence of the seventeenth century before 1688 is not the Civil
War or the execution of the King, but the intervention
of Cromwell in the European war. This act may almost
be regarded as the foundation of the English World-
Empire. It was of so much immediate importance that it
may be said to have decided the fall of the Spanish Power.
Spain, which less than a century before had overshadowed
the world, is found soon after lying a helpless prey to the
ambition of Louis XIV. Perhaps the turning-point is
marked by the Revolution of Portugal, which took place in
1640. Then began the fall of Spain. But for twenty years
from that time she struggled with her destiny, and the
internal troubles of her rival France caused a reaction in
her favour. At this crisis then the interference of Cromwell was decisive. Spain fell never to rise again, and no

measure taken by England had for centuries been so momentous.

But it marks the rise as well as the fall of a World-Power. England by this time has learned to profit by the example of Holland, and follows her in the path of commercial empire. The first Stuarts, though it was in their time that our first colonies were founded, show, I think, no signs of having entered into the new ideas. They abandon the Elizabethan system, and set their faces towards the Old World rather than the New. But this reaction comes to an end with the accession to power of the party of the Commonwealth. A policy now begins which is not, to be sure, very scrupulous, but is able, resolute and successful.

It is oceanic and looks westward, like the policy of the later years of Elizabeth. Here for the first time the New World reacts upon the Old by actual personal influence. Dr Palfrey has traced in a very interesting manner what I may call the New England element in our Parliamentary party. New England was itself the child of Puritanism, and of Puritanism in that second form of Independency to which Cromwell himself adhered. Accordingly it took a very direct part in the English Revolution. Several prominent English politicians of that time may be mentioned who had themselves lived in Massachusetts, e.g. Sir Henry Vane, George Downing, and Hugh Peters, Cromwell's chaplain. Now too the great English navy, so famous since, begins to rule the seas under the command of Robert Blake. The navy is now and henceforth the great instrument of England's power. The army—though it is more highly organised than ever before, and has in fact usurped the government of the country and placed its leader on the throne ; this army falls with a great catastrophe and is devoted to public execration, but the navy from this time forward is the nation's favourite. Henceforward it is a maxim that England is not a military state, that she ought to have either no army or the smallest army possible, but that her navy ought to be the strongest in the world.

From our point of view the colonial policy of Cromwell does not attract us by any marked superiority either in morality or success to that of the Restoration, but rather as the model which Charles II. imitates. Moral rectitude is hardly a characteristic of it, and if it is religious, this perhaps would have appeared, had the Protectorate lasted longer, to have been its most dangerous feature. Nothing is more dangerous than Imperialism marching with an idea on its banner, and Protestantism was to our Emperor Oliver what the ideas of the Revolution were to Napoleon and his nephew. The success too of this policy is of the same Napoleonic type. England had become for the moment a military State, and necessarily assumed a far grander position in the world than she could support when she disbanded her army and became constitutional again. The Protectorate was fortunate in coming to an end before its true character was understood. By the law of its nature it was drawn towards war. It is an illusion to suppose that the Puritanism of the Protector or of his party was analogous to modern Liberalism, and therefore inspired a repugnance to war. Read Marvell's panegyric on him. The virtuous poet predicts that Oliver will be ere long 'a Caesar to Gaul and a Hannibal to Italy.' Does the prospect shock him ? Not at all ; lest his hero should falter in the course, he exhorts him to 'march indefatigably on,' and bids him remember that 'the same acts that did gain a power must it maintain'. Nor when we examine the Protector's foreign policy do we find him unmindful of this

principle. He seems to look forward to a religious war, in
which England will play the same part in Europe that he
himself with his Ironsides has played in England. Some
of his modern admirers have perceived this. 'In truth,'
writes Macaulay, 'there was nothing which Cromwell had,
for his own sake and that of his family, so much reason to
desire as a general religious war in Europe... *Unhappily for
him* he had no opportunity of displaying his admirable
military talents except against the inhabitants of the British
isles.' We may well, I think, shudder at the thought of
the danger which was removed by the fall of the Protectorate.

On the side of the Continent this imperialist policy
was developed but imperfectly, but on the side of the New
World, where it was borne upon the tide of the time, it
went further and had more lasting consequences. Here
indeed Cromwell's policy is only that of the Long Parliament before him and of Charles II. after him. It has
indeed a peculiarly absolute and unscrupulous tinge. Of
his own pure will, without consulting directly or indirectly
the people, and in spite of opposition in his Council, he
plunges the country into a war with Spain. This war is
commenced after the manner of the old Elizabethan sea-
rovers by a sudden descent without previous quarrel or
declaration of war upon St Domingo. I remember hearing
a predecessor of my own, Sir J. Stephen, say in this
place that, if any of his hearers had a taste for iconoclasm,
he could recommend him to employ it upon the buccaneering Cromwell. Perhaps this may seem too severe, when
we remember the lawlessness of all maritime war at that
time. What I wish you to remark is the continuity that
holds together this Cromwellian policy with the Elizabethan, and equally with the policy which the nation
pursued in the eighteenth century, when in 1739 it went to

war again to break the Spanish monopoly. In all these
cases alike you see the close connexion which the old
colonial system established between war and trade.

But the great characteristic of this Commonwealth
period, indeed of the whole middle part of the seventeenth
century, is not war with Spain, but war with Holland. If
Cromwell's breach with Spain shows most strikingly by its
violent suddenness the spirit of the new commercial policy,
yet it is capable of being misinterpreted. For Spain was
the great Catholic Power, and therefore it might be
imagined that our war with her was caused by the other
great historic cause which then acted, by the Reformation,
and not by the New World. But what of our war with
Holland? Had the Reformation been the dominating
cause in the seventeenth century, we should have seen
England and Holland in permanent brotherly alliance. It
is the great proof that this cause is fast giving way to the
other, viz., the great trade-rivalry produced by the New
World, that all through the middle of the seventeenth
century England and Holland wage great naval wars of a
character such as had never been seen before. These wars
are seldom sufficiently considered as a whole, and therefore
are explained by causes which in fact were only secondary.
This is especially the case with the war of 1672, for which
Charles II. and the Cabal are responsible. It is cited as a
proof of the reckless immorality of that Government, that
it combined with the Catholic Government of Louis XIV.
to strike a deadly blow at the brother Protestant Power,
and that it did so for a dynastic interest, for the purpose
of overthrowing the oligarchic or Louvestein faction and
raising to power Charles II.'s nephew, the young Prince of
Orange. And no doubt Charles II. had this object.
Nevertheless there was nothing new at that time either in

war with Holland or alliance with France. Instead of
suddenly reversing the foreign policy of the country, Charles
here followed precedents set by the Commonwealth and
by Cromwell, for the former had waged fierce war with
Holland, and the latter had entered into alliance with
France. Accordingly the Government was supported by
some of those who inherited the tradition of the Commonwealth. Anthony Ashley Cooper, a man of Cromwellian
ideas, supported it by quoting the old words *Delenda est
Carthago.* In other words : ' Holland is our great rival in
trade, on the Ocean and in the New World. Let us
destroy her, though she be a Protestant Power, let us
destroy her with the help of a Catholic Power'. These
were the maxims of the Commonwealth and of the Protector, because, Puritans though they were and though
they had risen up against Popery, they understood that in
their age the struggle of the Churches was falling into
the background, and that the rivalry of the maritime
Powers for trade and empire in the New World was taking
its place as the question of the day.

And thus we are able to fill up the large outline of the
history of Greater Britain. We saw in the Elizabethan
war with Spain the movement, the fermentation out
of which it sprang. Under the first two Stuarts we see it
actually come into existence by the settlement of Virginia,
New England and Maryland. At a later time, in the
eighteenth century, it is seen to engage, now more mature,
in a long duel with Greater France. What occupies the
interval ? This is the foundation of the English navy and
the great duel with Holland. It covers the middle of the
seventeenth century, it embraces our first great naval wars,
and the following acquisitions ; Jamaica conquered under
Cromwell from Spain, Bombay received by Charles II.

from Portugal, New York acquired also by Charles II. from Holland.

This great struggle with Holland is followed by a period of close alliance with Holland, represented in the career of William of Orange. From our point of view this appears as a temporary revival of the Reformation-contest. By the Revocation of the Edict of Nantes the world is thrown back into the religious wars of the sixteenth century. The New World passes for a time into the background ; once more the question is of Catholicism or religious freedom. Once more therefore the two Protestant Powers stand shoulder to shoulder against France. William rules both countries and the trade-rivalry is adjourned for a time.

LECTURE VII.

THE object I professed to set before myself in these lectures was to present English history to you in such a light that the interest of it instead of gradually diminishing should go on increasing to the close. You will perceive by this time in what way I hope to do this. It is impossible that the history of any state can be interesting, unless it exhibits some sort of development. Political life that is uniform has no history, however prosperous it may be. Now it appears to me that English historians fail in the later periods of England, because they have traced one great development to its completion, and do not perceive that, if they would advance further, they must look out for some other development. More or less consciously, they have always before their minds the idea of constitutional liberty. This idea suffices until they reach the Revolution of 1688, perhaps even until they reach the accession of the House of Brunswick. But after this it fails them. Not that development ceases in the English Constitution at that point, nor even that to the political student it becomes less interesting. But it begins to be gradual and quiet; the tension is relaxed; dramatic incident henceforth must be looked for elsewhere. Our historians are not sufficiently alive to this. It may be true that George III.'s use of royal influence attained in an insidious way objects similar to those which the Stuarts tried to reach by prerogative or by military force. But when Wilkes and Horne Tooke, Chatham and Fox are brought forward to play the parts of Prynne and Milton, Pym and Shaftesbury, the interest of the reader grows languid. He seems to have before him the feeble second part of some striking story. Those parliamentary struggles which in the seventeenth century were so intense, seem, when repeated in the eighteenth, to have something conventional about them.

The mistake, according to me, lies in selecting these struggles to fill the foreground of the scene. It is a misrepresentation to describe England in George III.'s reign as mainly occupied in resisting the encroachments of a somewhat narrow-minded king. We exaggerate the importance of these petty struggles. England was then engaged in other and vaster enterprises. She was not wholly occupied in doing over again what she had done before; she was also doing new and great things. And these new things had vast consequences, which have changed and are at this day changing the face of the world. It is the historian's business then to open a new scene, and to bring into the foreground new actors.

I have now brought out in strong relief this new development in English history. I have shown that in the same seventeenth century, when England at home was victoriously reconciling her old Teutonic liberties to modern political conditions, and finding a place in England for the professional soldier and for the religious dissenter, she was also at work abroad. She, along with the other four

western States of Europe, was founding an empire in
the New World. I have shown also that, though she began
this work later than some other States, and did not for a
long time make strikingly rapid progress in it, yet in the
end she left all her rivals behind, so that she alone now
remains in possession of a great New World empire. Now
it was in the eighteenth century, just when the struggle for
liberty was over, that she began thus to take the lead in the
New World, and it is now, in the nineteenth century, that
she finds herself called upon to consider what new shape
she shall give to the Empire she possesses. It plainly
follows that here is the new development we are in search
of, the development which ought to make the principal
study of historians from the time when they find constitutional liberty a completed development and therefore an
exhausted topic. For here is a development which ever
since the seventeenth century has been steadily growing in
magnitude, here is a development which binds together
the future with the past.

If then we give it the principal place, we escape the
perplexity into which most historians fall, who strangely
find the history grow less and less interesting as England
grows greater and greater. But at the same time we
shall find much rearrangement necessary. For we shall
have adopted a new standard of importance for events,
and a new principle of grouping. Colonial affairs and
Indian affairs are usually pushed a little on one side by
historians. They are relegated to supplementary chapters.
It seems to be assumed that affairs which are remote from
England cannot deserve a leading place in a history of
England, as if the England of which histories are written
were the island so-called, and not the political union named
after the island, which is quite capable of expanding so as

to cover half the globe. To us England will be wherever English people are found, and we shall look for its history in whatever places witness the occurrences most important to Englishmen. And therefore, as in the periods when the liberties of England were in danger we seek it principally at Westminster in the Parliamentary debates, so in these periods, of which the characteristic is that England is expanding into Greater Britain, English history will be wherever this expansion is taking place, even when the scene is as remote as Canada or as India. We shall avoid the error commonly committed in these later periods of confounding the history of England with the history of Parliament. The rearrangement which such a change will involve may affect especially the nineteenth and eighteenth centuries. But in the seventeenth century also, though we may not wish to displace the accepted arrangement, which has reference to the struggle for liberty with the Stuart Kings, yet we must keep in our minds at the same time another arrangement, founded on the principle of marking the stages in the advance of Greater Britain.

The accepted arrangement is according to reigns and dynasties, and in each reign it ranks as the principal occurrences the dealings of the sovereign with Parliament. On this system the leading demarcations are the accession of the House of Brunswick, and beyond that the accession of the House of Stuart, and in the middle the Great Interregnum and the Revolution of 1688. We make far too much of these demarcations even when they are unobjectionable. We imagine a much greater difference than really existed between the age of George I. and that of Queen Anne, between that of William III. and that of Charles II., between the Restoration and the Commonwealth, between the age of James I. and the Elizabethan age. The Revolution was not nearly so revolutionary, nor the Restoration so reactionary as is commonly supposed. But if once we begin to think of England as a living organism, which in the Elizabethan age began a process of expansion, never intermitted since, into Greater Britain, we shall find these divisions altogether useless, and shall feel the want of a completely new set of divisions to mark the successive stages of the expansion.

I have already pointed out some of the principal of these divisions. But it will be well to present a connected view of English history as it appears when arranged on this principle.

The history of the expansion of England must necessarily begin with the two ever-memorable voyages of Columbus and Vasco da Gama in the reign of Henry VII. From that moment the position of England among countries was entirely changed, though almost a century elapsed before the change became visible to all the world. In our rearrangement this tract of time forms one period, the characteristic of which is that England is gradually finding out her vocation to the sea. We pass by the domestic disturbances, political religious and social, of that crowded age. We see nothing of the Reformation and its consequences. What we see is simply that England is slowly and gradually taking courage to claim her share with the Spanish and Portuguese in the new world that has been thrown open. There are a few voyages to Newfoundland and Labrador, then there is a series of bold adventures, which however proved not to have been happily planned. Our explorers, naturally but unfortunately, turned their attention to the Polar regions, and so discovered nothing but frozen Oceans, while their rivals were making a triumphal progress 'on from island unto island at the gateways of the day.' Next comes the series of buccaneering raids upon the Spanish settlements, in the course of which the English earned at least a character for seamanship and audacity.

The Spanish Armada marks the moment when this period of preparation or apprenticeship closes. The internal modification in the nation is now complete. It has turned itself round, and looks now no longer towards the Continent but towards the Ocean and the New World. It has become both maritime and industrial.

On the other system of arrangement the accession of the House of Stuart is thought to mark a decline. The Tudor sovereignty, popular and exercised with resolution and insight, makes way for a monarchy of divine right, pedantic and unintelligent. Nevertheless in our view there is no decline, there is continuous development. The personal unlikeness of James and Charles to Elizabeth is a matter of indifference. The foundation of Greater Britain now takes place. John Smith, the Pilgrim Fathers, and Calvert establish the colonies of Virginia, New England, and Maryland, of which the last marks its date by its name, taken from Queen Henrietta Maria.

Greater Britain henceforth exists, for henceforth Englishmen are living on both sides of the Atlantic Ocean. It received at once a peculiar stamp from the circumstances of the time. Greater Spain had been an artificial fabric, to which much thought and skilful contrivance had been applied by the Home Government. Authority, both civil and ecclesiastical, was more rigorous there than at home. This was because the Spanish settlements, as producing a steady revenue, were all-important to the mother-country. The English settlements, not being thus important, were neglected. This neglect had a momentous result owing to the

discord just then springing up in England. Colonies, if
not sources of wealth, might at least be useful as places of
refuge for unauthorised opinions. Half a century before
the voyage of the Mayflower Coligny [1] had given this turn
to colonisation. He had conceived that idea of toleration
along with local separation of rival religions, which was
afterwards realised within France itself by the Edict of
Nantes. How different, be it said in passing, would the
world now be, if a Huguenot France had sprung up beyond
the Atlantic! The idea of Coligny was now realised by
England.[2] As her settlements were made at a critical moment of dissension, an impulse to emigration was supplied
which would not otherwise have existed, but at the same
time there was introduced a subtle principle of opposition
between the New World and the Old. The emigrants
departed with a secret determination, which was to bear
fruit later, not of carrying England with them, but of
creating something which should not be England.

The second phase of Greater Britain was brought on by
the military revolution of 1648. After the triumph of the
Commonwealth at home, it had to wage a new war with
royalism by sea. From our point of view this second
contest is more important than the first; for the army
created by Cromwell was destined soon to dissolve again,
but the maritime power organised by Vane and wielded by
Blake is the English navy of all later time. Our maritime
ascendancy has its beginning here. 'At this moment,' says

---

[1] See an excellent account of his schemes in Mr Besant's *Coligny*.

[2] In the charter of Rhode Island 1663 it is expressed distinctly.
Religious liberty is granted 'for that the same by reason of the remote
distances of those places will, as We hope, be no breach of the unity
and uniformity established in this nation.' Charles II. in his religious
policy seems always to keep his maternal grandfather in view.

Ranke, 'England awoke more clearly than ever before to a consciousness of the advantage of her geographical position, of the fact that a maritime vocation was that to which she was called by nature herself.' Cromwell's attack upon the Spanish Empire and seizure of Jamaica, the most high-handed measure recorded in the modern history of England, is the natural effect of this new consciousness awakening at a moment when England found herself a military State.

The next phase is the duel with Holland. This belongs most peculiarly to the first half of the reign of Charles II., when it fills the foreground of the historic stage; but it had begun long before at the massacre of Amboyna in 1623, and had grown in prominence under the Commonwealth. It may be said to end in the year 1674, when Charles II. withdrew from the attack on Holland, which he had made in combination with Louis XIV. That was a great moment of glory for Holland, when in such extreme danger she found a new champion in the family which had saved her before, when a new Stadtholder, a second William the Silent, stood in the breach to withstand the new invasion. Nevertheless it was the beginning of the decline of Holland. For in this second great struggle of the Dutch Republic, though she showed the old heroism, she could not have all the old good fortune. She could not again positively prosper and grow rich by means of war, as she had done before. This time she was at war not with Spain, the possessor of infinite colonies, which she could plunder at leisure, but only with France; her fleet did not now sweep the seas unopposed, but was confronted with the powerful navy of England; and the very source of her wealth, her mercantile marine, was struck at by the English Navigation Act. Accordingly, though she saved herself and after-

wards had another age of great deeds, the decay of Holland
begins now to set in; it becomes visible to all the world
at the death of her great Stadtholder, the last of the old
line, our William III. England, richer by nature, and not
tried by invasion, begins now to draw ahead, and the
θαλασσοκρατία of Holland terminates.

The reign of Charles II. stands out in the history of
Greater Britain as a period of remarkable progress[1]. It
was then especially that the American Colonies took the
character which they had when they attracted so much
attention in the next century, of an uninterrupted series
of settlements extending from South to North along the
Atlantic coast. For it was in this reign that the Carolinas
and Pennsylvania were founded and that the Dutch were
expelled from New York and Delaware. Considered as a
whole and judged by the standard of the time, this American
settlement begins now to be most imposing. Its distinction is that it has a population which is at once large and
almost purely European. Throughout the Spanish settlements the Europeans were blended and lost in an ocean of
Indian and half-Indian population. The Dutch colonies
naturally wanted population, because the Dutch mother-
country was so small; they were generally little more than
commercial stations. The French colonies, which now
begin to attract attention, were also weak in this respect.
Already in the dawn of French colonial greatness might
be perceived a deficiency in genuine colonising power,
and perhaps also that slowness of multiplication which has
characterised the French since. The row of English colonies on the Atlantic was perhaps already the most solid

---

[1] 'The spirit of enterprise,' writes Mr Sainsbury, 'and the desire for
colonisation appear to have been almost as strong at that period as in the
days of Elizabeth and James.'

achievement in the way of colonisation that any European state could boast, though it would seem insignificant enough if judged by a modern standard. The whole population at the end of Charles II.'s reign was about two hundred thousand, but it was a population which doubled itself every quarter of a century.

What now is the next phase of Greater Britain? It enters now, in conjunction with Holland, upon a period of resistance to the aggressions of Greater France created by Colbert. From our point of view the administration of Colbert means the deliberate entrance of France into the competition of the Western States for the New World. France had not been much, if at all, behind England in her early explorations. Jacques Cartier had made himself a name earlier than Frobisher and Drake, Coligny had had schemes of colonisation earlier than Raleigh. Acadie and Canada were settled and the town of Quebec founded under the guidance of Samuel Champlain about the time of the voyage of the Mayflower. But, as usual, her European entanglements checked the progress of France in the New World. The Thirty Years' War had given her an opportunity of laying the foundation of a European Ascendancy. All through the middle of that century she was engaged in almost uninterrupted European war. Of the great Spanish estate which is in liquidation she leaves the colonial part to Holland and England, because she naturally covets for herself that which lies close to her frontier, the Burgundian part. In the days of Cromwell therefore she has fallen somewhat behind in the colonial race. Mazarin seems to have little comprehension of the oceanic policy of the age. But as soon as he is gone, and the war is over, and a tranquil period has set in, Colbert rises to guide her into this new path. He appropriates all the great commercial inventions

of the Dutch Republic, particularly the chartered Company.
He labours, and for a time with success, to give to France,
the State preeminently of feudalism, aristocracy and chivalry,
an industrial and modern character, such as the attraction
of the New World was impressing upon the maritime states.
He figures in Adam Smith as the representative statesman
of the mercantile system, and indeed, as the minister of
Louis XIV., he seemed to embody that perversion of the
commercial spirit which filled Europe with war, so that, as
Adam Smith himself says, 'commerce, which ought
naturally to be, among nations as among individuals, a
bond of union and friendship, has become the most fertile
source of discord and animosity.'

We have remarked that the seventeenth century is
controlled by two great forces, of which one, the Reformation, is decreasing, while the other, which is the attraction
of the New World, increases, and that the student must
continually beware of attributing to one of these forces
results produced by the other. Thus under Cromwell, as
under Elizabeth before him, the commercial influence works
disguised under the religious. When now, later in the
century, the duel between the two Sea-Powers is succeeded
by their alliance against France, we have once more to
unravel the same tangle of causation. This alliance en-
dured through two great wars and through two English
reigns, and it seems, when we trace the growth of it from
1674 to the Revolution of 1688, to be an alliance of the
two Protestant Powers against a new Catholic aggression.
For in those years there set in one of the strangest and most
disastrous reactions that history has to record. The Revocation of the Edict of Nantes revived the politics of the
sixteenth century. Coinciding nearly in time with the
accession of the Catholic James II. in England, it created

a world-wide religious panic. History seemed to be rolled
back just a century, the age of the League, of Philip II.
and William the Silent seemed to have returned, at a time
when it was thought that the balance of the Confessions
had been established firmly thirty years before in the
Treaty of Westphalia, and when the age had during those
thirty years been drifting in the other direction of colonial
expansion. The ideas of Colbert seem suddenly to be forgotten, the wealth he has amassed is wasted, the navy he
has founded is exposed to destruction at La Hogue. It is
against this Catholic Revival that England and Holland
first form their alliance.

But it was only for a moment, and less really than
apparently, that the New World was thus pushed into the
background. If we trace history upward instead of down-
ward, if we look from the Treaty of Utrecht back upon the
alliance of the Sea Powers which triumphed there, we see
an alliance of quite a different kind. There has been no
breach of continuity; Marlborough has the same position
as William, and the alliance is still directed against the
same Louis XIV. But the religious warmth has faded out
of the war, which now betrays by the settlement made at
Utrecht its intensely commercial character. That war has
such a splendour in our annals, and the title we give it,
'War of the Spanish Succession,' has such a monarchical
ring, that we think it a good sample of the fantastic, barbaric, wasteful wars of the olden time. It is of this war
that 'little Peterkin' desires to know 'what good came of
it at last.' In reality it is the most business-like of all our
wars, and it was waged in the interest of English and Dutch
merchants whose trade and livelihood were at stake. All
those colonial questions, which had been setting Europe at
discord ever since the New World was laid open, were

brought to a head at once by the prospect of a union
between France and the Spanish Empire, for such a union
would close almost the whole New World to the English
and Dutch, and throw it open to the countrymen of Colbert,
who were at that moment exploring and settling the
Mississippi. Behind all the courtly foppery of the Grand
Siècle commercial considerations now rule the world as they
had never ruled it before, and as they continued to rule it
through much of the prosaic century that was then opening.

In the midst of this war a memorable event befel,
which belongs to this development in the fullest sense, the
legislative union of England and Scotland. Read the history
of it in Burton; you will see that it marks the beginning
of modern Scottish history, just as the Armada that of
modern English history. It is the entrance of Scotland
into the competition for the New World. No nation has
since, in proportion to its numbers, reaped so much profit
from the New World as the Scotch, but before the Union
they had no position there. They were excluded from the
English trade, and the poverty of the country did not
allow them successfully to compete with the other nations
on their own account. In William III.'s reign they made
a great national effort on the plan then usual. They
tried to appropriate to themselves a territory in the New
World. They set up the Darien Company, which was to
carve a piece for the benefit of Scotland out of the huge
territory claimed by Spain as its own. This enterprise
failed, and it was out of the excitement and disappoint-
ment caused by the failure that the negotiations arose
which ended in the Union. England gained by the Union
security in time of war against a domestic foe; Scotland
gained admission into the New World.

In the history of the expansion of England one of the

greatest epochs is marked by the Treaty of Utrecht. In
our survey this date stands out almost as prominently as
the date of the Spanish Armada, for it marks the beginning of England's supremacy. At the time of the Armada
we saw England entering the race for the first time;
at Utrecht England wins the race. Then she had the
audacity to defy a power far greater than her own, and her
success brought her forward and gave her a place among
great states. She had advanced steadily since, but in the
first half of the seventeenth century Holland had attracted more attention and admiration, and in the second half
France. From about 1660 to 1700 France had been the
first state in the world beyond all dispute. But the Treaty
of Utrecht left England the first state in the world, and
she continued for some years to be first without a rival.
Her reputation in other countries, the respect felt for her
claims in literature, philosophy, scholarship and science
date from this period. If ever, it was after this time that
she held the same kind of intellectual primacy which France
had held before. Much of this splendour was transient,
but England has remained ever since that date on a higher
level than ever before. It has been universally allowed
ever since that no state is more powerful than England.
But especially it has been admitted that in wealth and
commerce and in maritime power, no state is equal to her.
This was partly because her rivals had fallen off in power,
partly because she herself had advanced.

The decline of Holland had by this time become
perceptible. So long as William lived, she enjoyed the
benefit of his renown. But in Marlborough's time and
from that time forward languor and the desire of repose
grow upon her. Her powers have been overstrained in war
with France and in competition with England. Never

again does she display her old energy. Thus the old
rival has fallen behind. The new rival, France, is for the
moment overwhelmed by the disasters of the war, and she,
whose affairs thirty years before had been set in order by
the greatest financier of the age, is now burdened with a
bankruptcy she will carry with her to the Revolution.
Her bold snatch at the trade of the New World has not
succeeded. She has in a sense won Spain, but not that
which made Spain valuable, viz., a share in the American
monopoly. Some part of the loss was indeed soon to
be repaired. France was soon to show much colonial
enterprise and intelligence. Dupleix in India, La
Galissonière in Canada, the Bailli Suffren on the sea, were
to carry the name of France high in the New World and
maintain for a long time an equal competition with
England. But at the moment of the Peace of Utrecht so
much could hardly have been foreseen. Fresh from her
victories, England seemed at that moment even greater
than she was.

The positive gains of England were Acadie, or Nova
Scotia, and Newfoundland (surrendered by France) and
the Asiento Compact granted by Spain. In other words,
the first step was taken towards the destruction of Greater
France by depriving her of one of her three settlements,
Acadie, Canada, and Louisiana, in North America. And
the first great breach was made in that intolerable Spanish
monopoly, which then closed the greater part of Central
and Southern America to the trade of the world. England
was allowed to furnish Spanish America with slaves, and
along with slaves she soon managed to smuggle in other
commodities.

I must pause here for a moment to make a general
observation. You will remark that in this survey of the

growth of Greater Britain I do not make the smallest
attempt, either to glorify the conquests made, or to justify
the means adopted by our countrymen, any more than, when
I point out that England outstripped her four rivals in the
competition, I have the smallest thought of claiming for
England any superior virtue or valour.   I have not called
upon you to admire or approve Drake or Hawkins or
the Commonwealth or Cromwell or the Government of
Charles II.   Indeed it is not easy to approve the conduct
of those who built up Greater Britain, though there is
plenty to admire in their achievements, and much less
certainly to blame or to shudder at than in the deeds of
the Spanish adventurers.   But I am not writing the
biography of these men; it is not as a biographer nor as a
poet nor as a moralist that I deal with their actions.   I am
concerned always with a single problem only, that of
causation.   My question always is, how came this enterprise to be undertaken, how came it to succeed ?   I ask it
not in order that we may imitate the actions we read of,
but in order that we may discover the laws by which
states rise, expand and prosper or fall in this world.   In
this instance I have also the further object, viz., to throw
light on the question whether Greater Britain, now that it
exists, may be expected to prosper and endure or to fall.
Perhaps you may ask whether we can expect or wish
it to prosper, if crime has gone to the making of it.   But
the God who is revealed in history does not usually
judge in this way.   History does not show that conquests
made lawlessly in one generation are certain or even
likely to be lost again in another : and, as government is
never to be confounded with property, it does not appear
that states have always even a right, much less that they
are bound, to restore gains that may be more or less ill-

gotten. The Norman conquest was lawless enough, yet it prospered and prospered permanently; we ourselves own this land of England by inheritance from Saxon pirates. The title of a nation to its territory is generally to be sought in primitive times, and would be found, if we could recover it, to rest upon violence and massacre; the territory of Greater Britain was acquired in the full light of history and in part by unjustifiable means, but less unrighteously than the territory of many other Powers, and perhaps far less unrighteously than that of those states whose power is now most ancient and established. If we compare it with other Empires in respect of its origin, we shall see that it has arisen in the same way, that its founders have had the same motives, and these not mainly noble, that they have displayed much fierce covetousness, mixed with heroism, that they have not been much troubled by moral scruples, at least in their dealings with enemies and rivals, though they have often displayed virtuous self-denial in their dealings among themselves. So far we shall find Greater Britain to be like other Empires, and like other states of whose origin we have any knowledge; but its annals are on the whole better, not worse, than those of most. They are conspicuously better than those of Greater Spain, which are infinitely more stained with cruelty and rapacity. In some pages of these annals there is a real elevation of thought and an intention at least of righteous dealing, which are not often met with in the history of colonisation. Some of these founders remind us of Abraham and Aeneas. The crimes on the other hand are such as have been almost universal in colonisation.

I make these remarks in this place because I have now before me the greatest of these crimes. England had taken some share in the slave-trade as early as Elizabeth's age, when John Hawkins distinguished himself as the first Englishman who stained his hands with its atrocity. You will find in Hakluyt his own narrative, how he came in 1567 upon an African town, of which the huts were covered with dry palm-leaves, how he set fire to it, and out of ' 8000 inhabitants succeeded in seizing 250 persons, men, women and children.' But we are not to suppose that from that time until the abolition of the slave trade England took a great or leading share in it. England had then, and for nearly half a century afterwards, no colonies in which there could be a demand for slaves, and when she acquired colonies they were not mining colonies like the first colonies of Spain, in which the demand for slaves had been urgent. Like our colonial empire itself, our participation in the slave-trade was the gradual growth of the seventeenth century. By the Treaty of Utrecht it was, as it were, established, and became ' a central object of English policy[1].' From this date I am afraid we took the leading share, and stained ourselves beyond other nations in the monstrous and enormous atrocities of the slave-trade.

This simply means that we were not better in our principles in this respect than other nations, and that, having now at last risen to the highest place among the trading-nations of the world and having extorted the Asiento from Spain by our military successes, we accidentally obtained the largest share in this wicked commerce. It is fair that we should bear this in mind while we read the horror-striking stories which the party of Abolition afterwards published. Our guilt in this matter

[1] The phrase is borrowed from Mr Lecky. See *History of England in the Eighteenth Century*, II. p. 13.

was shared by all the colonising nations; we were not the inventors of the crime, and, if within a certain period we were more guilty than other nations, it is some palliation that we published our own guilt, repented of it and did at last renounce it. But taken together the whole successful development which culminated at Utrecht secularised and materialised the English people as nothing had ever done before. Never were sordid motives so supreme, never was religion and every high influence so much discredited, as in the thirty years that followed. There has been a disposition to antedate this corruption, and to attribute it to the wrong cause. It was not so much after the Restoration, as after the Revolution, and especially after the reign of Queen Anne, that cynicism and corruption set in. In his well-known essay on 'the Comic Dramatists of the Restoration' Macaulay attributes to the Restoration the cynicism of four writers, Wycherley, Congreve, Vanbrugh, and Farquhar, of which writers three did not write a play till several years after the Revolution!

We have arrived then at the stage when England, in the course of her expansion, stands out for the first time as the supreme maritime and commercial Power in the World. It is evidently her connexion with the New World that has given her this character; nevertheless she did not yet appear at least to ordinary eyes as absolutely the first colonial Power. In extent her territories were still insignificant by the side of those of Spain and much inferior to those of Portugal. They were but a fringe on the Atlantic coast of North America, a few Western Islands and a few commercial stations in India. What was this compared with the mighty viceroyalties of Spain in Southern and Central America? And, as I have said before, France as a colonial Power might seem in some respects superior to England; her colonial policy might seem more able and likely in the end to be more successful.

The next stage in the history of Greater Britain is one which I have already surveyed. Holland being now in decline, the rivalry of England is henceforth with Spain and France, Powers henceforth united by a Family Compact. But the pressure of it falls mainly on France, since it is France, not Spain, that is neighbour to England both in America and in India. That duel of France and England begins, which I have already described. The decisive event of it is the Seven Years' War and the new position given to England by the Treaty of Paris in 1762. Here is the culminating point of English power in the eighteenth century; nay, relatively to other states England has never since been so great. For a moment it seems that the whole of North America is destined to be hers, and to make for ever a part of Greater Britain. Such an Empire would not have been greater in mere extent than that which Spain already possessed; but in essential greatness and power how infinitely superior! The Spanish Empire had the fundamental defect of not being European in blood. Not only did the part of the population which was European belong to a race which even in Europe appeared to be in decline, but there was another large part which had a mixture of barbarism in its blood, and another larger still whose blood was purely barbaric. The English Empire was throughout of civilised blood, except so far as it had a slave-population. But the example of antiquity shows that a separate slave-caste, discharging all drudgery and unskilled labour, is consistent with a very high form of civilisation. Much more serious is the deterioration of the national type by barbaric intermixture.

In this culminating phase England becomes an object

of jealousy and dread to all Europe, as Spain and afterwards France had been in the seventeenth century. It was about the time when she won her first victories in the colonial duel with France, that an outcry began to be raised against her as the tyrant of the seas. In 1745, just after the capture of Louisburg, the French Ambassador at St Petersburg handed in a note, in which he complained of the maritime despotism of the English, and their purpose of destroying the trade and navigation of all other nations; he asserted the necessity of a combination to maintain the maritime balance. England's former ally joins in the complaint, for there appeared about the same time a pamphlet entitled '*La voix d'un citoyen à Amsterdam*' in which the cry *Delenda est Carthago*, formerly raised by Shaftesbury against Holland, is now echoed back by a certain Maubert against England. 'Mettons nous,' he exclaims, 'avec la France au niveau de la Grande Bretagne, enrichissons-nous de ses propres fautes et du délire ambitieux de ses Ministres.' And then he suggests a Coalition for the purpose of procuring the repeal of the Navigation Act. From this time till 1815 jealousy of England is one of the great motive forces of European politics. It led to the intervention of France in America, and to the Armed Neutrality; later it became a kind of passion in the mind of the First Napoleon, and lured him gradually on, partly against his will, to make the conquest of Europe.

So far we have traced a course of uninterrupted continuous expansion. Slowly but surely England has grown greater and greater. But now occurs an event wholly new in kind, a sudden shock, proving that in the New World there might be other hostile Powers beside the rival States of Europe. The secession of the American colonies is one of those events, the immense significance of which could not even at the moment be overlooked. It was felt at the time to be pregnant with infinite consequences, and so it has proved, though the consequences have not been precisely of the kind that was expected. It was the first stirring of free will on the part of the New World which had remained, since Columbus discovered it, and since the Spanish Adventurers ruthlessly destroyed whatever germs of civilisation it possessed, in a kind of nonage. But now it asserts itself; it accomplishes a revolution in the European style, appealing to all the principles of European civilisation. This was in itself a stupendous event, perhaps in itself greater than that French Revolution, which followed so soon and absorbed so completely the attention of mankind. But it might have seemed at the moment to be the fall of Greater Britain. For the thirteen colonies which then seceded were almost all the then colonial Empire of Britain. And their secession seemed at the moment a proof demonstrative that any Greater Britain of the kind must always be unnatural and short-lived. Nevertheless a century has passed and there is still a Greater Britain, and on more than the old scale of magnitude.

This event will be the subject of the next lecture.

LECTURE VIII.

SCHISM IN GREATER BRITAIN.

As objects change their outline when the observer changes his point of view, so the history of a state may be made to take many forms. The outline I have given of English history in the seventeenth and eighteenth centuries is very different from that with which we are familiar, because I have taken a point of view from which many things seem great that before seemed small and many small that seemed great, while some things are now outline that were shading and others are shading that were outline.

And yet most people think of history as if its outline were quite fixed and unalterable. Details, they think, may be more or less accurate, more or less vivid, in this historian or in that, but the framework must be the same for all historians. In reality it is just this framework, the list of great events which children learn by heart, that is unfixed, unstable, alterable, though it seems made of cast-iron. For what makes an event great or little? Is the accession of a king necessarily a great event? At the moment it seems great, but when the excitement it causes has subsided, it may appear to have been in the history of the country no event at all. This principle consistently applied would produce a revolution in our ideas of history. It would show us that the real history of a state may be quite different from the conventional, since all or many of the events that have passed for great may be really unimportant, and the truly important events may be among those which have been slightly or not at all recorded.

We must have then a test for the historical importance of events, and to apply this test will be a principal part of the historian's task. Now what test shall we apply? Shall we say, 'The historian should make prominent those events which are *interesting?*' But surely an occurrence may be interesting biographically, or morally, or poetically, and yet not interesting historically. Shall we say then, 'He is to give to events the importance they were felt to have at the moment when they happened, he is to revive the emotion of the time'? I maintain that it is not the business of the historian, as we so often hear, to put his reader back in the past time, or to make him regard events as they were regarded by contemporaries. Where would be the use of this? Great events are commonly judged by contemporaries quite wrongly. It is in fact one of the chief functions of the historian to correct this contemporary judgment. Instead of making us share the emotions of the passing time, it is his business to point out to us that this event, which absorbed the public attention when it happened, was really of no great importance, and that event, though it passed almost unnoticed, was of infinite consequence.

Of all events of English history it is perhaps the American Revolution that has suffered most from the application of these wrong tests. Considered as a mere story or romance, it is not so very interesting. There is no very wonderful generalship, no very glorious victory on either side, and of all heroes Washington is the least dramatic. We forget that what is not very thrilling as *story* may be of profound interest as *history*. It marks our blindness to this distinction that we rank the French Revolution, because of its abundance of personal incidents, so much before the American. But I think the other cause of error I mentioned operates in this case even more fatally. The historian must not indeed be a novelist, but it is as bad, if not worse, for him to be a mere newspaper politician. The average contemporary view of a great event is almost certain to be shallow and false. And yet it seems to be the ambition of our historians to estimate the American Revolution just as they would have done had they been members of Parliament at the time of the administration of Lord North. Instead of trying to give the philosophy of it and to assign to the event its due importance in the history of the world, they seem always making up their minds how it would have been their duty to vote at this stage of the proceedings or at that, on the Repeal of the Stamp Act or the Boston Port Bill or the Compromise Act. I call this the newspaper treatment of affairs. It waits upon the parliamentary debates, and has an eye to the fate of the Ministry and to the result of the next division. In particular it takes up and dismisses questions as they come, and on each it contents itself with the smattering of information which may suffice for the short space that the question may remain under discussion. All this may be well enough in its place, but it produces the most melancholy effect in historical writing. And yet in the modern periods of England history seems to aim only at perpetuating such ordinary superficial views of the moment. It is deeply infected throughout with the commonplaces of party politics, and in discussing the greatest questions seems always to take for its model the newspaper leading-article.

What then is the true test of the historical importance of events? I say, it is their *pregnancy*, or in other words the greatness of the consequences likely to follow from them. On this principle I have argued that in the eighteenth century the expansion of England is historically far more important than all domestic questions and movements. Look at the great personage who dominates English politics through the whole middle period of that century, the elder Pitt. His greatness is throughout identified with the expansion of England; he is a statesman of Greater Britain. It is in the buccaneering war with Spain that he sows his political wild oats; his glory is won in the great colonial duel with France; his old age is spent in striving to avert schism in Greater Britain.

Look now at the American Revolution. In pregnancy this event is evidently unique. So it has always struck impartial observers at a distance. But the newspaper politicians of the day had no time for such large views. To them it presented itself only in detail, as a series of questions upon which Parliament would divide. These questions came before them mixed up inextricably with other questions, often of the pettiest kind, yet at the moment not less important as practical questions of party politics. It is well known that the Stamp Act passed at first almost without notice. A Parliament which discussed one night the Address, another night listened to declamations on the back-stairs influence of Bute and covert attacks on the Princess Dowager, another night excited itself over Wilkes and General Warrants, found on the Order of the Day a proposal for taxing the colonies, and passed it as a matter of course with as little attention

as is now given to the Indian Budget. This is deplorable
enough, though it may be difficult to remedy. But what
excuse can there be for introducing into history such a
preposterous confusion of small things with great? And
yet consider whether by our artless chronological method,
and by the slavish obsequiousness with which our historians follow the order of business fixed by Parliament, we
do not really make much the same mistake in estimating
the American Revolution that was made by those who passed the Stamp Act with scarcely a division. The American
question is introduced in our histories almost as irrationally
as it was introduced at the time into Parliament; it is
introduced without any preparation, and in mere chronological order among other questions wholly unlike it.
What is the use of history, if it does not protect us in
reviewing the past from those surprises which in the
politics of the day arise inevitably out of the vastness and
multiplicity of modern states? And yet the American
Revolution surprises us now in the reading as much as it
did our forefathers when it happened. We too, as we read,
have our heads full of Bute's influence, of the king's
marriage, of the king's illness, of Wilkes and General
Warrants, when suddenly emerges the question of taxing
the American colonies. Soon after we hear of discontent
in the colonies. And then we say, just as our forefathers
did, 'By the way what *are* these colonies, and how did they
come into existence, and how are they governed?' The
historian, just as a daily paper might do, undertakes to
post us up in the subject. He stops and inserts at this
point a retrospective chapter, in which he informs us that
the country really has, and has long had, colonies in North
America! He imparts to us just as much information
about these colonies as may enable us to understand the

debates now about to open on the repeal of the Stamp
Act, and then, apologising for his departure from chronological order, he hurries back to his narrative.   In this
narrative he seems always to watch proceedings from the
reporters' gallery in the House of Commons.   You would
think it was in Parliament that the Revolution took place.
America is the great question of the Rockingham Cabinet,
then later of the North Cabinet.   The final loss of America
is considered very important because it brings down the
North Cabinet!

When he relates the conclusion of the Treaty of 1783,
the historian will no doubt pause for a moment and insert
a solemn paragraph upon the event, which he will recognise as momentous.   He will explain that colonies
always secede as soon as they feel themselves ripe for
independence, and that the secession of America was no
loss but rather a gain for England.   Hereupon he dismisses
the subject, and henceforth you hear as little of America
from him as you heard before the troubles began.   New
subjects have cropped up in the House of Commons.   He
is busy with the stormy debates on the India Bill, the
struggle of young Pitt with the Coalition, the Westminster
Election, and a little later the Regency Debates.   For the
English historian is as much fascinated by Parliament, and
pursues all its movements with the same reverential attention, as the old historians of France show in following
the personal movements of Louis XIV.   When at last he
reaches the wars of the French Revolution, and the great
struggle of England with Napoleon, then indeed he leaves
behind him finally the inglorious campaigns of Burgoyne
and Cornwallis, and rejoices once more to have to record
really great events and the deeds of great men.

Now I do not think I risk anything by saying in con-

tradiction to all this that the American Revolution, instead
of being a tiresome unfortunate business which may be
despatched in a very brief narrative, is an event not only
of greater importance but on an altogether higher level
of importance than almost any other in modern English
history, and that it is intrinsically much more memorable
to us than our great war with Revolutionary France, which
indeed only arrives to be at all comparable to it through
the vast indirect consequences produced necessarily by a
war on so large a scale and continued so long. No doubt
it is much more stirring to read of the Nile, Trafalgar, the
Peninsula and Waterloo than of Bunker's Hill, Brandy-
wine, Saratoga and Yorktown, and this not only because we
like better to think of victory than of defeat, but also
because in a military sense the struggle with France was
greater and more interesting than that with America, and
Napoleon, Nelson, and Wellington were greater commanders
than those who appeared in the American Revolution. But
events take rank in history not as they are stirring or
exciting, much less as they are gratifying to ourselves,
but as they are pregnant with consequences.

The American Revolution called into existence a new
state, a state inheriting the language and traditions of
England, but taking in some respects a line of its own, in
which it departed from the precedents not only of England
but of Europe. This state was at the time not large in
population, though it was very large in territory, and there
were many chances that it would dissolve again and never
grow to be very powerful. But it has not dissolved; it
has advanced steadily, and is now, as I have said, superior
not only in territory but in population also to every
European state except Russia. Now it is by this result
that I estimate the historic importance of the Revolution,

since it is with the rise and development of states that history deals.

I have called attention to a series of events, the Spanish Armada, the colonisation of Virginia and New England, the growth of the English navy and trade, Cromwell's attack on Spain, the naval wars with Holland, the colonial expansion of France and decline of Holland, the maritime supremacy of England from the Peace of Utrecht, the duel of England and France for the New World. I have shown that these events taken together make up the expansion of England, that during the seventeenth century this development is necessarily somewhat hidden behind the domestic struggle of the nation with the Stuart kings, but that in the eighteenth century it ought to be brought into the foreground of history. Now in this series the next event is the Schism, the American Revolution, and the historic magnitude of this event is as much above that of most earlier events in our history as Greater Britain is greater than England. For its magnitude is not to be estimated by inquiring whether Howe and Cornwallis were great generals, or whether Washington was or was not a man of genius! And in universal history it is scarcely less great than in the history of England. The foundation in new territory of a state of fifty millions of men, which before many years will be a hundred millions, this by itself is far above the level of all previous history. No such event had occurred before in full daylight either in the New World or in the Old. Such a state has ten times the population that England had at the Revolution of 1688, and twice the population that France had at the Revolution of 1789. This fact, if it stood by itself, would be enough to show that time has brought us into a period of

greater magnitudes and higher numbers than past history
has dealt with.   But it does not stand by itself.   Bigness
no doubt is not necessarily greatness, and in Asiatic
history, though not in European, much larger figures may
be met with, for India and China have a population not
less than five times as large as the United States.   But
the peculiarity of this state lies as much in its quality as
in its magnitude.   Hitherto, unless we except the imperfectly known case of China, all states that have been of
very large extent have been of low organisation.

It had been the boast of England to show how liberty,
such as had been known in the city-states of Greece and
Italy, might be maintained in a nation-state of the modern
type.   Now the new state founded in America inherited
this discovery, both the theory and the practice of it, and
has devised all the modifications that were necessary for the
application of it to a still larger territory.   The consequence
is that this new large state, while in extent it belongs to
the same class as India or Russia, is in point of liberty at the
opposite end of the scale.   Hegel described the history of
the world as a gradual development of human free will.
According to him there are some states in which only one
man is free, others in which a few are free, others in
which many.   Now if we were to arrange states in a
series according to the extension of the spirit of freedom,
we should put most of the very large states of the world
at the lower end of such a scale.   But no one would
hesitate to put this very large state, the United States, at
the opposite end, as being beyond question the state in
which free will is most active and alive in every individual.

Here is a result which is great, and not merely big!
But to Englishmen the American phenomenon ought

to be infinitely more interesting and important than to the rest of mankind because of the unique relation in which they stand to it. There is no other example in history of two great states related to each other as England and the United States are related. True, the South American Republics have sprung from Spain, and Brazil from Portugal, in the same way, but they cannot be called great states; and besides, as I have said, the South American population is to a very large extent of Indian blood. But this great state, sprung from England and predominantly English in blood, is not practically separated from us, as their former colonies are separated from Spain and Portugal by remoteness of space, but by reason of the immense expansion and ubiquitous activity of both nations is always close to us, always in contact with us, exerts a strong influence upon us by the strange career it runs and the novel experiments it tries, while at the same time it receives from us a great influence in many ways, but principally through our literature.

There is no topic so pregnant as this of the mutual influence of the branches of the English race. The whole future of the planet depends upon it. But if so, what are we to think of the treatment which the American Revolution receives from our historians? One would think that the importance of the event in English history and in universal history were no concern of theirs. They despatch it very summarily. They treat us to a constitutional discussion of the right of taxation and to some glowing descriptions of Chatham's oratory; in due time they describe the war, apologise for our defeats, make the most of our successes, tell some anecdotes of Franklin, estimate the merits of Washington, and then dismiss the whole subject, as if it were tedious and did not interest them. A very minor question in the long Stuart controversy would occupy them longer, the adventures of Prince Charles Edward would rouse their imaginations more, the inquiry who was the author of Junius would excite a more eager curiosity. Is there not something wrong here ? Is it not evident that we have yet to learn what history is, that what we have hitherto called history is not history at all, but ought to be called by some other name, perhaps biography, perhaps party politics ? History, I say, is not constitutional law, nor parliamentary tongue-fence, nor biography of great men, nor even moral philosophy. It deals with states, it investigates their rise and development and mutual influence, the causes which promote their prosperity or bring about their decay.

But in these lectures on the Expansion of England the American Revolution is to be discussed in one aspect only, viz., as the end of our first experiment in expansion. Like a bubble, Greater Britain expanded rapidly and then burst. It has since been expanding again. Can we avoid the obvious inference ?

It is constantly repeated, as if it were beyond dispute, that the secession of the American colonies was an inevitable result of the natural law which prompts every colony, when it is ripe, to set up for itself, and that therefore the statesmen of George III.'s time who are responsible for it, George Grenville, Charles Townshend, and Lord North, can be charged with nothing more serious than hastening perhaps by a little an unavoidable catastrophe. Now on this head I need add but little to what I have said already. So long as a colony is regarded as a mere estate out of which the mother-country is to make a pecuniary profit, of course its allegiance is highly precarious, of course it will escape as soon as it can. In truth the illustration drawn from the grown-up son is not half strong enough for such a case. On that system a colony is not treated as a child but as a slave, and it will emancipate itself from such a yoke, not with gratitude as a grown-up son may do, but with indignation that it should ever, even in its weakness, have been treated so. The secession of the American colonies therefore was perhaps inevitable, but only because, and so far as, they were held under the old colonial system.

I have explained how difficult it was at that time to substitute a better system, but a better system exists, a better system is practicable now. There is now no reason why a colony after a certain time should desire emancipation; nay, even in that age the practice of our colonial government was much better than the theory. We are not to suppose that the colonies rebelled against English rule simply as such. The Government against which they rebelled was that of George III. in his first twenty years; now that period stands marked in our domestic annals too for the narrow-mindedness and perverseness of Government. There was discontent at home as well as in the colonies. Mansfield on the one side of politics and Grenville on the other had just at that time given an interpretation of our liberties which deprived them of all reality. It was this new-fangled system, not the ordinary system of English government, which excited discontent everywhere alike, which provoked the Wilkes agitation in England at the same time as the colonial agitation beyond the Atlantic. But the malecontents in England had no such simple remedy as lay at the command of the malecontents of Massachusetts and Virginia. They could not repudiate the Government which roused their sense of injury.

It was not then simply because they were colonies that

our colonies rebelled. It was because they were colonies under the old colonial system, and at a moment when that system itself was administered in an unusually narrow-minded and pedantic way. But I observe next that any general inference drawn from the conduct of these colonies is open to objection, because they were not normal but very peculiar colonies.

The modern idea of a colony is that it is a community formed by the overflow of another community. Over-crowding and poverty in one country causes, we think, emigration to another country which is emptier and richer. I have explained that this was not the nature of our American colonies. England[1] on the one hand was then not overcrowded. On the other hand the eastern coast of North America, where the colonies were settled, was not specially attractive by its wealth. It was no Eldorado, no Potosi, and in the northern part it was even poor. Why then did colonists settle in it? They had one predominant motive, and it was the same which Moses alleged to Pharaoh for the Exodus of the Israelites. 'We must go seven days' journey into the wilderness to offer a sacrifice unto the Lord our God.' Religion impelled them. They wished to live on beliefs and to practise rites which were not tolerated in England. This indeed was not the case everywhere alike. Virginia of course was Anglican. But the New England colonies were Puritan, Pennsylvania was Quaker, Maryland was Catholic, while of South Carolina we read[2] that 'the Churchmen were not a third part of the inhabitants' and that 'many various opinions had been taught by a multitude of teachers and ex-

[1] Compare the chapter in Adam Smith; Of the motives for establishing new colonies.
[2] Hildreth ii. p. 232

pounders of all sorts and persuasions.' Thus the old
emigration was a real exodus, that is, it was a religious
emigration. Now this makes all the difference. The
emigrant who goes out merely to make his fortune may
possibly in time forget his native land; but he is not likely
to do so; absence endears it to him, distance idealises it;
he desires to return to it when his money is made, he
would gladly be buried in it. There is scarcely more than
one thing that can break this spell, and that is religion.
Religion indeed may turn emigration into exodus. Those
who leave Troy carrying their gods with them can resist
no doubt the yearning that draws them back; they can
build with confidence their Lavinium or their Alba or
even their Rome in the new territory unhallowed before.
For I always hold that religion is the great state-building
principle; these colonists could create a new state because
they were already a church, since the church, so at least I
hold, is the soul of the state; where there is a church a
state grows up in time; but if you find a state which is
not also in some sense a church, you find a state which is
not long for this world.

Now in this respect the American colonies were very
peculiar. How is it possible to draw from their history
any conclusion about colonies in general? In particular
how can you argue from their case to the case of our
present colonies which have grown up since? In those
colonies there was from the outset a spirit driving them to
separation from England, a principle attracting them and
conglobing them into a new union among themselves. I
have remarked how early this spirit showed itself in the
New England colonies. No doubt it was not present in
all. It was not present in Virginia, but when the colonial
discontents, heated by the pedantry of Grenville and Lord

North, burst into a flame, then was the moment when
Virginia went over to New England, and the spirit of the
Pilgrim Fathers found the power to turn offended colonists
into a new nation.

But what is to be found similar to this in our present
colonies ? They have not sprung out of any religious
exodus. Their founders carried no gods with them. On
the contrary they go out into the wilderness of mere
materialism, into territories where as yet there is nothing
consecrated, nothing ideal. Where can their gods be but
at home ? If they in such circumstances can find within
them the courage to stand out as state-builders, if they
can have the heart to sever themselves from English
history, from all traditions and memories of the island
where their fathers lived for a thousand years, it will
indeed be necessary to think that England is a name which
possesses sadly little attractive power.

I think then that we mistake the moral of the
American Revolution, when we infer from it that all
colonies—and not merely colonies of religious refugees
under a bad colonial system—fall off from the tree as soon
as they ripen. And in like manner perhaps we draw a
wrong inference, and omit to draw the right inference,
from the prosperity which the United States have enjoyed
since the secession. I suppose there has never been in
any community so much happiness, or happiness of a kind
so little demoralising, as in the United States. But the
causes of this happiness are not political. They lie rooted
much deeper than the political institutions of the country.
If a philosopher were asked for a recipe to produce the
greatest amount of pure happiness in a community he
would say, Take a number of men whose characters have
been formed during many generations by rational liberty,

serious religion, and strenuous labour. Place these men in a wide territory, where no painful pressure shall reach them, and where prosperity shall be within the reach of all. Adversity gives wisdom and strength, but with pain ; prosperity gives pleasure, but relaxes the character. Adversity followed after a time by prosperity, this is the recipe for healthy happiness, for it gives pleasure without speedily relaxing energy. And it is a better recipe still if the prosperity at last given shall not be given too easily and unconditionally. Now these are the conditions which have produced American happiness. Characters formed in a temperate zone, by Teutonic liberty and Protestant religion ; prosperity conferred freely but in measure, and on the condition not only of labour but of the use of intelligence and ingenuity.

This recipe will produce happiness, but only for a time, only as long as the population bears a low proportion to the extent of territory. For a long time it was supposed that America had some magic secret by which she avoided all the evils of Europe. The secret was simple ; prosperous conditions of life and strong characters. Of late years the Americans themselves have awakened from the dream that their country is never to be soiled with the crimes and follies of Europe. They have no enemies, but yet they have had a war on a scale as gigantic as their territory, which Mr Wells reckons to have cost in four years a million lives and nearly two thousand millions of pounds sterling ; they have not kings, and yet we know that they have had regicide. Nevertheless the reputation and the greatness of the United States stand now perhaps higher than ever. But insensibly their pretensions have changed their character. Now it is said that no state was ever so powerful, that it is or will be the dominating state of the world ; in

other words it is classed among other states, but at the
head of them. Its pretension used to be wholly different.
It used to claim to be unique in kind; to be a visible
proof that the states of Europe with their vaunts of
power, their haughty Governments, their wars and their
debts, were on the wrong road altogether; that happiness
and virtue hold a more modest path; and that the best lot
for a state is not to be great in history, but rather to have
no history at all.

American happiness then is in no great degree the
consequence of secession. But does she owe to secession
her immense greatness?

When we look back over the stages of her progress we
are able easily to discover that she has been in several
points remarkably favoured by fortune. Imagine for instance that the original colonies, instead of lying in a compact group along the coast, had been scattered over the
Continent, and had been separated from one another by
other settlements belonging to other European states.
Such a difference might have made the growth of the
Union impossible. Imagine again that the French colony
of Louisiana, instead of failing miserably, had advanced
steadily in the hundred years between its foundation and
the American Revolution. This colony embraced the valley of the Mississippi. Had it been successful it might
easily have grown into a great French state, held together
through its whole length by its immense river. Or again
suppose it had passed into the hands of England! It was
Napoleon who, by selling Louisiana to the United States,
made it possible for the Union to develop into the gigantic
Power we see.

Still it is evident that the United States has found
the solution of that great problem of expansion on a

vast scale, which we have seen all the five Western nations of Europe in succession failing to solve. We saw them starting with the notion of an indefinite extension of the state, but we saw them almost in a moment lose their hold of this conception and take up instead an extremely opposite conception, out of which grew the old colonial system. We saw them treat their colonies as public estates, of which the profits were to be secured to the population of the mother country. We saw at the same time that this system could never be represented as anything but a makeshift, so that under it there always lurked the despair of any permanent possession of colonies. We saw, from this cause and from others, Empire after Empire in the New World dissolve. Our own first Empire was among these. But we have since come into possession of a new one. In the management of this we have been careful enough to avoid the old error. The old colonial system is gone. But in place of it no clear and reasoned system has been adopted. The wrong theory is given up, but what is the right theory? There is only one alternative. If the colonies are not, in the old phrase, possessions of England, then they must be a part of England; and we must adopt this view in earnest. We must cease altogether to say that England is an island off the north western coast of Europe, that it has an area of 120,000 square miles and a population of thirty odd millions. We must cease to think that emigrants, when they go to colonies, leave England or are lost to England. We must cease to think that the history of England is the history of the Parliament that sits at Westminster, and that affairs which are not discussed there cannot belong to English history. When we have accustomed ourselves to contemplate the whole Empire together and call it all England, we shall see that here too

is a United States. Here too is a great homogeneous
people, one in blood language religion and laws, but dispersed over a boundless space. We shall see that, though
it is held together by strong moral ties, it has little that
can be called a constitution, no system that seems capable
of resisting any severe shock. But if we are disposed to
doubt whether any system can be devised capable of holding
together communities so distant from each other, then is
the time to recollect the history of the United States of
America. For they have such a system. They have
solved this problem. They have shown that in the present
age of the world political unions may exist on a vaster
scale than was possible in former times. No doubt our
problem has difficulties of its own, immense difficulties.
But the greatest of these difficulties is one which we make
ourselves. It is the false preconception which we bring to
the question, that the problem is insoluble, that no such
thing ever was done or ever will be done; it is our
misinterpretation of the American Revolution.

From that Revolution we infer that all distant colonies,
sooner or later, secede from the mother-country. We
ought to infer only that they secede when they are held
under the old colonial system.

We infer that population overflowing from a country
into countries on the other side of an ocean must needs
break the tie that binds them to their original home,
acquire new interests, and make the nucleus of a new
State. We ought to infer only that refugees, driven across
the ocean by religious exclusiveness and carrying with them
strong religious ideas of a peculiar type, may make the
nucleus of a new state. This remark is confirmed in an un-
expected manner by the history of the secession of Southern
and Central America from Spain and Portugal. Here, to

be sure, there was Catholicism on both sides of the ocean
but Gervinus remarks that in reality the religion of the
regions was Jesuitism, and that accordingly the suppressi
of the Jesuits gave a moral shock to the population wh
he reckons among the leading causes of disruption.

Lastly, we infer from the greatness of the Uni
States since their secession that the division of sta
when they become overlarge, is expedient. But
greatness of the United States is the best proof tha
state may become immensely large and yet prosper. T
Union is the great example of a system under which
indefinite number of provinces is firmly held toget
without any of the inconveniences which have been felt
our Empire. It is therefore the visible proof that the
inconveniences are not inseparable from a large Empi
but only from the old colonial system.

But the expansion of England has been twofo
Hitherto we have considered only the expansion of
English nation and state together by means of colo
What are we to think of that other and much str
expansion by which India with its vast population
passed under the rule of Englishmen?

SECOND COURSE.

LECTURE 1.

HISTORY AND POLITICS.

Historians are sometimes ridiculed for indulging in conjectures about what would have followed in history if some one event had fallen out differently. 'So gloriously unpractical!' we exclaim. Now it is not for the sake of practice, but for the sake of theory that such conjectures are hazarded, and I think historians should deal in them much more than they do. It is an illusion to suppose that great public events, because they are on a grander scale, have something more fatally necessary about them than ordinary private events; and this illusion enslaves the judgment. To form any opinion or estimate of a great national policy is impossible so long as you refuse even to imagine any other policy pursued. This remark is especially applicable to an event so vast and complex as the Expansion of England. Think for a moment, if there had been no connexion of England with the New World! How utterly different would have been the whole course of English history since the reign of Queen Elizabeth! No Spanish Armada would have come against us, and there would have been no Drake and

11—2

Hawkins to withstand it. No great English navy would
have grown up. Blake would not have fought with Van
Tromp and De Ruyter. The wars of the Long Parliament
and Charles II. with Holland, the war of Cromwell with
Spain, would never have taken place. The country would
not have amassed the capital which enabled it to withstand
and at last to humble Louis XIV. The great commercial
corporations would not have arisen to balance the landed
interest and transform the policy of the state. England
would not have stood at the head of all nations in Queen
Anne's reign, and we should have had a wholly and entirely
different eighteenth century. Everything in short would
be utterly unlike what it is; and you may be tempted to
ridicule the whole speculation as unprofitable, because
infinite.

But yet it is the most practical of all speculations,
and for this reason. All this vast expansion, all these
prodigious accretions which have gathered round the
original England in three centuries, are yet not so completely incorporate with England that we cannot contemplate shaking ourselves free from them and becoming
again the plain England of Queen Elizabeth. The growth
of our Empire may indeed have been in a certain sense
natural; Greater Britain, compared to old England, may
seem but the full-grown giant developed out of the sturdy
boy; but there is this difference, that the grown man does
not and cannot think of becoming a boy again, whereas
England both can and does consider the expediency of
emancipating her colonies and abandoning India. We do
not, as a matter of fact, think of Canada as we think of
Kent, nor of Nova Scotia as of Scotland, nor of New South
Wales as of Wales, nor of India as of Ireland. We can
most easily conceive them separated from us, and, if we

chose, we could most easily bring about the separation. Nay more, many authorities actually recommend us to do so. We are forced then to pass some judgment on the expansion of England considered as a whole. Is it a transient development, like the expansion of Spain? Was it even a mistake from the beginning, a product of mis- directed energy? Nations can and *do* make mistakes. They are guided often by blind passion or instinct, and there is no reason in the nature of things why their aberrations should not continue for ages and lead them infinitely far. And thus it is conceivable that England ought from the beginning to have resisted the temptations of the New World, that she ought to have remained the self-contained island she was in Shakspeare's time—'in a great pool a swan's nest'; or at least that it would have been fortunate for her to have lost her Empire as France did, or when she lost her first colonial Empire not to have founded a new one.

But if this be so, or even if it may be so, what an enormous, intricate, and at the same time what a momentous problem is before us! If we have thus wandered from the right path, or if only we ought now to strike into a wholly new path, how prodigiously important is the fact! How much it surpasses in importance all those questions of home politics which absorb our attention so much! Many of us elude this consideration by a very confused argument. We say 'Let us mind our own affairs and not concern ourselves with remote countries, which are beyond our comprehension, and which it was a misfortune for us ever to become connected with.' But if this really was a misfortune, if our empire really is so much too large for us, then the question is infinitely more urgent and instant than if it were otherwise. For then we cannot too soon resolve to free ourselves from an encumbrance which will assuredly entail disaster upon us, then we ought to devote ourselves to the vast and delicate problem of destroying our Empire, until it is fairly achieved. And thus in any case we have here by far the largest of all political questions, for if our Empire is capable of further development, we have the problem of discovering what direction that development should take, and if it is a mischievous encumbrance, we have the still more anxious problem of getting rid of it, and in either case we deal with territories so vast and populations which grow so rapidly that their destinies are infinitely important.

I say, this is a political problem, but is it not also a historical problem? Yes, and the main reason why I have chosen this subject is that it illustrates better than any other subject my view of the connexion between history and politics. The ultimate object of all my teaching here is to establish this fundamental connexion, to show that politics and history are only different aspects of the same study. There is a vulgar view of politics which sinks them into a mere struggle of interests and parties, and there is a foppish kind of history which aims only at literary display, which produces delightful books hovering between poetry and prose. These perversions, according to me, come from an unnatural divorce between two subjects which belong to each other. Politics are vulgar when they are not liberalised by history, and history fades into mere literature when it loses sight of its relation to practical politics. In order to show this clearly, it has seemed to me a good plan to select a topic which belongs most evidently to history and to politics at once. Such a topic preeminently is Greater Britain. What can be more plainly

political than the questions What ought to be done with
India? What ought to be done with our Colonies? But
they are questions which need the aid of history. We
cannot delude ourselves here, as we do in home questions
of franchise or taxation, so as to fancy that common sense
or common morality will suffice to lead us to a true
opinion. We cannot suppose ourselves able to form a
judgment, for example, about Indian affairs without some
special study, because we cannot help seeing that the races
of India are far removed from ourselves in all physical,
intellectual, and moral conditions. Here then we see how
politics merge into history. But I am even more anxious
to show you by this example how history merges into
politics. The foundation of this Empire of ours is a
comparatively modern event. If we leave out of account
the colonies we have lost and think only of the Empire
we still possess, we think of an Empire which was founded
almost entirely in the reigns of George II. and George III.
Now this is the period which students avoid as being
too modern for study; this is the period which classic
historians neglect, and which accordingly passes in the
popular mind for an uneventful period of uniform prosperity and civilisation. I have complained that our
historians all grow languid as they approach this period,
that their descriptions of it are featureless, and that
accordingly they lead their readers to think of English
history as leading up to nothing, as a story without a
moral, or as like the Heart of Midlothian, of which the
whole last volume is dull and superfluous. You see then
how I think this evil may be cured. I show you mighty
events in the future, events of which, as future, we know
as yet nothing but that they must come and that they
must be mighty. These events are some further develop-

ment in the relation of England to her colonies and
also in her relation to India. Some further development, I say, for evidently the present phase is not
definitive; but what the development will be we cannot
yet know. Will there be a great disruption? Will
Canada and Australia become independent States? Shall
we abandon India, and will some native Government at
present almost inconceivable take the place of the Viceroy
and his Council? Or will the opposite of all this happen?
Will Greater Britain rise to a higher form of organisation?
Will the English race, which is divided by so many oceans,
making a full use of modern scientific inventions, devise
some organisation like that of the United States, under
which full liberty and solid union may be reconciled with
unbounded territorial extension? And secondly shall we
succeed in solving a still harder problem? Shall we
discover some satisfactory way of governing India, some
modus vivendi for two such extreme opposites as a ruling
race of Englishmen in a country which they cannot
colonise, and a vast population of Asiatics with imme-
morial Asiatic traditions and ways of life? We do not
know, I say, how these problems will be solved, but we
may be certain that they will be solved somehow, and we
may be certain from the nature of the problems that the
solution of them will be infinitely momentous. This
then is the goal towards which England is travelling.
We are not then to think, as most historians seem to
do, that all development has ceased in English history, and
that we have arrived at a permanent condition of security
and prosperity. Not at all; the movement may be less
perceptible because it is on a much larger scale; but the
changes and the struggles when they come—and they
will come—will be on a larger scale also. And when

the crisis arrives, it will throw a wonderful light back upon our past history. All that amazing expansion which has taken place since the reign of George II., and which we read of with a kind of bewildered astonishment, will begin then to impress us differently. At present when we look at the boundless extent of Canada and Australia given up to our race, we are astonished, but form no definite opinion. When we read of the conquest of India, two hundred millions of Asiatics conquered by an English trading company, we are astonished and admire, but we form no definite opinion. All seems so strange and anomalous that it almost ceases to be interesting. We do not know how to judge of it nor what to think of it. It will be otherwise then. Time will reveal what was really solid in all this success, and what was not so. We shall know what to think of that great struggle of the eighteenth century for the possession of the New World, when the event has shown, either that a great and solid World-State has been produced, or that an ephemeral trade-empire, like that of old Spain, rose to fall again, either that a solid union between the West and East, fruitful in the greatest and profoundest results, was effected in India, or that Clive and Hastings set on foot a monstrous enterprise which, after a century of apparent success, ended in failure.

This lesson time will teach to all alike. But history ought surely in some degree, if it is worth anything, to anticipate the lessons of time. We shall all no doubt be wise after the event; we study history that we may be wise before the event. Why should we not now form an opinion about the destiny of our colonies and of our Indian Empire? That destiny, we may be sure, will not be decreed arbitrarily. It will be the result of the working of those laws which it is the object of political science to discover. When the event takes place, this will be visible enough; all will see more or less clearly that what has happened could not but happen. But if so, the students of political science ought to be able to foresee, at least in outline, the event while it is still future.

Now do not these considerations set the more recent history of England in a new light? I have shown you England in the latter part of the sixteenth century entering upon a wholly new path. I have traced the stages of its progress in this path through the seventeenth century and the prodigious results which followed in the eighteenth. I have pointed out that we are still in a state of things which is evidently provisional, of which some great modification is evidently at hand. It follows from all this that the modern part of English history presents to us a great problem, one of the greatest problems, in political science. And thus I show you history merging in politics. I show you the reigns of George II. and George III. not as a mere by-gone period, whose quaint manners and fashions it is a delightful amusement to revive with the imagination, but as a storehouse of the materials by which we are to solve the greatest and most urgent of all political problems. In order to understand what is to become of our Empire we must study its nature, the causes which support it, the roots by which its life is fed; and to study its nature is to study its history, and especially the history of its beginning.

We have been told for a long time past by fashionable writers that history has made itself too solemn and pompous, that it ought to deal in minute, familiar, vivid details, in fact that it ought to be written just in the style of a novel. I will pause once more to tell you what I

think of this view, which has been of late so prevalent. I
do not deny the criticism on which it is founded. I fully
admit that history should not be solemn and pompous,
and I admit that for a long time it was both. But
solemnity is one thing, and seriousness is quite another.
This school argue that because history should not be
solemn, therefore it should not be serious. They deny
that history can establish any solid or important truths;
they have no conception that any great discoveries can
ever come out of it. They can only see that it is ex-
quisitely entertaining and delightful to call the past into
life again, to see our ancestors in their costume as they
lived, and to surprise them in the very act of doing
their famous deeds. I find their theory stated with the
most ingenuous frankness by Thackeray in the opening to
his lecture on Steele, a passage which almost every one
has read and I fancy almost every one has thought very
shrewd and true.

He says, 'What do we look for in studying the history
of a past age ? Is it to learn the political transactions and
characters of the leading public men ? is it to make ourselves acquainted with the life and being of the time ? If
we set out with the former grave purpose, where is the
truth, and who believes that he has it entire ? ' And then
he goes on to declare that in his opinion the solemn
statements which we find in books of history about public
affairs are all nonsense, and would not bear any sceptical
examination. He refers by way of example to Swift's
Conduct of the Allies and Coxe's Life of Marlborough, and
you see that it is from works of that extremely old-
fashioned cast that he has formed his idea of what history
is. But now, political history being all nonsense, what are
we to substitute for it ?

Thackeray tells us that we are 'to make ourselves acquainted with the life and being of the time.' What does this mean? He goes on to explain. 'As we read in these delightful volumes of the Tatler and Spectator, the past age returns, the England of our ancestors is revivified. The Maypole rises in the Strand again in London, the churches are thronged with daily worshippers; the beaux are gathering in the coffee-houses, the gentry are going to the drawing-room, the ladies are thronging to the toy-shops, the chairmen are jostling in the streets, the footmen are running with links before the chariots or fighting round the theatre doors. I say the fiction carries a greater amount of truth in solution than the volume which purports to be all true. Out of the fictitious book I get the expression of the life of the time; of the manners, of the movement, the dress, the pleasures, the laughter, the ridicules of society—the old times live again and I travel in the old country of England. Can the heaviest historian do more for me?'

That a great novelist should think thus is in itself almost a matter of course. The great engineer Brindley, being asked for what purpose he supposed rivers to have been created, answered without the least hesitation, To feed canals! Thackeray, being asked why Queen Anne lived and the English under the Duke of Marlborough fought the French, answers candidly, It was that I might write my delightful novel of Esmond. Of course he thought so, but how could he, with his keen sense of humour, venture to say so? You see, he appeals to our scepticism. He does not deny that history might be important if it were true, but he says it is not true. He does not believe a word of it.

Well! if so, what should we do? Must we take the

course he points out to us ? Must we give up history as a
serious study but keep it as a delightful amusement,
turn away from European wars and watch the ladies
thronging to the toy-shops, cease studying what sort of
government our ancestors had and inquire rather what they
had for dinner ? I tell you there is another and a much
better course, which leads in quite the opposite direction.
If history for a long time has been, as it has been, untrue
and unsatisfactory, correct it, amend it. Make it true and
trustworthy. There is no reason in the world why this
should not be done, or rather it has been done already for
the greater part of history, and only remains undone in
those more recent periods which students have neglected.
It seems not to be generally known how much the study of
history has been transformed of late years. Those charges of
untrustworthiness, of pompous and hollow conventionality,
which are vulgarly made against history, used to be well-
grounded once, but are in the main groundless now. History
has been in great part rewritten ; in great part it is now
true, and lies before science as a mass of materials out of
which a political doctrine may be deduced. It is not now
pompous and solemn, but it is thoroughly serious, much
more serious than ever. Here then is the alternative
which lies before you. Instead of ceasing to regard history
seriously, as Thackeray advises you, regard it more
seriously than before. Instead of holding that you cannot
find the truth and therefore may as well cease to seek it,
consider that the truth is hard to find and therefore must
be sought all the more diligently, all the more laboriously.

For observe that if once we grant that historic truth is
attainable, and attainable it is, then there can be no further
dispute about its supreme importance. It deals with facts
of the largest and most momentous kind, with the causes of

the decay and growth of Empires, with war and peace, with the sufferings or happiness of millions. It is by this consideration that I merge history in politics. I tell you that when you study English history you study not the past of England only, but her future. It is the welfare of your country, it is your whole interest as citizens, that is in question while you study history. How it is so I illustrate by putting before you this subject of the Expansion of England. I show you that there is a vast question ripening for decision, upon which almost the whole future of our country depends. In magnitude this question far surpasses all other questions which you can ever have to discuss in political life. And yet it is altogether a historical question. The investigation of it requires not only some knowledge, but I may almost say a full knowledge of the modern history of England. For, as I have pointed out, England has been entirely engaged for the last three centuries in this expansion into Greater Britain. If therefore you would discern in outline the future of Greater Britain, you will have to master almost the whole history of England in the last three centuries. Only enter upon these inquiries, only undertake to make up your minds upon the colonial question and the Indian question; you will find that you are led back from question to question and from one department of affairs to another, until you discover that these two questions bring the whole modern history of England in their train. And not only is this one way of grasping English history, but it is the best way. For in history everything depends upon turning narrative into problems. So long as you think of history as a mere chronological narrative, so long you are in the old literary groove which leads to no trustworthy knowledge, but only to that pompous conventional romancing of which all serious men are tired. Break the drowsy spell of narrative; ask yourself questions; set yourself problems; your mind will at once take up a new attitude; you will become an investigator; you will cease to be solemn and begin to be serious. Now modern English history breaks up into two grand problems, the problem of the colonies and the problem of India.

Moreover all those considerations which make the universal study of history imperative in all countries where there is popular government, operate in England far more strongly than in any other country. For this immense expansion of our race has the effect of making English politics most bewilderingly difficult. I take it that every other country, France, Germany, the United States, every country except perhaps Russia, has a simple problem to solve compared with that which is set before England. Most of those states are compact and solid, scarcely less compact, though so much larger, than the city-states of antiquity. They can only be attacked at home, and therefore their armies are a kind of citizen soldiery. Now distant dependencies destroy this compactness, and make the national interest hard to discern and hard to protect. Because of our scattered colonies it is easy for an enemy to strike at us. If we were at war with the United States, we should feel it in Canada; if with Russia, in Afghanistan. But this external difficulty is less serious than the internal difficulties which arise in a scattered empire. How to give a moral unity to vast countries separated from each other by half the globe, even when they are inhabited in the main by one nation! But even this is not the greatest of the anxieties of England. For besides the colonies, we have India. Here at least there is no community of race or of religion. Here that solid basis which is formed by immigration and colonisation is almost entirely wanting. Here you have another problem not less vast, not less difficult, and much less hopeful than that of the colonies. Either problem by itself is as much as any nation ever took in hand before. It seems really too much that both should fall on the same nation at the same time.

Consider how distracting must be the effect upon the public mind of these two opposite questions. The colonies and India are in opposite extremes. Whatever political maxims are most applicable to the one, are most inapplicable to the other. In the colonies everything is brand-new. There you have the most progressive race put in the circumstances most favourable to progress. There you have no past and an unbounded future. Government and institutions are all ultra-English. All is liberty, industry, invention, innovation, and as yet tranquillity. Now if this alone were Greater Britain, it would be homogeneous, all of a piece; and, vast and boundless as the territory is, we might come to understand its affairs. But there is at the same time another Greater Britain, surpassing this in population though not in territory, and it is everything which this is not. India is all past and, I may almost say, has no future. What it will come to the wisest man is afraid to conjecture, but in the past it opens vistas into a fabulous antiquity. All the oldest religions, all the oldest customs, petrified as it were. No form of popular government as yet possible. Everything which Europe, and still more the New World, has outlived still flourishing in full vigour; superstition, fatalism, polygamy, the most primitive priestcraft, the most primitive despotism; and threatening the northern frontier the vast Asiatic steppe with its Osbegs and Turcomans. Thus the same nation which reaches one hand towards the future of the globe and assumes the position of mediator between Europe and the New World, stretches the other hand towards the remotest past, becomes an Asiatic conqueror, and usurps the succession of the Great Mogul.

How can the same nation pursue two lines of policy so radically different without bewilderment, be despotic in Asia and democratic in Australia, be in the East at once the greatest Mussulman Power in the world and the guardian of the property of thousands of idol-temples, and at the same time in the West be the foremost champion of free thought and spiritual religion, stand out as a great military Imperialism to resist the march of Russia in Central Asia at the same time that it fills Queensland and Manitoba with free settlers? Never certainly did any nation, since the world began, assume anything like so much responsibility. Never did so many vast questions in all parts of the globe, questions calling for all sorts of special knowledge and special training, depend upon the decision of a single public. It must be confessed that this public bears its responsibility lightly! It does not even study colonial and Indian questions. It does not consider them interesting, except in those rare cases when they come to the foreground of politics. When the fate of a Ministry is concerned they are found intensely interesting, but the public does not consider them interesting so long as only the population of India, the destiny of a vast section of the planet, and the future of the English state itself, are concerned. As to India, Macaulay writes thus: 'It might have been expected that every Englishman who takes any interest in any part of history would be anxious to know how a handful of his countrymen separated from their home by an immense ocean, subjugated in the course of a few years one of the greatest empires in the world. Yet unless we greatly err, this subject is to most readers not only insipid but positively distasteful.'

The acquisition of India by England, as part of that expansion which in the last two centuries has so profoundly modified our state, will be examined in the succeeding lectures.

LECTURE II.

As formerly the Colonial Empire, so now the Indian Empire is to be considered only so far as it illustrates the general law of expansion which prevails in the modern part of English history. It will be considered not in itself, but only in its relation to our own state. It will be considered historically, that is, in the causes which produced it, but also politically, that is, in regard to its value or stability.

From this point of view we shall not find it convenient to observe chronological order. Our acquisition of India was made blindly. Nothing great that has ever been done by Englishmen was done so unintentionally, so accidentally, as the conquest of India. There has indeed been little enough of calculation or contrivance in our colonisation. When our first settlers went out to Virginia and New England, it was not intended to lay the foundations of a mighty republican state. But here the event has differed from the design only in degree. We did intend to establish a new community, and we even knew that it would be republican in its tendency; what was hidden from us was

12—2

only its immense magnitude. But in India we meant one thing, and did quite another. Our object was trade, and in this we were not particularly successful. War with the native states we did not think of at all till a hundred years after our first settlement, and then we thought only of such war as might support our trade; after this time again more than half a century passed before we thought of any considerable territorial acquisitions; the nineteenth century had almost begun before the policy of acquiring an ascendency over the native states was entered upon; and our present supreme position cannot be said to have been attained before the Governor-Generalship of Lord Dalhousie little more than a quarter of a century ago. All along we have been looking one way and moving another. In a case like this the chronological method of study is the worst that can be chosen. If we were to trace the history of the East India Company from year to year, carefully putting ourselves at the point of view of the Directors, we should be doing all in our power to blind ourselves. For it has not been the will of the Directors, but other forces overruling their will, forces against which they struggled in vain, by which the Indian Empire has been brought into existence. For this reason it is almost necessary, as for other reasons it is convenient, to begin at the other end, and before considering how the Empire grew to its present greatness to inquire what at the present moment it actually is.

We call this Empire a conquest, in order to mark the fact that it was not acquired in any degree by settlement or colonisation, but by a series of wars ending in cessions of territory by the native Powers to the East India Company. But let us be careful how we take for granted that it is a conquest in any more precise sense of the word.

Above I criticised the term 'possessions of England,' which is so commonly applied to the colonies. I asked, if by England be meant the people inhabiting England and by the colonies certain English people living beyond the sea, in what sense can one of these populations be said to belong to the other? Or if by England you mean the English Government, which is also ultimately the Government of the colonies, why should we speak of the subjects of a Government as its possession or property, unless indeed they became its subjects by conquest? Now this criticism does not directly apply to India, because India did come under the Queen's government by conquest. India therefore may be called a possession of England in a sense which is not applicable to the colonies. Nevertheless the word conquest, which, like most of the vocabulary of war, has come down to us from primitive barbaric times, may easily be misunderstood. We may still ask in what sense England can be said to possess India. What we possess we devote in some manner to our own enjoyment. If I own land, I either take the profits of the harvest, or, if I let the land to a farmer, I get rent from it. And in primitive times the conquest of a country was usually followed by possession in some literal sense. Sometimes the conquerors actually became landlords of the conquered territory or of part of it, as in that conquest of Palestine which we read of in the Book of Joshua, or in those Roman conquests where a certain extent of confiscated land was often granted out to a number of Roman citizens. Now assuredly India is not a conquered country in this sense. England has not seized lands in India, and after displacing the native proprietors assigned them to Englishmen.

There is another sense in which we may conceive the condition of a conquered country. We may think of it as tributary or paying tribute. Only we must be careful how we understand the expression. If it merely means that the people pay a tax, in other words that they meet the expense of their own government or of the army that protects their frontier, there is nothing in this peculiar to a conquered people. Almost every people in some form or other pays the expense of its own government. If the word 'tributary' is to be equivalent to 'conquered' or 'dependent,' it must mean paying something over and above the expense of its government. We have an example of such a tribute in modern Egypt. The government of Egypt is in the hands of a Khedive who pays himself handsomely out of the pockets of the people, but Egypt is tributary to the Sultan of Turkey, that is, it pays to him a sum which does not in any shape return to the country, but simply marks its relation of dependence upon the Sultan.

Such a tribute as this would mark that the country which paid it was a possession of the country which received it, because it seems analogous to the rent which a tenant farmer pays to the landowner. Is India then tributary in this sense to England? Certainly not, at least not directly or avowedly. Taxes are raised of course in India, as taxes are raised in England, but India is no more tributary than England itself. The money drawn from India is spent upon the government of India, and no money is levied beyond what is supposed to be necessary for this purpose.

Of course it may be and often has been argued that India is in many ways sacrificed to England, and in particular that money is under colourable pretexts extorted from her. I am not now concerned with this question, because I am inquiring simply what is the relation

established by law between India and England, and not
how far that relation may by abuse have been perverted.
India then is not a possession of England in the sense of
being legally tributary to England, any more than any of
our colonies are so.

The truth is that, though the present relation between
India and England was historically created by war, yet
England does not, at least openly, claim any rights over
India in virtue of this fact.   In the Queen's proclamation
of November 1st, 1858, by which the open assumption of
the government by the Queen was announced, occur the
express words 'We hold ourselves bound to the natives
of our Indian territories by the same obligations of duty
which bind us to all our other subjects.'   That is, conquest
confers no peculiar rights, or India is not for practical
purposes a conquered country.

In fact, though the advance of civilisation has not
as yet abolished wars nor even perhaps diminished the
frequency of them, yet it has very much transformed
their character.   Conquest is nominally still possible, but
the word has changed its meaning.   It does not now mean
spoliation or the acquisition of any oppressive lordship, so
that the temptation to make conquests is now very much
diminished.   Thus our possession of India imposes upon
us vast and almost intolerable responsibilities; this is
evident; but it is not at once evident that we reap any
benefit from it.

We must therefore dismiss from our minds the idea
that India is in any practical sense of the word a possession of England.   In ordinary language the two notions of
property and government are mixed up in a way that
produces infinite confusion.   When we speak of India as
'our magnificent dependency' or 'the brightest jewel in

the English diadem,' we use metaphors which have come
down to us from primitive ages and from a state of society
which has long passed away. India does indeed depend
on England in the sense that England determines her
condition and her policy and that she is governed by
Englishmen, but not in the sense that she renders service
to England or makes England directly richer or more
powerful. And thus with respect to India as with respect
to the colonies the question confronts us on the threshold
of the subject, What is the use of it ? Why do we take
the trouble and involve ourselves in the anxiety and
responsibility of governing two hundred millions of people
in Asia ?

Now in respect to the colonies I argued that this
question, however naturally it may suggest itself, is perverse,
unless it can be shown that our colonies are too remote
either to give or receive any advantage from their
connexion with us. For they are of our own blood, a mere
extension of the English nationality into new lands. If
these lands were contiguous to England, it would seem a
matter of course that the English population as it increases
should occupy them, and evidently desirable that it should
do so without a political separation. As they are not
contiguous but remote, a certain difficulty arises, but it is
a difficulty which in these days of steam and electricity
does not seem insurmountable. Now you see that this
argument rests entirely upon the community of blood
between England and her colonies. It does not therefore
apply to India. Two races could scarcely be more alien
from each other than the English and the Hindus.
Comparative philology has indeed discovered one link that
had never been suspected before. The language of the
prevalent race of India is indeed of the same family as

our own language.   But in every other respect there is
extreme alienation.   Their traditions do not touch ours at
any point.   Their religion is further removed from our
own even than Mohammedanism.

Our colonies, as I pointed out, were in the main planted
in the emptier parts of the globe, so that their population
is for the most part either entirely English or predominantly so.   I pointed out that this was not the case with
the colonies of Spain in Central and Southern America,
where the Spanish settlers lived in the midst of a larger
population of native Indians, whom they reduced to a kind
of serfdom.   Here then are two kinds of dependency, of
which the one is much more closely cognate to the mother
country than the other.   But both are connected by real
ties of blood with the mother country.   Now India belongs
to neither class, because its population has no tie of blood
whatever with the population of England.   Even if colonies
had gone out from England to India, they must have
continued insignificant in comparison to the enormous
native population; but there have been no such colonies.
England is separated from India by one of the strongest
barriers that nature could set up between the two countries.
Nature has made the colonisation of India by Englishmen
impossible by giving her a climate in which, as a rule,
English children cannot grow up.

And thus, while the connexion of England with her
colonies is in the highest degree natural, her connexion
with India seems at first sight at least to be in the highest
degree unnatural.   There is no natural tie whatever
between the two countries.   No community of blood; no
community of religion, for we come as Christians into
a population divided between Brahminism and Mohammedanism.   And lastly no community of interest, except

so much as there must be between all countries, viz. the interest that each has to receive the commodities of the other. For otherwise what interest can England and India have in common? The interests of England lie in Europe and in the New World. India, so far as so isolated a country can have foreign interests at all, looks towards Afghanistan, Persia and Central Asia, countries with which except through India we should scarcely ever have had any communication.

The English conquest of India has produced results even more strange than the Spanish conquest of America, though the circumstances of it were, I think, considerably less astonishing and romantic. Whether we think of it with satisfaction or not, it is the most striking and remarkable incident in the modern part of the history of England. In a history of modern England it deserves a prominent place in the main narrative, and not the mere digression or occasional notice which our historians commonly assign to it. But how important it is we shall not see so long as we only consider its strangeness; we must also bear in mind its enormous magnitude. Much has been written to show the immensity of the task we have undertaken in India; yet with surprisingly little effect. Figures seem only to paralyse the imagination when they pass a certain magnitude, and thus while in our domestic politics we grow the more interested the larger the question at issue is shown to be, we cease to be interested when our Empire with its much vaster questions is brought before us. Point out that this Indian Empire is something like what the Roman Empire was at its greatest extension, and that we are responsible for it; the only effect produced is a disinclination to attend to the subject. Can we seriously justify this? I fancy we are in some degree misled by an impres-

sion that in the outlying parts of the world large dimensions
are a matter of course and make no difference. Thus if
India is large, Canada and Australia are still larger, and yet
we do not find that the affairs of Canada and Australia
require much of our attention. True, but we overlook an
important distinction. In Canada and Australia the territory
is vast, but the population exceedingly small; the country
also is not merely distant from us, as India is, but also
distant from all the great Powers with which we might
possibly engage in war. India really belongs to quite a
different category of countries. It is a country as populous
and in some large regions more populous than the most
thickly peopled parts of Europe. It is a country in which
we have over and over again had to wage war on a grand
scale. Thus in the second Mahratta war of 1818 Lord
Hastings brought into the field more than a hundred
thousand men. And, distant as it may seem, it is by no
means out of the range of European politics. Thus throughout the eighteenth century it was part of the chess-board
on which France and England played out their game of
skill. Again since about 1830 India, and India almost
alone, has involved us in differences with Russia, and given
us a most intimate interest in the solution of the Eastern
Question.

India therefore is rather to be compared to the
countries of Europe than to the outlying, thinly peopled
countries of the New World. Let us then contemplate a
little the magnitude of this Empire, and take some pains
to realise it by comparing it to other magnitudes with
which we are familiar. Let us think then of Europe
without Russia, that is, of all that system of countries
which a few centuries ago formed almost the whole scene
of civilised history, all the European countries of the

Roman Empire *plus* the whole of Germany, the Slavonic
countries which are outside Russia, and the Scandinavian
countries.   India may be roughly said to be about equal
both in area and population to all these countries taken
together.   This Empire, which we now govern from Downing Street and whose budget forms the annual annoyance
and despair of the House of Commons, is considerably
larger and more populous than the Empire of Napoleon
when it had reached its utmost extent.   And, as I have
said already, it is an Empire of the same kind, not some
vast empty region like the old Spanish Dominion in South
America, but a crowded territory with an ancient civilisation, with languages, religions, philosophies and literatures
of its own.

I think perhaps it may assist conception if I split up
this immense total into parts.   The reason, no doubt, why
the thought of all Europe together impresses us so much,
is that there passes before the mind a series of six or seven
great states which must be added together to make up
Europe.   Our conception of Europe is the sum of our
conceptions of England, France, Germany, Austria, Italy,
Spain, and Greece.   Perhaps the name India would strike
as majestically upon the ear, if in like manner it were to
us the name of a grand complex total. Let me say then that
in the first place it has one region which in population far
exceeds any European State except Russia, and exceeds
the United States.   This is the region governed by the
Lieutenant-Governor of Bengal.   Its population is stated
actually to exceed 66,000,000 on an area considerably less
than that of France.   Then come two other regions which
may be compared with European States.   These are the
North West Provinces, which answer pretty well to Great
Britain without Ireland, being in area somewhat smaller,

but somewhat more populous. Next comes the Madras Presidency, larger in area—being about equal to Great Britain with Ireland—but less populous, being about equal in population to the Kingdom of Italy. The population in all these three cases rises far above 20,000,000. Then come two provinces in which it approaches 20,000,000, the Punjab, which is somewhat superior in population to Spain, and the Bombay Presidency which is slightly inferior, though in area it is equal to Great Britain and Ireland. In the next class come Oude, which is rather superior, and the Central Provinces, which are about equal, to Belgium and Holland taken together. These provinces, together with some others of less importance, make up that part of India which is directly under English government. But the region which is practically under English supremacy is still larger. When we speak of the Empire of Napoleon, we do not think only of the territory directly governed by his officials; we reckon-in States nominally sovereign, which were practically under his ascendancy. Thus the Confederation of the Rhine consisted of a number of German states, which had by a formal act consented to regard Napoleon as their Protector. Now England has a similar dependent confederation in India, and this makes an additional item which, reckoned by population, is superior to the United States.

Is it possible that besides our terrible hive of population at home, giving rise to most anxious politics, and besides our vast colonial Empire, we are also responsible for another Empire densely peopled and about equal to Europe? Is it possible that about this Empire we neither have, nor care to acquire, the most rudimentary information? Would it be possible for us, even if we did try to acquire such information, to form a rational opinion about affairs so remote and complicated?

There have been great Empires before now, but the government of them has generally been in the hands of a few experts. Rome was forced to commit her Empire to the care of a single irresponsible statesman, and could not even reserve for herself her old civic liberties. In the United States we do indeed see a boundless dominion successfully guided under a democratic system. But the territory in this case, extensive though it be, is all compact and continuous, and the population however large it may come to be, will still be in the main homogeneous. If the United States should come into the possession of countries separated from her by the sea and of different nationality, her position in the world would be at once essentially altered. What is unprecedented in the relation of England to India is the attempt to rule, not merely by experts, but by a system founded on public opinion, a population not merely distant, but wholly alien, wholly unlike in ways of thinking, to the sovereign public. Public opinion is necessarily guided by a few large, plain, simple ideas. When the great interests of the country are plain and the great maxims of its government unmistakable, it may be able to judge securely even in questions of vast magnitude. But public opinion is liable to be bewildered when it is called on to enter into subtleties, draw nice distinctions, apply one set of principles here and another set there. Such bewilderment our Indian Empire produces. It is so different in kind both from England itself and from the Colonial Empire that it requires wholly different principles of policy. And therefore public opinion does not know what to make of it, but looks with blank indignation and despair upon a Government which seems utterly un-English, which is bureaucratic and in the hands of a ruling race, which rests mainly on military force, which raises its revenue, not in the European fashion, but by monopolies of salt and opium and by taking the place of a universal landlord, and in a hundred other ways departs from the traditions of England.

And it may be asked, For what end? As I have remarked, the connexion itself is not directly profitable to England. We must look therefore to advantages which may come to us from it indirectly. We find then that the trade between the two countries has gradually grown to be very great indeed. The loss of the Indian trade which might follow if the country fell again into anarchy or under a Government which closed its harbours to our merchants, would amount to £60,000,000 annually. But we are to set over against this advantage the great burden which is imposed by India upon our foreign policy. In the present state of the world a dependency held by military force may easily be like a mill-stone round the neck of a nation. For it may lock up an army which the nation may grievously need for other purposes or even for defence. We all conceive with what satisfaction Bismarck at the present moment sees France undertaking schemes of conquest in Africa and Asia. Now if England, which is not a military state, had in reality to hold down by English military force a population of two hundred millions, it is needless to say that such a burden would overwhelm us. This is not so, owing to a fundamental peculiarity of the Indian Empire, upon which I shall enlarge later, the peculiarity namely that in the main England conquered India and now keeps it by means of Indian troops paid with Indian money. We keep there only an English army of 65,000 men. But this is by no means the whole of the burden which India lays upon us. India, at the same time that she locks up an army, more than doubles the difficulty of our foreign policy. The supreme happiness for a country of course is to be self-contained, to have no need to inquire what other nations are doing. Very wisely did Washington advise his countrymen to retain this happiness as long as they could. England cannot well enjoy it, but if she did not possess India she might enjoy it comparatively. Her colonies as yet have for the most part only peaceful or insignificant or barbarous neighbours, and our old close interest in European struggles has passed away. But we continue to be anxiously interested in the East. Every movement in Turkey, every new symptom in Egypt, any stirring in Persia or Transoxiana or Burmah or Afghanistan, we are obliged to watch with vigilance. The reason is that we have possession of India. Owing to this we have a leading position in the system of Asiatic Powers, and a leading interest in the affairs of all those countries which lie upon the route to India. This and this only involves us in that permanent rivalry with Russia, which is to England in the nineteenth century what the competition with France for the New World was to her in the eighteenth.

My object in this lecture is to lay before you the Indian question in its broad outlines. I have put together at the outset some considerations which might incline us to take an anxious or desponding view of it. If it is doubtful whether we reap any balance of advantage from our Indian Empire, and if it is not doubtful that it involves us in enormous responsibilities and confuses our minds with problems of hopeless difficulty, may we not feel tempted to exclaim that it was an evil hour for England when the daring genius of Clive turned a trading company into a political Power, and inaugurated a hundred years of continuous conquest? Must we not at least hold, as many among the distinguished statesmen who have devoted their lives to Indian affairs have held, that the Empire is ephemeral, and that the time is not far off when we must withdraw from the country?

On the other hand the wisest men may easily be mistaken when they speculate on such a subject. The end of our Indian Empire is perhaps almost as much beyond calculation as the beginning of it. There is no analogy in history either for one or the other. If the government of India from a remote island seems a thing which can never be permanent, we know that it once seemed a thing which could never take place, until it did take place. At any rate if the Empire is to fall, we ought to be able to point already to proofs of its decline. Proofs certainly we can show of the immense difficulties it has to contend with, but scarcely symptoms of anything which can be called decline. And again if we should admit, or not deny, that England has not been repaid in any way for the trouble that this dependency has cost her, the admission by itself would have no practical importance. Between such an admission and any practical project, such as that of abandoning the Empire, there is a gulf fixed.

It is possible to hold that England would be better off now had she founded no such Empire at all, had she remained standing, as a mere merchant, on the threshold of India, as she stands now on that of China. But the abandonment of India is an idea which even those who believe that we shall one day be driven to it are not accustomed to contemplate as a practical scheme. There are some deeds which, though they had been better not done, cannot be undone. A time may conceivably

S. L.   13

come when it may be practicable to leave India to
herself, but for the present it is necessary to govern her
as if we were to govern her for ever. Why so? Not
mainly on our own account. Some tell us that our
honour requires us to maintain the acquisition which our
fathers made with their blood, and which is the great
military trophy of the nation. To my mind there is
something monstrous in all such notions of honour; they
belong to that primitive and utterly obsolete class of
notions, of which I have spoken before, which rest upon a
confusion between the ideas of government and property.
Nothing is to be considered for a moment but the well-
being of India and England, and of the two countries
India, as being by much the more nearly interested, by
much the larger, and by much the poorer, is to be considered before England. But on these very principles,
and especially on account of the interest of India, it is
impossible for the present to think of abandoning the
task we have undertaken there. We might do so if our
own interest alone were considered. Not that it would
be easy, now that such a vast trade has grown up and such
vast sums of English money, particularly in these latest
years, have been invested in the country. But it would be
possible. On the other hand if we consider the interest
of India, it appears wholly impossible. Much may be
plausibly alleged against the system under which we
govern India. It may be doubted whether it is altogether
suited to the people, whether it is not needlessly expensive,
and so forth. We may feel a reasonable anxiety as to
what will come in the end of this unparalleled experiment.
But I think it would be a very extreme view to deny that
our Government is better than any other which has existed
in India since the Mussulman conquest. If it should

ultimately fail more than any one imagines, we could
never leave the country in a state half so deplorable as
that in which we found it. A very moderately good
Government is incomparably better than none. The
sudden withdrawal even of an oppressive Government
is a dangerous experiment. Some countries, no doubt,
there are, which might pass through such a trial without
falling into anarchy. Thinly peopled countries, or countries whose inhabitants had been long accustomed to
much freedom of action, might be trusted to devise for
themselves very speedily as much government as might
be necessary. But what a mockery to lay down such pro-
positions with India in view! When we began to take
possession of the country, it was already in a state of
wild anarchy such as Europe has perhaps never known.
What government it had was pretty invariably despotic,
and was generally in the hands of military adventurers,
depending on a soldiery composed of bandits whose whole
vocation was plunder. The Mahratta Power covered the
greater part of India and threatened at once Delhi
and Calcutta, while it had its head-quarters at Poonah,
and yet this power was but an organisation of pillage.
Meanwhile in the North Nadir Shah rivalled Attila or
Tamerlane in his devastating expeditions. It may be
said that this was only a passing anarchy produced by the
dissolution of the Mogul Empire. Even so, it would show
that India is not a country which can endure the withdrawal of Government. But have we not a somewhat
exaggerated idea of the Mogul Empire? Its greatness
was extremely shortlived, and in the Deccan it seems
never really to have established itself. The anarchy
which Clive and Hastings found in India was not so
exceptional a state of things as it might seem. Probably

13—2

it was much more intense at that moment than ever before, but a condition of anarchy seems almost to have been chronic in India since Mahmoud, and to have been but suspended for a while in the Northern half by Akber and Shah Jehan.

India then is of all countries that which is least capable of evolving out of itself a stable Government. And it is to be feared that our rule may have diminished what little power of this sort it may have originally possessed. For our supremacy has necessarily depressed those classes which had anything of the talent or habit of government. The old royal races, the noble classes, and in particular the Mussulmans who formed the bulk of the official class under the Great Moguls, have suffered most and benefited least from our rule. This decay is the staple topic of lamentation among those who take a dark view of our Empire; but is it not an additional reason why the Empire should continue? Then think of the immense magnitude of the country; think too that we have undermined all fixed moral and religious ideas in the intellectual classes by introducing the science of the West into the midst of Brahminical traditions. When you have made all these reflexions, you will see that to withdraw our Government from a country which is dependent on it and which we have made incapable of depending upon anything else, would be the most inexcusable of all conceivable crimes and might possibly cause the most stupendous of all conceivable calamities.

Such then in its broad outline is the Indian Question of the present day. In what way did such a question grow up? How did we come into possession of a dependency so enormous?

LECTURE III.

THE question how we conquered India does not at all resemble the questions which I raised in the last course. Our colonists in the new world occupied, to be sure, a vast territory, but it was comparatively an empty territory. The difficulties they encountered arose not so much from the natives, as from the rivalry of other European nations. By what degrees and from what causes we gained the advantage over these rivals, I partly discussed. It was a question to which the answer was not at once obvious, but at the same time not extremely difficult to find. On the other hand it is at first sight extremely perplexing to understand how we could conquer India. Here the population was dense, and its civilisation, though descending along a different stream of tradition, was as real and ancient as our own. We have learnt from many instances in European history to think it almost impossible really to conquer an intelligent people wholly alien in language and religion from its invaders. The whole power of Spain could not in eighty years conquer the Dutch provinces with their petty population. The Swiss could not be conquered in old time, nor the Greeks the other day. Nay, at the very time when we made the first steps in the conquest of India, we showed ourselves wholly unable to reduce to obedience three millions of our own race in America, who had thrown off their allegiance to the English Crown. What a singular contrast is here! Never did the English show so much languid incompetence as in the American War, so that it might have seemed evident that their age of greatness was over, and that the decline of England had begun. But precisely at this time they were appearing as irresistible conquerors in India, and showing a superiority which led them to fancy themselves a nation of heroes. How is the contradiction to be explained?

History is studied with so little seriousness, with so little desire or expectation of arriving at any solid result, that the contradiction passes almost unremarked, or at most gives occasion to a triumphant reflexion that after all there was life in us yet. And indeed it may seem that, however difficult of explanation the fact may be, there can be no doubt of it. Over and over again in India, at Plassey, at Assaye, and on a hundred other battle-fields, our troops have been victorious against great odds, so that here at least it seems that we may indulge our national self-complacency without restraint, and feel that at any rate in comparison with the Hindu races we really are terrible fellows!

But does this hypothesis really remove the difficulty? Suppose that one Englishman is really equal as a soldier to ten or twenty Hindus, can we even then conceive the whole of India conquered by the English? There were not more than twelve millions of Englishmen at the time when the conquest began, and it was made in a period when England had other wars on her hands. Clive's career falls partly in the Seven Years' War of Europe, and the great annexations of Lord Wellesley were made in the midst of our war with Napoleon. We are not a military state. We did not in those times profess to be able to put on foot at any moment a great expeditionary army. Accordingly in our European wars we usually confined ourselves to acting with our fleet, while for hostilities on land it was our practice to subsidise any ally we might have among the military states, at one time Austria, at another Prussia. How then in spite of all this weakness by land could we manage to conquer during this time the greater part of India, an enormous region of nearly a million square miles and inhabited by two hundred millions of people? What a drain such a work must have made upon our military force, what a drain upon our treasury! And yet somehow the drain seems never to have been perceived. Our European wars involved us in a debt that we have never been able to pay. But our Indian wars have not swelled the National Debt. The exertions we had to make there seem to have left no trace behind them.

It seems then that there must be something wrong in the conception which is current, that a number of soldiers went over from England to India and there by sheer superiority in valour and intelligence conquered the whole country. In the last great Mahratta war of 1818 we had, it appears, more than a hundred thousand men in the field. But what! that was the time of mortal exhaustion that succeeded the great Napoleonic War. Is it possible that only three years after the battle of Waterloo we were at war again on a vast scale and had a much greater army in India than Lord Wellington had in Spain? Again at the present moment the army kept in foot in India amounts to two hundred thousand men. What! two

hundred thousand English soldiers! And yet we are not a
military State!

You see of course what the fact is that I point at.
This Indian army, we all know, does not consist of English
soldiers, but mainly of native troops.   Out of 200,000 only
65,000, or less than a third, are English.   And even this
proportion has only been established since the mutiny,
after which catastrophe the English troops were increased
and the native troops diminished in number.   Thus I find
that at the time of the mutiny there were 45,000 European
troops to 235,000 native troops in India, that is, less than
a fifth.   In 1808 again I find only 25,000 Englishmen to
130,000 natives, that is, somewhat less than a fifth.   The
same proportion obtained in 1773 at the time of the
Regulating Act, when British India first took shape.
At that date the Company's army consisted of 9000
Europeans and 45,000 natives.   Before that I find the
proportion of Europeans even lower, about a seventh; and
if we go back to the very beginning we find that from the
first the Indian army was rather a native than a European
force.   Thus Colonel Chesney opens his historical view of
it in these words: 'The first establishment of the
Company's Indian Army may be considered to date from
the year 1748, when a small body of sepoys was raised at
Madras after the example set by the French, for the
defence of that settlement....At the same time a small
European force was raised, formed of such sailors as could
be spared from the ships on the coast and of men
smuggled on board the Company's vessels in England by
the crimps.'

In the early battles of the Company by which its
power was decisively established, at the siege of Arcot,
at Plassey, at Buxar, there seem almost always to

have been more sepoys than Europeans on the side of the Company. And let us observe further that we do not hear of the sepoys as fighting ill, or of the English as bearing the whole brunt of the conflict. No one who has remarked the childish eagerness with which historians indulge their national vanity, will be surprised to find that our English writers in describing these battles seem unable to discern the sepoys. Read Macaulay's Essay on Clive; everywhere it is 'the imperial people,' 'the mighty children of the sea,' 'none could resist Clive and his Englishmen.' But if once it is admitted that the sepoys always outnumbered the English, and that they kept pace with the English in efficiency as soldiers, the whole theory which attributes our successes to an immeasurable natural superiority in valour falls to the ground. In those battles in which our troops were to the enemy as one to ten, it will appear that if we may say that one Englishman showed himself equal to ten natives, we may also say that one sepoy did the same. It follows that, though no doubt there was a difference, it was not so much a difference of race as a difference of discipline, of military science, and also no doubt in many cases a difference of leadership.

Observe that Mill's summary explanation of the conquest of India says nothing of any natural superiority on the part of the English. 'The two important discoveries for conquering India were: 1st, the weakness of the native armies against European discipline, 2dly, the facility of imparting that discipline to natives in the European service.' He adds: 'Both discoveries were made by the French.'

And even if we should admit that the English fought better than the sepoys, and took more than their share in those achievements which both performed in common, it

remains entirely incorrect to speak of the English nation
as having conquered the nations of India. The nations of
India have been conquered by an army of which on the
average about a fifth part was English. But we not only
exaggerate our own share in the achievement; we at
the same time entirely misconceive and misdescribe the
achievement itself. For from what race were the other
four-fifths of the army drawn? From the natives of India
themselves! India can hardly be said to have been conquered at all by foreigners; she has rather conquered
herself. If we were justified, which we are not, in personi-
fying India as we personify France or England, we could
not describe her as overwhelmed by a foreign enemy; we
should rather have to say that she elected to put an
end to anarchy by submitting to a single Government, even
though that Government was in the hands of foreigners.

But that description would be as false and misleading
as the other, or as any expression which presupposes India
to have been a conscious political whole. The truth is
that there was no India in the political, and scarcely in
any other, sense. The word was a geographical expression, and therefore India was easily conquered, just as
Italy and Germany fell an easy prey to Napoleon, because
there was no Italy and no Germany, and not even any
strong Italian or German national feeling. Because there
was no Germany, Napoleon was able to set one German
state against another, so that in fighting with Austria or
Prussia he had Bavaria and Württemberg for allies. As
Napoleon saw that this means of conquest lay ready to
his hand in Central Europe, so the Frenchman Dupleix
early perceived that this road to empire in India lay
open to any European state that might have factories
there. He saw a condition of chronic war between one

Indian state and another, and he perceived that by interfering in their quarrels the foreigner might arrive to hold
the balance between them.   He acted upon this view, and
accordingly the whole history of European Empire in India
begins with the interference of the French in the war of
succession in Hyderabad that broke out on the death of
the great Nizam ul Mulk (1748).

The fundamental fact then is that India had no
jealousy of the foreigner, because India had no sense whatever of national unity, because there *was* no India and
therefore, properly speaking, no foreigner.   So far, as I
have pointed out, parallel examples may be found in
Europe.   But we must imagine a much greater degree of
political deadness in India than in Germany eighty years
ago, if we would understand the fact now under consideration, the fact namely that the English conquered India by
means of a Sepoy army.   In Germany there was scarcely
any German feeling, but there was a certain amount, though
not a very great amount, of Prussian feeling, Austrian
feeling, Bavarian feeling, Suabian feeling.   Napoleon is
able to set Bavaria against Austria or both against Prussia,
but he does not attempt to set Bavaria or Austria or
Prussia against itself.   To speak more distinctly, he
procures by treaties that the Elector of Bavaria shall
furnish a contingent to the army which he leads against
Austria; but he does not, simply by offering pay, raise an
army of Germans and then use them in the conquest of
Germany.   This would be the exact parallel to what has
been witnessed in India.   A parallel to the fact that India
has been conquered by an army of which four-fifths were
natives and only one-fifth English, would be found in
Europe, if England had invaded France and then by offering good pay had raised an army of Frenchmen large

enough to conquer the country. The very idea seems
monstrous. What! you exclaim, an army of Frenchmen
quietly undertake to make war upon France! And yet, if
you reflect, you will see that such a thing is abstractedly
quite possible, and that it might have been witnessed if
the past history of France had been different. We can
imagine that a national feeling had never sprung up in
France; this we can easily imagine, because we know that
the twelfth century is full of wars between a king who
reigned at Paris and another who reigned at Rouen. But
let us imagine further that the different Governments
established in different parts of France were mostly foreign
Governments, that in fact the country had been conquered
before and was still living under the yoke of foreign rulers.
We can well understand that if in a country thus broken
to the foreign yoke a disturbed state of affairs supervened,
making mercenary war a lucrative profession, such a
country might come to be full of professional soldiers
equally ready to take service with any Government and
against any Government, native or foreign.

Now the condition of India was such as this. The
English did not introduce a foreign domination into it, for
the foreign domination was there already. In fact we
bring to the subject a fixed misconception. The homogeneous European community, a definite territory possessed
by a definite race, in one word, the Nation-State, though
we assume it as if it were a matter of course, is in fact
much more exceptional than we suppose, and yet it is upon
the assumption of such a homogeneous community that all
our ideas of patriotism and public virtue depend. The
idea of nationality seems in India to be thoroughly confused. The distinction of national and foreign seems to be
lost. Not only has a tide of Mussulman invasion covered

the country ever since the eleventh century, but even if we go back to the earliest times we still find a mixture of races, a domination of race by race. That Aryan, Sanscrit-speaking race which, as the creators of Brahminism, have given to India whatever unity it can be said to have, appear themselves as invaders, and as invaders who have not succeeded in swallowing up and absorbing the older nationalities. The older, not Indo-Germanic race, has in Europe almost disappeared, and at any rate has left no trace in our European languages, but in India the older stratum is everywhere visible. The spoken languages there are not mere corruptions of Sanscrit, but mixtures of Sanscrit with older languages wholly different, and in the south not Sanscrit at all. Brahminism too, which at first sight seems universal, turns out on examination to be a mere vague eclecticism, which has given a show of unity to superstitions wholly unlike and unrelated to each other. It follows that in India the fundamental postulate cannot be granted, upon which the whole political ethics of the West depend. The homogeneous community does not exist there, out of which the State properly so called arises. Indeed to satisfy ourselves of this it is not necessary to travel so far back into the past. It is enough to notice that since the time of Mahmoud of Ghazni a steady stream of Mussulman invasion has poured into India. The majority of the Governments of India were Mussulman long before the arrival of the Mogul in the sixteenth century. From this time therefore in most of the Indian States the tie of nationality was broken. Government ceased to rest upon right; the State lost its right to appeal to patriotism.

In such a state of affairs what is called the conquest of India by the English can be explained without supposing

the natives of India to be below other races, just as it
does not force us to regard the English as superior to other
races. We regard it as the duty of a man to fight for his
country against the foreigner. But what is a man's
country ? When we analyse the notion, we find it presupposes the man to have been bred up in a community
which may be regarded as a great family, so that it is
natural for him to think of the land itself as a mother.
But if the community has not been at all of the nature of
a family, but has been composed of two or three races
hating each other, if not the country, but at most the
village has been regarded as a home, then it is not the
fault of the natives of it that they have no patriotism but
village-patriotism. It is one thing to receive a foreign
yoke for the first time, and quite a different thing to
exchange one foreign yoke for another.

But, as I have pointed out, the surprising feature in the
English conquest of India is not so much that it should
have been made, as that it should have cost England no
effort and no trouble. The English people have not paid
taxes, the English Government has not opened loans, no
conscription was ever introduced, nay no drain of men was
ever perceived, and no difficulty was ever felt in carrying
on other wars at the same time, because we were engaged
in conquering a population equal to that of Europe. This
seems at first sight incredible, but I have already given the
explanation of it. As to the finance of all these wars, it
falls under the general principle which applies to all wars
of conquest. Conquest pays its own expenses. As
Napoleon had never any financial difficulties, because he
lived at the expense of those whom he vanquished in war,
so the conquest of India was made, as a matter of course,
at the expense of India. The only difficulty then is to

understand how the army could be created. And this difficulty too disappears, when we observe that four-fifths of this army was always composed of native troops.

If we fix our attention upon this all-important fact we shall be led, if I mistake not, to perceive that the expression 'conquest', as applied to the acquisition of sovereignty by the East India Company in India, is not merely loose but thoroughly misleading, and tempts us to class the event among events which it in no way resembles. I have indeed remarked more than once before that this expression, whenever it is used, requires far more definition than it commonly receives, and that it may bear several different meanings. But surely the word is only applicable at all when it refers to some action done to one state by another. There is war between two states; the army of the one state invades the other and overturns the Government of it, or at least forces the Government to such humiliating terms that it is practically deprived of its independence; this is conquest in the proper sense. Now when we say that England has conquered India, we ought to mean that something of this sort has happened between England and India. When Alexander the Great conquered the Persian Empire, there was war between the Macedonian state and the Persian, in which the latter was subjugated. When Caesar conquered Gaul, he acted in the name of the Roman Republic, holding an office conferred on him by the senate and commanding the army of the Roman state. But nothing of this sort happened in India. The King of England did not declare war upon the Great Mogul or upon any Nawab or Rajah in India. The English state would perhaps have had no concern from first to last in the conquest of India but for this circumstance, that it engaged five times in war with

France after the French settlements in India had become considerable, and that these wars, being partly waged in India, were in a certain degree mixed up with the wars between the East India Company and the native Powers of India. If we wish clearly to understand the nature of the phenomenon, we ought to put this circumstance, which was accidental, on one side. We shall then see that nothing like what is strictly called a conquest took place, but that certain traders inhabiting certain seaport towns in India, were induced, almost forced, in the anarchy caused by the fall of the Mogul Empire, to give themselves a military character and employ troops, that by means of these troops they acquired territory and at last almost all the territory of India, and that these traders happened to be Englishmen, and to employ a certain, though not a large, proportion of English troops in their army.

Now this is not a foreign conquest, but rather an internal revolution. In any country when government breaks down and anarchy sets in, the general law is that a struggle follows between such organised powers as remain in the country, and that the most powerful of these sets up a Government. In France for instance after the fall of the House of Bourbon in 1792 a new Government was set up chiefly through the influence of the Municipality of Paris; this Government having fallen into discredit a few years later was superseded by a military Government wielded by Bonaparte. Now India about 1750 was in a condition of anarchy caused by a decay in the Mogul Empire, which had begun at the death of Aurungzebe in 1707. The imperial authority having everywhere lost its force over so vast a territory, the general law began to operate. Everywhere the minor organised powers began to make themselves supreme. These powers, after the fashion of India, were most commonly mercenary bands of soldiers, commanded either by some provincial governor of the falling Empire, or by some adventurer who seized an opportunity of rising to the command of them, or lastly by some local power which had existed before the establishment of the Mogul supremacy and had never completely yielded to it. To give an example of each kind of power, the state of Hyderabad was founded by the satrap of the Great Mogul called the Nizam, the state of Mysore was founded by the Mussulman adventurer Hyder Ali, who rose from the ranks by mere military ability, the great Mahratta confederacy of chieftains headed by the Peishwa, a Brahminical not a Mussulman Power, represented the older India of the time before the Mogul. But all these powers alike subsisted by means of mercenary armies, they lived in a state of chronic war and mutual plunder such as, I suppose, has hardly been witnessed in Europe except perhaps in the dissolution of the Carolingian Empire.

Such a state of affairs was peculiarly favourable to the rise of new powers. In other circumstances conquest presupposes what I may call a capital fund of power. No one can undertake it that does not already possess a recognised authority and an army. In those circumstances it was otherwise. Hyder Ali had nothing but his head and his right arm, and he became Sultan of Mysore. For mercenary armies were everywhere; they were at the service of every one who could pay them or win an influence over them; and any one who commanded a mercenary army was on a level with the greatest potentates of India, since in the dissolution of authority the only force left was military force.

Now among the different local powers in India, which in such peculiar circumstances might strike for empire

with some chance of success, were certain merchants who
had factories in the seaport towns. They were foreigners
indeed, but, as I have pointed out, this could make no
difference in India, where most Governments were foreign,
where the Great Mogul himself was a foreigner. Much
rhetoric has been spent on the miraculousness of the
fortune of the East India Company. It is true that there
had been no previous example of such a fortune, and that
for this reason it would not have occurred to any one to
predict such a fortune. But it was not miraculous in the
sense of being hard to account for or having no visible
cause. For the East India Company had really some
capital to start with. It had a command of money, it had
two or three fortresses, the command of the sea, and it
had the advantage of being a corporation, that is, it was
not liable to be killed in battle or to die of a fever.
We are not much astonished when an individual rises
from some private station into empire over a great
territory, because this has happened often. And yet
intrinsically it is much more astonishing. That the
younger son of a poor nobleman in Corsica should control
the greater part of Europe with despotic power, is intrinsically far more wonderful than that the East India
Company should conquer India, for Bonaparte began
without interest, without friends, without a penny in his
pocket, and yet he not only gained his empire but lost
it again in less than twenty years. In like manner the
rise of Hyder Ali, or of Scindiah, or of Holkar, was more
wonderful and demanded more of the special favour of
fortune than the rise of the East India Company. You
see that I wish you to place this event in a different class
of events from that in which it is commonly placed.
It is not the conquest of one state by another. It is

not an event in which two states are concerned, at least directly ; it is not an event belonging to the foreign department. It is an internal revolution in Indian society, and is to be compared to one of those sudden usurpations or *coups d'état*, by which a period of disturbance within a community is closed. Let us imagine for a moment that the merchants who rose to power had not been foreign at all, the nature of the event is not thereby altered. We may suppose that a number of Parsee merchants in Bombay, tired of the anarchy which disturbed their trade, had subscribed together to establish fortresses and raise troops, and then that they had had the good fortune to employ able generals. In that case they too might have had their Plassey and their Buxar; they too might have extorted from the Great Mogul the Dewannee, or financial administration of a province, and so laid the foundations of an Empire, which might in time have extended over all India. In that case we should have had substantially the same event, but it would have appeared clearly in its true light. We should have recognised it as having the nature of an internal revolution, as being the effect of the natural struggle which every community makes to put down the anarchy which is tearing it to pieces.

In such an event as that there would have been nothing very miraculous, and yet the rise of the East India Company was much less miraculous. For the Company was closely connected with Europe, and could call in the military science and discipline of Europe, which was evidently superior to that of India. That same Frenchman Dupleix, who laid down so clearly the theory of the conquest of India, perceived that the native armies could not for a moment stand before European troops.

14—2

but he perceived also that the native of India was quite
capable of receiving European discipline and learning to
fight with European efficiency. This then was the talis-
man which the Company possessed, and which enabled it
not merely to hold its own among the Powers of India but
to surpass them,—not some incommunicable physical or
moral superiority, as we love to imagine—but a superior
discipline and military system, which *could* be communi-
cated to the natives of India.

Beyond this they had another great advantage. They
did not, to be sure, represent the English State, but yet
their connexion with England was of infinite service to
them. They had indeed to procure in the main for
themselves the money and the men by which India was
conquered. But as a chartered Company which had the
monopoly of English trade in India and China, they were
an object of interest to the English Government and to
Parliament. It several times happened that the war by
which they acquired Indian territory wore the appearance
before the English public of a war between England and
France, and was therefore heartily supported by the nation.
This is a fact of fundamental importance, which has not
often been sufficiently considered. The English conquest
of India began not in some quarrel between the Company
and a native Power. It began in an alarming attempt
made by the French to get control over the Deccan, and so
among other things to destroy the English settlements at
Madras and Bombay, by interfering in the question of the
Hyderabad succession. Our first military step in the East
was to defend ourselves against the French attack. And
from that time for nearly seventy years, that is, to the end
of the war with Napoleon, our wars in India never ceased
to wear more or less the appearance of defensive wars

against France. The effect of this was that, though they were not waged in the name or at the expense of the State, yet they seemed to a certain extent national wars, wars in which England was deeply concerned. To a considerable extent therefore the Company's troops were aided by Royal troops, and from 1785, when Lord Cornwallis went out as Governor-General, an English statesman of mark was sent out to preside over the political and military affairs. The attacks that were made upon the Company in Parliament, the vote of censure moved against Lord Clive, the impeachment brought against Hastings, the successive ministerial schemes for regulating the Company's affairs, one of which in 1783 convulsed the whole political world of England, all these interferences contributed to make our Indian wars seem national wars, and to identify the Company with the English nation. In this way the Company was practically backed by the credit and renown of a first-class European state, though at the same time that state contributed little to the wars by which the Company acquired territory.

The words 'wonderful,' 'strange,' are often applied to great historical events, and there is no event to which they have been applied more freely than to our conquest of India. But an event may be wonderful or strange without being necessarily at all difficult to account for. The conquest of India is very wonderful in the sense that nothing similar to it had ever happened before, and that therefore nothing similar could be expected by those who for the first century and a half administered the affairs of the Company in India. No doubt Job Charnock, or Josiah Child, or Governor Pitt of Madras (grandfather of the great Lord Chatham) or perhaps Major Lawrence, never dreamed that we should one day suppress the authority

alike of the Peishwa of the Mahrattas and of the Great
Mogul himself. But the event was not wonderful in the
sense that it is difficult to discover adequate causes by
which it could have been produced. If we begin by
remarking that authority in India had fallen on the ground
through the decay of the Mogul Empire, that it lay there
waiting to be picked up by somebody, and that all over
India in that period adventurers of one kind or another were
founding Empires, it is really not surprising that a mercantile corporation which had money to pay a mercenary
force, should be able to compete with other adventurers,
nor yet that it should outstrip all its competitors by
bringing into the field English military science and
generalship, especially when it was backed over and over
again by the whole power and credit of England and
directed by English statesmen.

The sum of what I have urged is that the conquest of
India is not in the ordinary sense a conquest at all, because
it was not the act of a state and was not accomplished by
the army and the money of a state. I have pointed this
out in order to remove the perplexity which must be
caused by the statement that England conquered India,
that is, a population as large as that of Europe and many
thousand miles off, and yet that England is not a military
state, though this enormous conquest was achieved by
England without any exhausting effort and without any
expense. The explanation of this contradiction is that
England did not in the strict sense conquer India, but that
certain Englishmen, who happened to reside in India at
the time when the Mogul Empire fell, had a fortune like
that of Hyder Ali or Runjeet Singh and rose to supreme
power there.

But yet of course in its practical result the event has

proved to be a conquest of India by England. For now
that the process is complete and the East India Company
has been swept away we see that Queen Victoria is
Empress of India, and that a Secretary, who is a member
of the English Cabinet and sits in the English Parliament,
is responsible for the administration of India. England
as a state did not make the acquisition, yet it has fallen
to England. This is merely an exemplification of the
general principle, which, as I pointed out above, has
governed all the settlements of Europeans outside Europe
since the time of Columbus. However far they roamed,
however strange and wonderful was their success, they
were never able at the outset to shake off their European
citizenship. Cortez and Pizarro trampled under their
feet the Governments they found in America. With
scarcely an effort they made themselves supreme wherever
they came. But though they could set at nought in
Mexico the authority of Montezuma, they could not resist
or dream of resisting the authority of Charles V. who was
on the other side of the Atlantic. The consequence was
that whatever conquests they made by their own unassisted
audacity and effort were confiscated at once and as a
matter of course by Spain. So with the English in India.
After 1765 the East India Company held nominally a high
office in the Empire of the Great Mogul. But it was
asserted at once by the English Parliament that whatever
territorial acquisitions might be made by the Company
were under the control of Parliament. The Great Mogul's
name was scarcely mentioned in the discussion, and the
question seems never to have been raised whether he
would consent to the administration of his provinces
of Bengal, Behar and Orissa being thus conducted under
the control of a foreign Government. The Company

made part of two states at once. It was a Company
under a Charter from the King of England; it was a
Dewan under the Great Mogul. But it swept away the
Great Mogul, as Cortez swept away Montezuma; on the
other hand it submitted all its boundless acquisitions
meekly to the control of England, and at last, when a
century was completed from the battle of Plassey, it
suffered itself to be abolished and surrendered India to the
English Government.

LECTURE IV.

HOW WE GOVERN INDIA.

I HAVE considered the nature of the relation in which India stands to England and have tried to explain how this relation could spring up without a miracle. We may now advance a step and form some opinion on the question whether that relation can endure without a miracle, as it was created without one, or whether we ought to regard the government of India by the English as a kind of political *tour de force,* a matter of astonishment while it lasts, but certain not to last very long. For the great difficulty which the student has to contend with in studying Indian affairs is the dazzling effect of events so strange, so remote, and on a scale so large, by which he is led to think that ordinary causation is not to be expected in India, and that in that region all is miraculous. The rhetorical tone ordinarily adopted in history favours this illusion; historians are fond of parading all the strange and marvellous features of the Indian Empire, as if it were less their business to account for what happens than to make it seem more unaccountable than before.

Thus we come to think of our ascendancy in India as an exception to all ordinary rules, a standing miracle in

politics, only to be explained by the heroic qualities of
the English race and their natural genius for government.
So long as we take this view, it is of course impossible
for us to form any opinion concerning the duration of it.
What was a miracle at the beginning is likely to continue
so to the end. If ordinary laws are suspended, who shall
say how long the suspension is likely to last? Now I have
tried to look calmly at our Empire in its beginning. I have
examined the conquest of India, and have found that it is
indeed miraculous in the sense of being unlike our experience—the revolutions of Asiatic society would naturally
be unlike those of Europe—but that it is not miraculous
in the sense of being unaccountable, or even difficult to
account for. I now inquire whether our government of
India is miraculous in this sense.

It must certainly appear so, if we assume that India is
simply a conquered country and the English its conquerors.
Who does not know the extreme difficulty of repressing the
disaffection of a conquered population? Over and over
again it has been found impossible, even where the
superiority both in the number and efficiency of troops
has been decidedly on the side of the conquerors. When
the Spaniards failed in the Low Countries, they were
the best soldiers and Spain by far the greatest state in
Christendom. For the instinct of nationality or of separate religion more than supplies the place of valour or
of discipline, being diffused through the whole population
and not confined to the fighting part of it. Let us compare
the parallel case of Italy. Italy corresponds in the map of
Europe to India in that of Asia. It is a similar peninsula
at the south of the Continent with a mighty mountain
range above it and below this a great river flowing from
west to east. It is still more similar in the circumstance

that for many centuries it was a prey to foreign invaders. No long time ago Italy was subject to the ascendancy and partly to the actual rule of Austria. Its inhabitants were less warlike, its armies much less efficient than those of Austria, and Austria was close at hand. And yet, though fighting at so much disadvantage, Italy has made herself free. In the field she was generally defeated, but the feeling of nationality was so strong within and attracted so much sympathy without, that she has had her way, and the foreigner has left her to herself. Now in every point India is more advantageously situated with respect to England than Italy with respect to Austria. She has a population about eight times as great as that of England; she is at the other side of the globe; and then England does not profess to be a military state. Yet to all appearance she submits to the yoke; we do not hear of rebellions. In conducting the government of India we meet with difficulties, but they are chiefly financial and economical. The particular difficulty which in Italy was too much for Austria we do not encounter; we do not feel the difficulty of repressing the disaffection of a conquered nationality. Is not this miraculous? Does it not seem as if all ordinary laws were suspended in this case, or as if we might assume that there are no bounds either to the submissiveness of the Hindu or to the genius for government of the English?

What I urged above may partly prepare you for the answer which I make to this question. In the question it is assumed, first, that India constitutes a nationality, secondly, that this nationality has been conquered by England; now both these assumptions are wholly unfounded.

First the notion that India is a nationality rests

upon that vulgar error which political science principally
aims at eradicating. We in Europe, accustomed to see
the map of Europe divided into countries each of which
is assigned to a peculiar nationality, of which a special
language is the badge, fall into a profound misconception. We assume that wherever, inside or outside
of Europe, there is a country which has a name, there
must be a nationality answering to it. At the same time
we take no pains to conceive clearly or define precisely
what we call a nationality. We content ourselves with
remarking that we in England should be most unwilling
to be governed by the French, and that the French would
be sorry to be governed by the Germans, and from these
examples we draw the conclusion that the people of India
must in like manner feel it a deep humiliation to be
governed by the English. Such notions spring from mere
idleness and inattention. It does not need proving, it is
sufficient merely to state, that it is not every population
which constitutes a nationality. The English and the
French are not mere populations; they are populations
united in a very special way and by very special forces.
Let us think of some of these uniting forces, and then ask
whether they operate upon the populations of India.

The first is community of race, or rather the belief in a
community of race. This, when it appears on a large scale,
is identical with community of language. The English are
those who speak English, the French those who speak
French. Now do the inhabitants of India speak one
language ? The answer is, No more, but rather less, than the
inhabitants of Europe speak one language ! So much has
been said by philologers about Sanscrit and its affinities
with other languages, that it is necessary to remark that it
is an obvious community of language, of which the test

is intelligibility, and not some hidden affinity, that acts as a uniting force. Thus the Italians regarded the Austrians as foreigners because they could not understand German, without troubling themselves to consider that German as well as Italian is an Indo-European language. There is affinity among several of the languages of India, as among those of Europe. The Hindi languages may be compared with the Romance languages of Europe, as being descendants of the ancient language, but the mutual affinity of the Bengali, the Marathi, the Guzerati does not help to make those who speak them one nation. The Hindustani has sprung out of the Mussulman conquest, by a mixture of the Persian of the invaders with the Hindi languages of the natives. But in the South we find a linguistic discrepancy in India greater than any which exists in Europe, for the great languages of the South, Tamil, Telugu, Canarese, are not Indo-European at all, and they are spoken by populations far larger than those Finns and Magyars of Europe whose language is not Indo-European.

This fact is enough by itself to show that the name India ought not to be classed with such names as England or France, which correspond to nationalities, but rather with such as Europe, marking a group of nationalities which have chanced to obtain a common name owing to some physical separation. Like Europe it is a mere geographic expression, but even so, it has been much less uniformly used than the name Europe. Europe at any rate has been used in much the same sense since the time of Herodotus, but our present use of the word India is not perhaps very old. To us indeed it seems natural that the whole country which is marked off from Asia by the great barrier of the Himalaya and the Suleiman range should have a single name. But it has not always seemed so. The Greeks had

but a very vague idea of this country. To them for a long
time the word India was for practical purposes what it was
etymologically, the province of the Indus. When they say
that Alexander invaded India, they refer to the Punjab.
At a later time they obtained some information about the
valley of the Ganges, but little or none about the Deccan.
Meanwhile in India itself it did not seem so natural as
it seems to us to give one name to the whole region.
For there is a very marked difference between the northern and southern parts of it. The great Aryan community which spoke Sanscrit and invented Brahminism
spread itself chiefly from the Punjab along the great valley
of the Ganges, but not at first far southward. Accordingly
the name Hindostan properly belongs to this Northern
region. In the South or peninsula we find other races and
non-Aryan languages, though Brahminism has extended
itself there too. Even the Mogul Empire in its best time
did not much penetrate into this region.

It appears then that India is not a political name, but
only a geographical expression like Europe or Africa. It
does not mark the territory of a nation and a language, but
the territory of many nations and many languages. Here
is the fundamental difference between India and such
countries as Italy, in which the principle of nationality has
asserted itself. Both India and Italy were divided among
a number of states, and so were weak in resistance to the
foreigner. But Italy, though divided by organisation, was
one by nationality. The same language pervaded it, and
out of this language had sprung a great literature, which
was the common possession of the whole peninsula. India,
as I have pointed out, is no more united by language than
Europe is.

But nationality is compounded of several elements, of

which a sense of kindred is only one. The sense of a
common interest and the habit of forming a single political
whole constitute another element. This too has been very
weak, though perhaps it has not been altogether wanting
in India. The country might seem almost too large for
it, but the barrier which separates India from the rest of
the world is so much more effective than any barrier
between one part of India than another, that in spite of all
ethnical and local divisions some vague conception of India
as at least a possible whole has existed from a very ancient
time. In the shadowy traditionary history of the times
before Mahmoud of Ghazni it is vaguely related of this
king and that king that he was lord of all India; the dominion of some historical princes in the first Mohammedan
period, and finally the Mogul Empire, were approximately
universal. But we must not exaggerate the greatness of
the Mogul Empire, or imagine that it answers in India to
the Roman Empire in Europe. Observe how short its
duration was. We cannot put the very commencement of
it earlier than 1524, the date of the capture of Lahore by
Baber, that is, in Henry VIII.'s reign. When Vasco da
Gama landed in India it had not begun to exist, and its
marked and rapid decline begins in 1707, that is in Queen
Anne's reign. Between these dates there is less than two
centuries. But next observe that the Mogul Empire cannot
be properly said to have existed from the moment when
Baber entered India, but only from the moment when the
Indian dominion of the Moguls became extensive. Now
at the accession of Akber, which was in 1559 or the year
after that of Queen Elizabeth, this Empire consisted simply
of the Punjab and the country round Delhi and Agra. It
was not till 1576 that Akber conquered Bengal, and he
conquered Sind and Guzerat between 1591 and 1594.

His empire was now extensive, but if we consider 1594 instead of 1524 as the date of the commencement of the Mogul Empire, we reduce its duration to little more than a century.

Next observe that even at this time it by no means includes all India. To imagine this is to confuse India with Hindostan. Akber's dominion in 1595 was limited by the Nerbudda, and he had not yet set foot in the Deccan. He was Emperor of Hindostan, but by no means of India. In his later years he invaded the Deccan, and from this time the Mogul pretensions began to extend to the Southern half of India. But it cannot be said that anything like a conquest of the Deccan was made before the great expedition of Aurungzebe in 1683. From this time we may, if we choose, speak of the Mogul Empire as including the Deccan, and therefore as uniting all India under one Government, though the subjection of the Deccan was chiefly nominal, for the Mahratta Power was already rising fast. But thus the duration of the Empire is reduced to a mere moment, for the Mogul Emperors purchased this extension of their dominion by the ruin of the Empire. Within twenty-four years decay had become visible, and, as I take it, directly in consequence of this ambitious expedition. The Empire had always wanted a sufficient nucleus, and its powers were exhausted by this unwise attempt to extend it.

On the whole then it may be said that India has never really been united so as to form one state except under the English. And they cannot be said to have accomplished the work until the Governor-Generalship of Lord Dalhousie thirty years ago, when the Punjab, Oude and Nagpore were incorporated with the English dominions.

Another leading element of nationality is a common

religion. This element is certainly not altogether wanting in India. The Brahminical system does extend over
the whole of India. Not of course that it is the only
religion of India. There are not less than fifty millions of
Mussulmans, that is, a far greater number than is to be
found in the Turkish Empire. There is also a small
number of Sikhs, who profess a religion which is a sort of
fusion of Mohammedanism and Brahminism; there are
a few Christians, and in Ceylon and Nepaul there are
Buddhists. But Brahminism remains the creed of the
enormous majority, and it has so much real vitality that
it has more than once resisted formidable attacks. One of
the most powerful of all proselytising creeds, Buddhism,
sprang up in India itself; it spread far and wide; we have
evidence that it flourished with vigour in India two
centuries before Christ, and that it was still flourishing
in the seventh century after Christ. Yet it has been
conquered by Brahminism, and flourishes now almost in
every part of Asia more than in the country which produced it. After this victory Brahminism had to resist the
assault of another powerful aggressive religion, before
which Zoroastrianism had already fallen and even Christianity had in the East had to retreat some steps, Mohammedanism. Here again it held its own; Mussulman
Governments overspread India, but they could not convert
the people.

Now religion seems to me to be the strongest and most
important of all the elements which go to constitute
nationality; and this element exists in India. When it
is said that India is to be compared rather to Europe than
to France or England, we may remember that Europe,
considered as Christendom, has had and still has a certain
unity, which would show itself plainly and quickly enough

if Europe were threatened, as more than once it was
threatened in the Middle Ages, by a barbarian and heathen
enemy. It may seem then that in Brahminism India has a
germ, out of· which sooner or later an Indian nationality
might spring. And perhaps it is so; but yet we are to
observe that in that case the nationality ought to have
developed itself long since. For the Mussulman invasions,
which have succeeded each other through so many centuries, have supplied precisely the pressure which was most
likely to favour the development of the germ. Why did
Brahminism content itself with holding its own against
Islam, and not rouse and unite India against the invader ?
It never did so. Brahminical Powers have risen in India.
A chieftain named Sivaji arose in the middle of the
seventeenth century, and possessing himself of one or two
hill-forts in the highlands behind Bombay, founded the
Mahratta Power. This was a truly Hindu organisation,
and, as its power increased, it fell more and more under the
control of the Brahmin caste. The decline of the Mogul
Empire favoured its advance, so that in the middle of the
eighteenth century the· ramifications of, the Mahratta
confederacy covered almost the whole of India. It might
appear that in this confederacy there lay the nucleus of an
Indian nationality, that Brahminism was now about to do
for the Hindus !what has been done for so many other
races by their religion. But nothing of the kind happened.
Brahminism did not pass into patriotism. Perhaps its
facile comprehensiveness, making it in reality not a
religion but only a loose compromise between several
religions, has enfeebled it as a uniting principle. At any
rate it appears that in the Mahratta movement there
never was anything elevated or patriotic, but that it continued from first to last to be an organisation of plunder.

There is then no Indian nationality, though there are some germs out of which we can conceive an Indian nationality developing itself. It is this fact, and not some enormous superiority on the part of the English race, that makes our Empire in India possible. If there could arise in India a nationality-movement similar to that which we witnessed in Italy, the English Power could not even make the resistance that was made in Italy by Austria, but must succumb at once. For what means can England have, which is not even a military state, of resisting the rebellion of two hundred and fifty millions of subjects? Do you say, as we conquered them before, we could conquer them again? But I explained that we did not conquer them. I showed you that of the army which won our victories four-fifths consisted of native troops. That we were able to hire these native troops for service in India, was due to the fact that the feeling of nationality had no existence there. Now if the feeling of a common nationality began to exist there only feebly, if, without inspiring any active desire to drive out the foreigner, it only created a notion that it was shameful to assist him in maintaining his dominion, from that day almost our Empire would cease to exist. For of the army by which it is garrisoned two-thirds consist of native soldiers. Imagine what an easy task the Italian patriots would have had before them, if the Austrian Government which they desired to expel had depended not upon Austrian but upon Italian soldiers! Let us suppose—not even that the native army mutinied —but simply that a native army could not any longer be levied. In a moment the impossibility of holding India would become manifest to us. For it is a condition of our Indian Empire that it should be held without any great effort. As it was acquired without much effort on the

15—2

part of the English state, it must be retained in the same way. We are not prepared to bury millions upon millions or army upon army in defending our acquisition. The moment India began really to show herself what we so idly imagine her to be, a conquered nation, that moment we should recognise perforce the impossibility of retaining her.

And thus the mystic halo of marvel and miracle which has gathered round this Empire disappears before a fixed scrutiny. It disappears when we perceive that, though we are foreign rulers in India, we are not conquerors resting on superior force, when we recognize that it is a mere European prejudice to assume that since we do not rule *by* the will of the people of India, we must needs rule *against* their will. The love of independence presupposes political consciousness. Where this is wanting, a foreign Government will be regarded passively, and such a Government may continue for a long time and prosper without exerting any extraordinary skill. Such a passive feeling towards Government becomes inveterate in a country that has been frequently conquered. Governments most oppressive have often continued for centuries, and that though they had no means of resisting rebellion if it should arise, simply because it did not enter into the habits of the people to rebel, because they were accustomed to obedience. Read the history of the Russian Czars in the sixteenth century. Why did a great population submit to the furious caprices of Ivan the Terrible? The answer is plain. They had been trampled under foot for two centuries by the Tartars, and during that period they had acquired the habit of passive submission.

Now ought we not to expect the population of India to be in a similar condition of feeling? Of liberty, of

popular institutions, there exists scarcely a trace in the
whole extent of Indian history or tradition.　The Italians
had the Roman Republic behind them, and it was by
reading Livy to the people that Rienzi roused them to
rebellion.　No Indian demagogue could find anything
similar to read to the people.　And for seven hundred
years when the English arrived, they had been governed
not only by despots but by foreign despots.　It would be
marvellous indeed if in such a country the feeling could
have sprung up that Government exists for and depends on
the people, if a habit of criticising Government, of medita-
ting its overthrow, or of organising opposition against
it, could have sprung up.　Nations have, as it were, very
stiff joints.　They do not easily learn a new kind of movement; they do what their fathers did, even when they
fancy themselves most original.　It has been pointed out
that even the French Revolution strangely resembled some
earlier chapters in the history of France.　Certainly the
Italian nationality-movement resembles earlier Italian
movements that go back beyond the age of Dante.　Now
by this rule we should expect to find the Indian population silently submitting to whatever Government had the
possession of power, even though it were foreign, as our
Government is, and even though it were savagely oppressive, which we think our Government is not.

Our Government of India would be a miracle on two
conditions.　First, if the Hindus had been accustomed to
be ruled only by their own countrymen, and were familiar
with the idea of resisting authority.　This is not the case
of the Hindus, and accordingly they submit, as throughout history vast populations have been in the habit of
submitting to Governments which they could easily overthrow, as the Chinese at the present day submit to a

Tartar domination, as the Hindus themselves submitted to the Mogul domination before the English came. Indeed this example of the Moguls is well adapted to show that our ascendancy over the Hindus is no proof of any supernatural statesmanship in us. For one cannot read the Mogul history without being struck with the very same fact which surprises us in the history of the English rule, viz., that the Moguls too conquered almost without apparent means. Baber, the founder of the Empire, did not come with a mighty nation at his back, or leaning on the organisation of some powerful state. He had inherited a small Tartar kingdom in Central Asia, but he had lost this by an invasion of Osbegs. He wandered for a while as a homeless adventurer, and then got possession of another small kingdom in Afghanistan. Nothing could be slighter than this first germ of empire. This Tartar adventurer ruling Afghans in Cabul founded an Empire which in about seventy years extended over half India, and in a hundred years more extended nominally at least over the whole. I do not say that the Mogul Empire was ever comparable for greatness or solidity to that which we have established, but like our own, even more than our own, it seems built up without hands. The Company had at least English money, English military science, and the immortality of a corporation. Baber and his successors had none of these resources. It is difficult to discover any causes which favoured the growth of their Empire. All we can say is that Central Asia swarmed with a wandering population much inclined to the vocation of mercenary soldiers, which passed very readily for pay and plunder into the service of the ruler of Cabul.

Secondly our rule would be wonderful if the two hundred million Hindus had the habit of thinking all

together, like a single nation. If not, there is nothing
wonderful in it. A mere mass of individuals, unconnected
with each other by any common feelings or interests, is
easily subjected, because they may be induced to act
against each other. Now I have pointed out how weak
and insufficient are the bonds which unite the Hindus. If
you wish to see how this want of internal union has
operated in favour of our rule, you have only to read the
history of the great Mutiny. It may have occurred to you
when I said that a mutiny or even less than a mutiny on
the part of our native troops would be instantly fatal to our
Empire, that just such a mutiny actually happened in 1857,
and yet that our Empire still flourishes. But you are to
observe that I spoke of a mutiny caused by a nationality-
movement spreading among the people and at last gaining
the army. The mutiny of 1857 was not of this kind. It
began in the army and was regarded passively by the
people; it was provoked by definite military grievances,
and not by any disaffection caused by the feeling of
nationality against our Government as foreign. But now
let us ask; in what way was this mutiny, when once it had
broken out, put down? I am afraid the only opinion
that has ever obtained in England has been that it was
crushed by the prodigious heroism of the English and
their infinite superiority to the Hindus. Let me read
you the account which Col. Chesney gives of the matter
in his 'Indian Polity.' After remarking that an intensely
strong *esprit de corps* had sprung up in the Bengal Army
—for observe that the Bombay and Madras armies were very
slightly concerned in the mutiny—an *esprit de corps* which
was purely military and actually opposed to the feeling of
nationality, since it welded together the Hindu and the
Mussulman elements, (so that Col. Chesney remarks: 'In

ill-discipline, bitterness of feeling against their masters, and confidence in their power to overthrow them, there was nothing to choose between Hindu or Mussulman') he goes on to point out by what counter-movement this movement was met. 'Fortunately the so-called Bengal Presidency was not garrisoned wholly by the regular army. Four battalions of Goorkhas, inhabitants of the Nepalese Himalaya, who had been kept aloof from the rest of the army, and had not imbibed the class-feeling which animated that body, with one exception stood loyal; the conspicuous gallantry and devotedness to the British cause displayed by one of these regiments especially won the admiration of their English comrades.   Two extra-regiments of the line, which had been recruited from the Punjab and its neighbourhood, also stood firm.   But the great help came from the Punjab Irregular Force, as it was termed, a force however which was organised on quite as methodical and regular a footing, was quite as well-drilled and vastly better disciplined, than the regular army. This force consisted of six regiments of infantry and five of cavalry, to which may be added four regiments of Sikh local infantry, usually stationed in the Punjab. These troops were directly under the orders of the Government of that province, and not subject to that centralised system of administration which had a share in undermining the discipline of the regular army. It was with these troops and the handful of Europeans quartered in the upper part of India that the rebellion was first met.   Meanwhile the sympathies of the people of the Punjab were enlisted on behalf of their rulers. A lately conquered people, whose accustomed occupation had been superseded by the disbandment of their army, they entertained no good will to the Hindustani garrisons which occupied their country, and welcomed with alacrity the appeal to arms made them to join in the overthrow of their hereditary enemies. Any number of men that could be required was forthcoming, and the levies thus raised were pushed down to the seat of war as fast as they could be equipped and drilled. And on the reorganisation of the Bengal army these Punjab levies have formed a large component part of it.'

You see, the mutiny was in a great measure put down by turning the races of India against each other. So long as this can be done, and so long as the population have not formed the habit of criticising their Government, whatever it be, and of rebelling against it, the government of India from England is possible, and there is nothing miraculous about it. But, as I said, if this state of things should alter, if by any process the population should be welded into a single nationality, if our relation to it should come to resemble even distantly the relation of Austria to Italy, then I do not say we ought to begin to fear for our dominion, I say we ought to cease at once to hope for it. I do not imagine that the danger we have to apprehend is that of a popular insurrection. In some of the alarmist literature, for instance, in Mr Elliot's book entitled, 'Concerning John's Indian Affairs', I find harrowing pictures of the misery of the poor ryot, and then the conclusion drawn as a matter of course that this misery must lead to an explosion of despair, by which we shall be expelled. Whether the descriptions are true this is not the place to inquire; but granting the truth of them for argument's sake I do not find in history that revolutions are caused in this way. I find great populations cowering in abject misery for centuries together, but they do not rise in rebellion; no, if they cannot live they die, and if they can only just live, then they just live, their sensibilities dulled and their very wishes crushed out by want. A population that rebels is a population that is looking up, that has begun to hope and to feel its strength. But if such a rising took place, it would be put down by the native soldiery so long as they have not learned to feel themselves brothers to the Hindu and foreigners to the Englishman that commands them. But on the other hand if this feeling ever does spring up, if India does begin to breathe as a single national whole—and our own rule is perhaps doing more than ever was done by former Governments to make this possible—then no such explosion of despair, even if there were cause for it, would be needed. For in that case the feeling would soon gain the native army, and on the native army ultimately we depend. We could subdue the mutiny of 1857, formidable as it was, because it spread through only a part of the army, because the people did not actively sympathise with it, and because it was possible to find native Indian races who would fight on our side. But the moment a mutiny is but threatened, which shall be no mere mutiny, but the expression of a universal feeling of nationality, at that moment all hope is at an end, as all desire ought to be at an end, of preserving our Empire. For we are not really conquerors of India, and we cannot rule her as conquerors; if we undertook to do so, it is not necessary to inquire whether we could succeed, for we should assuredly be ruined financially by the mere attempt.

LECTURE V.

MUTUAL INFLUENCE OF ENGLAND AND INDIA.

In the last two lectures I was engaged in showing that the conquest of India and the government of it by the English have in a certain sense nothing wonderful about them. We may fairly be proud of many particular deeds done by our countrymen in India and of many men who in India have shown a rare energy and talent for government, but it is a mistake to suppose that the Empire itself is a standing proof of some vast superiority in the English race over the races of India. Without assuming any such vast superiority we are able to assign causes, which are sufficient to account alike for the growth and for the continuance of that Empire. It is not then wonderful, if by wonderful be meant simply miraculous, or difficult to account for by ordinary causation.

Nevertheless there is a sense in which it is not only wonderful, but far more wonderful than is commonly understood. It is wonderful rather in its consequences than in its causes. In other words, it is great in the peculiarly historical sense, for the pregnancy of events, as we re-

marked, is what gives them historical rank. By applying
this test we raised the rank of several events in English
history, especially the American Revolution, which for
want of dramatic or romantic interest are too little studied.
Let us now remark that the Indian Empire, however it
may seem less marvellous on close examination than at
first sight, will be found to gain in historic interest, as
much as it loses in romantic.

A vast Oriental Empire is not necessarily at all an
interesting or a particularly important thing.   There
have been many such Empires in Asia, which historically
are less important than a single Greek or Tuscan city-
republic.   That they have been of wide extent, or even of
long duration, does not make them interesting. Generally
when we examine them we find that they are of a low
organisation, and that under their weight the individual
is crushed, so that he enjoys no happiness, makes no
progress, and produces nothing memorable. And perhaps
when first we turn our thoughts towards our Indian
Empire, we may receive the impression that it is not
intrinsically more interesting than the average of such
overgrown Asiatic despotisms. We trust indeed that,
thanks to the control of English public opinion, it may
stand at a higher level of intelligence, morality, and philan-
thropy than the Mogul Empire which it has succeeded.
But at best we think of it as a good specimen of a bad political system.   We are not disposed to be proud of the succession of the Great Mogul. We doubt whether with all the
merits of our administration the subjects of it are happy.
We may even doubt whether our rule is preparing them for a
happier condition, whether it may not be sinking them
lower in misery, and we have our misgivings that perhaps
a genuine Asiatic Government, and still more a national

Government springing up out of the Hindoo population itself, might in the long run be more beneficial because more congenial, though perhaps less civilised, than such a foreign unsympathetic government as our own.

But let us consider that it is not quite every Empire which is thus uninteresting. The Roman Empire for example is not so. I may say this now without fear, because our views of history have grown considerably less exclusive of late years. There was a time no doubt when even the Roman Empire, because it was despotic and in some periods unhappy and half-barbarous, was thought uninteresting. A generation ago it was the reigning opinion that there is nothing good in politics but liberty, and that accordingly in history all those periods are to be passed over and, as it were, cancelled, in which liberty is not to be found. Along with this opinion there prevailed a habit of reading history, as we read poetry, only for an exalted kind of pleasure, and this habit led us, whenever we came to a period in which there was nothing glorious or admirable, to shut the book. In those days no doubt the Roman Empire too was condemned. The Roman Republic was held in honour for its freedom; the earlier Roman Empire was studied for the traces of freedom still discernible in it. But we used to shut the book at the end of the second century, as if all that followed for some ten centuries were decay and ruin; and we did not take up the story again with any satisfaction until the traces of liberty began to reappear in England and in the Italian republics. I suppose I may say that this way of regarding history is now obsolete. We do not now read it simply for pleasure, but in order that we may discover the laws of political growth and change, and therefore we hardly stop to inquire whether the period before us is glorious or dismal. It is

enough if it is instructive and teaches lessons not to be
learned from other periods. We have also learnt that there
are many other good things in politics besides liberty; for
instance there is nationality, there is civilisation. Now
it often happens that a Government which allows no
liberty is nevertheless most valuable and most favourable to progress towards these other goals. Hence the
Roman Empire—not only in its beginnings but in its
later developments up to the thirteenth century—is now
regarded, in spite of all the barbarism, all the superstition,
and all the misery, as one of the most interesting of
all historical phenomena. For it is perceived that this
Empire is by no means without internal progress, without
creative ideas, or without memorable results. We discern in
it the embryo of that which is greatest and most wonderful, namely, the modern brotherhood or loose federation of
civilised nations. And therefore, though it was a great
Empire and though it was despotically governed, it is
studied with infinite curiosity and attention.

This difference between the Roman Empire and other
Empires founded on conquest, arises from the superiority in
civilisation of the conquerors to the conquered. A great
conquering race is not usually advanced in civilisation.
The typical conqueror is some Cyrus or Zinghis Khan, that
is, the chieftain of a hardy tribe, which has been steeled by
poverty and is tempted by plunder. Before such an assailant
the advanced civilisation is apt to go down, so that in history
we see civilisation often conquered, sometimes holding its
ground, but not very often making great conquests, until
in recent times the progress of invention strengthened
it by giving it new weapons. The great conquering
race of history has been one of the least progressive,
the Turcomans. It was from this race mainly, from

the hive of tribesmen, who in Central Asia furnished mercenary armies to all the ambitious kings of Asia, that Baber and Akber drew the force with which they conquered India. Such is the ordinary rule, but when an exceptional case does occur, when high civilisation is spread by conquest over populations less advanced, the Empire thus formed has a very peculiar interest. Of such a nature for instance was the conquest of the East by Alexander the Great, because the Macedonians through their close relationship with the Greeks brought all Hellenism in their train. Accordingly, though the kingdoms of the Diadochi were in themselves but military despotisms of a low type, yet the strangest and most memorable effects were produced by the fusion of Greek with Oriental thought. Still more remarkable, because it lasted much longer and because it is much better known, was the effect produced upon the nations of Europe by the Roman Empire. In fact this great phenomenon stands out in the very centre of human history, and may be called the foundation of the present civilisation of mankind.

Now it will make all the difference if the English conquest of India is to be classed along with the Greek conquest of the East and the Roman conquest of Gaul and Spain and not along with those of the Great Turk and the Great Mogul. If it belongs to the latter class, we shall not be misled by any mere splendour or magnitude, but shall pronounce it to be a phenomenon of secondary interest, belonging to the history of barbarism rather than to that of civilisation. But if it belongs to the former, we shall be prepared to place it among the transcendent events of the world, those events which rise as high above the average of civilised history as an ordinary Oriental conquest falls below it.

There need be no question about the general fact that the ruling race in British India has a higher and more vigorous civilisation than the native races. We may say this without taking too much to ourselves. The English, as such, are perhaps not a race of Hellenic intelligence or genius, but the civilisation they inherit is not simply their own. It is European civilisation, the product of the united labour of the European races held together and animated by the spirit of the ancient world. What do we see on the other side? What estimate shall we form of the native civilisation of India?

As I have said so often, India is not one country, and therefore it has not one civilisation. It has not even so much unity as it seems to have, for Brahminism by its peculiar trick of absorption and assimilation has brought together under one name forms of civilisation which are really diverse. If we look below the surface, we find two distinct layers of population, a fair-skinned and a dark-skinned race. The two layers are visible almost everywhere; the dark layer preponderates in the South; it is outnumbered but clearly visible in Bengal; it is evanescent perhaps higher up the Ganges; but that the two races did really blend almost all over India appears from the fact that no language is now spoken which is a mere corruption or dialect of Sanscrit, as French and Italian are dialects of Latin. Every Hindi language, even when its vocabulary is most exclusively Sanscrit, has inflexions and forms which are non-Aryan[1]. Now in estimating the civilisation of India we must begin by taking account of this fundamental distinction of race. The dark-skinned race is in many parts not civilised, and ought to be classed as barbarous. Mr B. H. Hodgson says, 'In every extensive jungly or hilly tract throughout the vast continent of India there exist

[1] Stated on the authority of Professor Cowell.

hundreds of thousands of human beings in a state not materially different from that of the Germans as described by Tacitus'.

We are to distinguish again between the Hindu races proper and the great Mussulman immigration. There are not less than fifty millions of Mussulmans in India, and of these a large proportion consists of Afghans or Pathans, Arabs, Persians, and Turcomans or Tartars who have at different times entered India either with, or in order to join, the armies of the Mussulman conquerors. Here we may expect to find, as everywhere in the Mussulman world, a sort of semi-civilisation, certain strong virtues but of a primitive kind, in short an equipment of ideas and views not sufficient for the modern forms of society.

Then finally we come to the characteristically Indian population, the Aryan race which descended from the Punjab with the Sanscrit language on its lips, which spread itself mainly along the valley of the Ganges, but succeeded in spreading its peculiar theocratic system over the whole of India. Perhaps no race has shown a greater aptitude for civilisation. Even its barbarism, as reflected in the Vedic literature, is humane and intelligent. And after its settlement in India it advanced normally along the path of civilisation. Its customs grew into laws, and were consolidated in codes. It imagined the division of labour. It created poetry and philosophy and the beginnings of science. Out of its bosom sprang a mighty religious reform called Buddhism, which remains to this day one of the leading religious systems of the world. So far then it resembled those gifted races which created our own civilisation.

But the Aryan race did not make so much progress in India as in Europe. As it showed in India an extreme incapacity for writing history, so that no record of it remains except where it came in contact with Greek or Mussulman invaders, we can only conjecture the causes that may have retarded its progress. But the great religious reform after some centuries of success for some reason or other failed; Buddhism was expelled. The tyranny of the priestly caste was firmly established. No great and solid political system grew up; there was little city-civilisation. And then came the scourge of foreign conquest.

Subjection for a long time to a foreign yoke is one of the most potent causes of national deterioration. And the few facts we know about the ancient Hindus confirm what we should conjecture about the moral effects produced upon them by their misfortunes[1]. We have in the Greek writer Arrian a description of the Indian character, which we read with surprise. He says, 'they are remarkably brave, superior in war to all Asiatics; they are remarkable for simplicity and integrity; so reasonable as never to have recourse to a law-suit and so honest as neither to require locks to their doors nor writings to bind their agreements. No Indian was ever known to tell an untruth.' This description has no doubt an air of exaggeration about it, but, as Elphinstone remarks, it shows that an extraordinary change has passed over the Hindu character since it was written. Exaggeration consists in exhibiting the real features larger than they ought to be. But this description exhibits on an unnatural scale precisely the features that are wanting in the modern Hindu character. Modern travellers therefore are found to exaggerate the very opposite features. They accuse the Hindu of want

[1] See this subject treated at much greater length by Professor Max-Müller in his recently published volume, *'What can India teach us ?'*

of veracity, want of valour, and extreme litigiousness. But the change is precisely such as might naturally be produced by a long period of submission to the foreigner.

On the whole then we find in India three stages of civilisation, first that of the hill-tribes, which is barbarism, then that which is perhaps sufficiently described as the Mussulman stage, and thirdly the arrested and half-crushed civilisation of a gifted race, but a race which has from the beginning been in a remarkable manner isolated from the ruling and progressive civilisation of the world. Whatever this race achieved it achieved a long time ago. Its great epic poems, which some would compare to the greatest poems of the West, are ancient, though perhaps much less ancient than has been thought, so too its systems of philosophy, its scientific grammar. The country has achieved nothing in modern times. It may be compared to Europe, as Europe would have been if after the irruption of barbarians and the fall of ancient civilisation it had witnessed no revival, and had not been able to protect itself against the Tartar invasions of the tenth and thirteenth centuries. Let us suppose Europe to have vegetated up to the present time in the condition in which the tenth century saw it, exposed to periodical invasions from Asia, wanting in strongly marked nations and vigorous states, its languages mere vernaculars not used for the purposes of literature, all its wisdom enshrined in a dead language and doled out to the people by an imperious priesthood, all its wisdom too many centuries old, sacred texts of Aristotle, the Vulgate, and the Fathers, to which nothing could be added but in the way of commentary. Such seems to be the condition of the Aryans of India, a condition which has no resemblance

16—2

whatever to barbarism, but resembles strikingly the
medieval phase of the civilisation of the West.

The dominion of Rome over the western races was the
empire of civilisation over barbarism. Among Gauls and
Iberians Rome stood as a beacon-light; they acknowledged its brightness, and felt grateful for the illumination
they received from it. The dominion of England in India is
rather the empire of the modern world over the medieval.
The light we bring is not less real, but it is probably less
attractive and received with less gratitude. It is not a
glorious light shining in darkness, but a somewhat cold daylight introduced into the midst of a warm gorgeous twilight.

Many travellers have said that the learned Hindu,
even when he acknowledges our power and makes use of
our railways, is so far from regarding us with reverence
that he very sincerely despises us. This is only natural.
We are not cleverer than the Hindu; our minds are not
richer or larger than his. We cannot astonish him, as
we astonish the barbarian, by putting before him ideas that
he never dreamed of. He can match from his poetry
our sublimest thoughts; even our science perhaps has
few conceptions that are altogether novel to him. Our
boast is not that we have more ideas or more brilliant
ideas, but that our ideas are better tested and sounder.
The greatness of modern, as compared with medieval or
ancient, civilisation is that it possesses a larger stock of
demonstrated truth, and therefore infinitely more of practical power. But the poetical or mystic philosopher is by
no means disposed to regard demonstrated truth with
reverence; he is rather apt to call it shallow, and to sneer
at its practical triumphs, while he revels for his part in
reverie and the luxury of unbounded speculation.

We in Europe however are pretty well agreed that the

treasure of truth which forms the nucleus of the civilisation
of the West is incomparably more sterling not only than
the Brahminic mysticism with which it has to contend,
but even than that Roman enlightenment which the old
Empire transmitted to the nations of Europe.   And therefore we shall hold that the spectacle now presented by
India of a superior civilisation introduced by a conquering
race is equal in interest and importance to that which the
Roman Empire presented.   Moreover the experiment is
tried on a scale equally large.   This Empire is usually judged
by its immediate effect on the welfare of the inhabitants.
It has removed evils of long standing, says one; it has
introduced new evils, says another.   This whole controversy puts on one side the most characteristic work of our
Empire, which is the introduction in the midst of Brahminism of European views of the Universe.   No experiment
equally interesting is now being tried on the surface of the
globe.   And when we consider how seldom it is put in the
power of a nation to accomplish a task so memorable, we
shall learn to take an eager interest in the progress of the
experiment, and to check the despondency which might
lead us to ask what profit accrues to ourselves from all
this labour that we have undertaken under the sun.

And now let us take note of a great advantage which
we enjoy in working at this task.   It comes to light when we
compare our Empire with the Roman.   Rome was placed
in the midst of its Empire, was subject to an overwhelming
reaction from it, and was exposed to all the dangers which
threatened it.   England on the other hand is singularly
disengaged from this enormous Empire which it governs,
and feels but a slight reaction from it.

Every historical student knows that it was the incubus
of the Empire which destroyed liberty at Rome.   Those

old civic institutions, which had nursed Roman greatness
and to which Rome owed all the civilisation which she
was to transmit to the countries of the West, had to be
given up as a condition of transmitting it. She had to
adopt an organisation of, comparatively, a low type. Her
civilisation, when she transmitted it, was already in decay.
In a great part of the Empire her very language was
worsted in the competition by the Greek, so that the
Emperor M. Aurelius himself writes his Meditations in
Greek. The Roman religion instead of making converts
fell into neglect, and in the end gave way to a religion
which had sprung up in a distant province of the
Empire. There came a time when almost all that was
Roman in thought and feeling seemed to be dead in the
Empire of Rome, when its Emperors were like Oriental
kings and wore the diadem. We know now that this was
not so, and that Roman influence, the Roman tradition
continued to sway the European mind for many centuries.
But this sway was exerted secretly, through law and
through Catholicism, at a later time through the Renaissance in literature and art. Think how different would
have been the course of modern European history if
the mother-city of its civilisation, instead of being in
the midst of the nations it educated, instead of suffering
in their discords and convulsions, instead of receiving as
much barbarism from them as it gave civilisation to them,
had stood outside, enjoying an independent prosperity,
developing its own civilisation further with an unabated
vigour of youth all the while that it guided the subject
nations.

The Roman Empire is in this respect a somewhat
extreme case, because the conquering Power was so remarkably small compared to the empire it attached to

itself. The light radiated not from a country but from a city, which was not so much a shining disk as a point of intense light. The Roman Republic had institutions which were essentially civic, and which began to break down as soon as they were extended even to the whole of Italy. But even where the conquering Power has a much broader basis, it is commonly altogether transformed by the effort of conquest. The wars by which the conquest is made, and then the establishments necessary to maintain the conquest, call for a new system of government and finance. Of all the unparalleled features which the English Empire in India presents, not one is so unique as the slightness of the machinery by which it is united to England and the slightness of its reaction upon England. How this peculiarity has been caused I have already explained. I have shown that our acquisition of India was made by a process so peculiar that it cost us nothing. Had England as a state undertaken to subvert the Empire of the Great Mogul, she would have destroyed her own constitution in the process, no less than Rome did by the conquest of Europe. For she would evidently have been compelled to convert herself into a military state of the most absolute type. But as England has merely inherited the throne which was founded in India by certain Englishmen who rose to the head of affairs in time of anarchy, she has been but very slightly disturbed in her domestic affairs by this acquisition. It has modified no doubt, as I have said, her foreign policy in a great degree, but it has produced no change in the internal character of the English state. In this respect India has produced as little effect upon England as those Continental States which have been in modern times connected with England in what is called a personal union, Hannover under the

Georges, or Holland under William III. The consequence is that in this instance the operation of the higher civilisation on the lower is likely to be far more energetic and continuous than in those ancient examples of the Roman Empire or the Greek Empire in the East. In those cases the lower civilisation killed the higher in the same moment that the higher raised the lower towards its own level. Hellenism covered the East, but the greatness of Greece came to an end. All nations crowded into the Roman citizenship; but what became of the original Romans themselves? England on the other hand is not weakened at all by the virtue that goes out from her. She tries to raise India out of the medieval into the modern phase, and in the task she meets with difficulties and even incurs dangers, but she incurs no risk whatever of being drawn down by India towards the lower level, or even of being checked for a moment in her natural development.

This has been the result; but for a long time it was uncertain that the result would be such. In the history of British India there are two most interesting chapters—I should say that in the whole history of the world there are no chapters more instructive—in which we learn, first how a mischievous reaction from India upon England was prevented, secondly how European civilisation was after much delay and hesitation resolutely brought to bear upon India. The first chapter embraces chronologically the first half of George III.'s reign, that stormy period of transition in English history when at the same time America was lost and India won. It covers the two great careers of Clive and Hastings, and the end of the struggle is marked by the reign of Lord Cornwallis, which began in 1785. The second chapter embraces about the first forty years of the present century, and the crowning point of this

development is the Governor-Generalship of Lord William
Bentinck.   For in the Indian Empire Lord Cornwallis and
Lord W. Bentinck have been the two great legislators
after Hastings, as Lord Wellesley, Lord Hastings and Lord
Dalhousie have been, after Clive, the great conquerors,
and when we consider, as we are doing now, the progress
of civilisation in the Empire, the great legislators naturally
demand our attention most.

First then let us consider the reaction which at the
beginning India threatened to have upon England, and
how this danger was averted.   The literature of the
seventies and the eighties of the eighteenth century is
full of that alarm which found its strongest expression in
the speeches of Burke against Warren Hastings.   England
had taken a sudden plunge into the unknown abyss of
Hindu politics.   Englishmen were becoming finance
ministers or commanders of mercenary troops to Mussulman Nawabs, and were bringing back to England the
plunder of the Mogul Empire, acquired no one knew how.
There were two dangers here, first lest the English
character should be corrupted, for those who take the
most favourable view of the Hindu character would admit
that Hindu politics in the last century were unspeakably
corrupt, secondly, lest the wealthy adventurers, returning
to England and entering into English political life with
ideas formed in Asia, should upset the balance of the
constitution.   This was particularly to be feared under
the old electoral system, which allowed so many seats in
Parliament to be put up to sale.   Moreover in an age when
Government derived its chief power from patronage, there
was a danger lest one of the contending parties should
make a snatch at the vast patronage of India, a prize
which, whether it fell to the King or to the Whig party,
would probably make its possessor supreme in the State.

To give you a specimen of the fears which were entertained by leading men, I will read a passage from William Pitt's motion for parliamentary reform made in 1782. He said, 'Our laws have with a jealous care provided that no foreigner shall give a single vote for a representative in Parliament; and yet we now see foreign princes not giving votes but purchasing seats in this House, and sending their agents to sit with us as representatives of the nation. No man can doubt what I allude to. We have sitting among us the members of the Rajah of Tanjore and the Nawab of Arcot, the representatives of petty Eastern despots; and this is notorious, publicly talked of and heard with indifference; our shame stalks abroad in the open face of day, it is become too common even to excite surprise. We treat it as a matter of small importance that some of the electors of Great Britain have added treason to their corruption and have traitorously sold their votes to foreign Powers; that some of the members of our Senate are at the command of a distant tyrant; that our Senators are no longer the representatives of British virtue but of the vices and pollutions of the East'.

The great incidents of this struggle are, the fall of the Coalition Ministry on the India Bill of Fox and the passing of the India Bill of Pitt, the trial of Warren Hastings, the succession of Lord Cornwallis to the Governor Generalship, and the administrative reform carried out by him in India. I merely touch these great occurrences to mark their significance and to show what results flowed from them. If I went into detail, I might show that much was unreasonable in the clamour raised against the India Bill of Fox, and that there was much unreasonable violence in the attacks made upon Hastings. I might also criticise the double system introduced by the

India Bill of Pitt. But, taking a broad view, it must be said that the particular dangers feared were very success-fully averted, that Lord Cornwallis established a title to gratitude and Edmund Burke to immortal glory. For the stain of immorality *did* pass away as by magic from the administration of the Company under the rule of Lord Cornwallis, a lesson never to be forgotten was taught to Governors General, and at the same time the political danger from the connexion with India passed away.

England had broken the toils that threatened to imprison her. But how far was she, who had so stoutly refused to be influenced by India, entitled to influence India in her turn? We could not fail to see the enormous differ-ence between our civilisation and that of India, we could not fail on the whole greatly to prefer our own. But had we any right to impose our views upon the natives? We had our own Christianity, our own views of philosophy, of history and science; but were we not bound by a sort of tacit contract with the natives to hold all these things officially in abeyance? This was the view which was taken at first. It was not admitted that England was to play the part of Rome to her empire; no; she was to put her civilisation on one side and govern according to Indian ideas. This view was the more winning as the new and mysterious world of Sanscrit learning was revealing itself to those first generations of Anglo-Indians. They were under the charm of a remote philosophy and a fantastic history. They were, as it was said, Brahminised, and would not hear of admitting into their enchanted Oriental enclosure either the Christianity or any of the learning of the West.

I have not space left in this lecture to do more than indicate how we were gradually led to give up this view and to stand out boldly as teachers and civilisers. The change began in 1813 when on the renewal of the Company's charter a sum was directed to be appropriated to the revival of learning and the introduction of useful arts and sciences. Over this enactment an Education Committee wrangled for twenty years. Were we to use our own judgments, or were we to understand learning and science in the Oriental sense? Were we to teach Sanscrit and Arabic, or English?

Never on this earth was a more momentous question discussed. Under Lord William Bentinck in 1835 the discussion came to a head, and by a remarkable coincidence a famous man was on the spot to give lustre to and take lustre from a memorable controversy. It was Macaulay's Minute that decided the question in favour of English. In that Minute or in Sir C. Trevelyan's volume on Education in India you can study it. Only remark a strange over-sight that was made. The question was discussed as if the choice lay between teaching Sanscrit and Arabic on the one hand, or English on the other. All these languages alike are to the mass of the population utterly strange. Arabic and English are foreign, and Sanscrit is to the Hindus what Latin is to the natives of Europe. It is the original language out of which the principal spoken languages have been formed, but it is dead. It has been dead a far longer time than Latin, for it had ceased to be a spoken language in the third century before Christ. By far the greater part of the famous Sanscrit poems and writings, philosophical or theological, were written artificially and by a learned effort, like the Latin poems of Vida and Sannazaro. Now over Sanscrit Macaulay had an easy victory, for he had only to show that English had poetry at least as good, and phi-losophy history and science a great deal better. But why should there be no choice but between dead languages? Could Macaulay really fancy it possible to teach two hundred and fifty millions of Asiatics English? Probably not, probably he thought only of creating a small learned class. I imagine too that his own classical training had implanted in his mind a fixed assumption that a dead language is necessary to education. But if India is really to be enlightened, evidently it must be through the medium neither of Sanscrit nor of English, but of the vernaculars, that is Hindustani, Hindi, Bengali &c. These, under some vague impression that they were too rude to be made the vehicles of science or philosophy, Macaulay almost refuses to consider, but against these his arguments in favour of English would have been powerless.

But though this great oversight was made—it has since been remarked and, since the education dispatch of Sir Charles Wood in 1854, in some measure repaired—the decision to which Macaulay's minute led remains the great landmark in the history of our Empire, considered as an institute of civilisation. It marks the moment when we deliberately recognised that a function had devolved on us in Asia similar to that which Rome fulfilled in Europe, the greatest function which any Government can ever be called upon to discharge.

LECTURE VI.

PHASES IN THE CONQUEST OF INDIA.

THE sum of what I have laid before you up to this point is that in India a result has been produced by causes less wonderful than is commonly supposed, which result is in magnitude more wonderful, and in the consequences which may possibly flow from it far more wonderful and great, than is imagined. But in showing how such a result could be produced without a miracle I have laid stress upon another peculiarity of this Empire, which is of fundamental importance, namely the slightness of the machinery which connects it with England. Let us now remark that in this respect our Indian Empire resembles our colonies. There is of course this vast difference, that our chief colonies determine in most matters their own policy through Governments which spring up by a constitutional process out of the colonial assembly, and that India has no such independent initiative, the Viceroy himself being liable to be overruled by the Indian Secretary at home. But at the same time there is this great resemblance, that India, like the colonies, has been held at arm's length, that its Government has never been suffered to approach the Home Government so closely as to blend with it, or to modify its character, or to hamper its independent development. India is both constitutionally and financially an independent Empire. If the Empire of the Great Mogul had continued in its original vigour up to the present time, no doubt in foreign affairs the history of England would differ considerably from what it is. Several of our wars with France would have taken a different turn, especially that war of which the Egyptian expedition of Bonaparte was a main incident. We can imagine too that the Crimean War would not have happened, and that we should not have taken the interest we did in the recent Russo-Turkish War. But the constitution of the English state would have been precisely what it is, and our domestic history would have run almost exactly the same course. Only once, I think, namely in 1783, has India come quite into the foreground of parliamentary debate and absorbed the attention of the political world. Even in the Mutiny of 1857, deeply as our feelings were stirred, the course of home politics was not affected by the affairs of India.

Accordingly if the Indian Empire were lost, the immediate and purely political effects of the change would not be great. A Secretaryship of State would disappear; the work of Parliament would be lightened. Our foreign policy would be relieved of a great burden of anxiety. Otherwise little would immediately be changed. In this respect I say the Indian Empire resembles the colonies, and we are led to perceive a universal characteristic of that expansion of England which is the subject of these lectures. I have remarked before that this expansion does not seem at first sight to be of the nature of organic growth. When the boy expands into the man, the boy disappears. He does not increase by an accretion visibly different from the original boy and attached to him so as to be easily peeled off. But it *is* in such a way that England seems to have increased. For the original England remains distinctly visible at the heart of Greater Britain, she still forms a distinct organism complete in herself, and she has not even formed the habit of thinking of her colonies and her Indian Empire along with herself.

Turgot compared colonies to fruit which hangs on the tree only till it is ripe. And indeed it might seem natural to picture the aggregate of English communities rather as a family than as an individual. We may say that the England of Queen Elizabeth's time has now a large family scattered over distant seas, that this family consists for the most part of thriving colonies, but that it includes also a corporation which had the good luck in the course of its trade to become ruler of a vast country. There is no objection to such an image, provided it is regarded only as an image, and is not converted by sleight of hand into an argument. But we know that a family, at least in the present state of society, is always tending towards practical dissolution. It is a close union so long as the children are young; it becomes a federation, and at last a loose federation, as they grow up; finally, in the present state of society, as the grown-up sons disperse or emigrate in quest of a livelihood and the daughters are married, it often ceases practically to be a federation or even a permanent alliance. Now we may call our Empire a family, but we must not without further investigation assume that it will have the fate which cannot even be said generally to attend literal families, but which attends them in the very peculiar form of society in which we happen to live. The dissolving causes which act upon families do not act in an equal degree upon states, and, what is especially to be observed, they do not act upon them nearly so much as they used to do. In the time of Turgot and of the American Revolution there was much force in the comparison between a distant dependency and a son who had left home and so practically passed out of the family. But there is much less force in it at the present day, when inventions have drawn the whole globe close together, and a new form of state on a larger scale than was known in former ages has appeared in Russia and the United States.

This consideration should make us hesitate in drawing the obvious conclusion from the great fact that the connexion of England with her colonies and her Indian Empire has been all along so remarkably slight. Above I pointed out with respect to the colonies that, though their connexion with the mother-country was loose at the outset, so that the secession of the American colonies was a natural effect of the causes then in operation, yet the connexion does not steadily grow slighter and slighter, but on the contrary increases and becomes closer. The colonies have practically approached much nearer to us, all that was invidious in the old colonial system has been repealed, and they have now become a natural outlet for a superfluous population, whereas in the old time, when there was as yet no surplus population, they were peopled principally by discontented refugees, who bore a grudge against the country they had left. A similar law governs our connexion with India. The machinery by which the connexion is maintained is slight. England has not allowed herself to be hampered by her relation to India. Enormous as the dominion is, England remains what she was before she acquired it, so that, as I have said, the connexion

could be broken any day, though it has lasted a hundred
years, without any violent wrench or any dislocation in our
domestic system.   But if it be inferred from this that a
connexion so slight must sooner or later snap, before we can
admit such an inference we must consider another question,
In which direction is the tendency ?   Does the slight connexion grow looser and looser, or does it on the other hand
tighten with time ?   And here again, as in the case of the
colonies, we shall find that the general tendency of our age,
which brings together what is remote and which favours
large political unions, operates to strengthen rather than
to weaken the connexion between England and India.

Macculloch, in the Note on India in his edition of
Adam Smith, speaks of the trade between England and
India about 1811, that is in the days of the monopoly, as
being utterly insignificant, of little more importance than
that between England and Jersey or the Isle of Man.
Now if trade be one of the principal bonds which unite
communities together, we shall have some criterion of the
tendency and of the strength of the tendency, whether
towards union or towards separation, between England and
India, by comparing the present with the former state
of the trade between the two countries.   It was supposed
in old times that the Hindus had unalterable habits, and
therefore that they would never become consumers of
European produce.   But now instead of Jersey or the Isle
of Man we compare our trade with India to that with the
United States and France, that is, with the greatest
commercial communities, and we find that though indeed
we receive from India much less than from them (thirty-
two millions, as against thirty-nine from France and not
less than a hundred and three from America in 1881) yet
India comes next to them as an exporting country, and on

the other hand India heads France and all other nations except the United States as an importer from England, for she took in the same year twenty-nine millions, whereas the countries which came next, that is, Australia and Germany, took twenty-one and seventeen respectively.

Now here is a prodigious advance which has been made in the present century, and it measures, you will observe, the gradual approach of the two populations towards each other, not their gradual separation from each other. And thus, though politically the direct effects of disruption would not be great, economically they would be enormous. For we are to remember that it is owing to the political connexion between the two countries that this commercial intercourse has been allowed to exist, and that it would cease perhaps if India became independent, and certainly if she passed into the hands of another European Power such as Russia. At the beginning of the century indeed we might have severed ourselves from India with little anxiety, and those struggles with France about our commercial factories at Madras, Bombay and Calcutta may seem to have had no sufficient motive, since the trade carried on at those stations was but insignificant. It is no longer so; the commercial stake we have in India is now very large; that is, we are more closely bound to India than we were. Look again at the moral approach that England has made towards India during the same time. Originally we had no sort of interest in the affairs of the Hindus among whom we had stationed commercial agencies. The Mogul Empire or the dissolution of the Mogul Empire did not concern us. It was no affair of ours whether the Hindus had a bad Government, or had no Government at all and were merely the prey of armed plunderers. Even when we began to conquer them, it was not on their

17—2

account but partly to resist the French, partly to protect
our factories from sudden attack. For a long time after
the Company had become a sovereign Power, this indifference on our part to the welfare of the natives continued. Adam Smith, writing in the eighties or about the
end of the reign of Warren Hastings, says that there
never was a Government so wholly indifferent to the
welfare of its subjects. This was only the natural consequence of the false position in which a trading company
suddenly turned into a Government found itself. The
anomaly and the effect of it could not but last as long
as the Company. But since 1858 it has been removed.
The very appearance of a selfish object is gone. The
Government is now as sincerely paternal as any Government
can be, and, as I explained, it has abandoned the affec-
tation of not imparting the superior enlightenment we
know ourselves to possess on the ground that the Hindus
do not want it.

At the same time the introduction of the telegraph
and the shortening of the voyage to India, first by the
overland route and since by the Suez Canal, has brought
India much more within reach of England. It has often
been contended that the effect of this change is bad, that
the constant interference of Downing Street and still
more of English public opinion is mischievous. Let this be
granted for argument's sake. Whether it be desirable or
undesirable that India should be more closely united with
England, is not now the question. What concerns us at
present is the fact that, for good or for evil, the connexion
of England with India does not diminish but increases.

Once more, let us remark the speed with which our
intercourse with India increases. Mr Cunningham in his
volume lately published, entitled 'British India and its

Rulers' compares the increase of the foreign trade of India between 1820 and 1880 with that of the foreign trade of Great Britain itself in the same period. This last increase has often excited astonishment: English foreign trade rose from about 80 to about 650 millions sterling. But Mr Cunningham points out that the increase of Indian trade in the same period has been even greater, and, as of course the foreign trade of India is principally with England, it follows that the tendency to commercial union between the two countries is prodigiously strong, so that fifty years hence, if no catastrophe takes place, the union will be infinitely closer than it is now.

If we combine all the facts I have hitherto adduced in order to form a conception of our Indian Empire, the result is very singular. An Empire similar to that of Rome, in which we hold the position not merely of a ruling but of an educating and civilising race (and thus, as in the marriage of Faust with Helen of Greece, one age is married to another, the modern European to the medieval Asiatic spirit); this Empire held at arm's length, paying no tribute to us, yet costing nothing except through the burden it imposes on our foreign policy, and neither modifying nor perceptibly influencing our busy domestic politics; this Empire nevertheless held firmly and with a grasp which does not slacken but visibly tightens; the union of England and India, ill-assorted and unnatural as it might seem to be, nevertheless growing closer and closer with great rapidity under the influence of the modern conditions of the world, which seem favourable to vast political unions; all this makes up the strangest, most curious, and perhaps most instructive chapter of English history. It has been made the subject of much empty boasting, while those who have looked deeper have often been disposed to regard the whole enterprise with despondency, as a kind of romantic adventure which can lead to nothing permanent.   But, as time passes, it rather appears that we are in the hands of a Providence which is greater than all statesmanship, that this fabric so blindly piled up has a chance of becoming a part of the permanent edifice of civilisation, and that the Indian achievement of England as it is the strangest, may after all turn out to be the greatest, of all her achievements.

At this point again we are led to turn our eyes from the present to the past, and to inquire how it could happen to us to undertake such an enterprise.   I devoted a lecture to the historical question by what force we were able to subdue the people of India to our government; but this question is different.   That was the question, how ? this is the question, why ?   We see that without any supernatural force or genius it was possible to raise such an Empire, but what was the motive which impelled us to do it ?   How many lives, some of them noble and heroic, many of them most laborious, have been spent in piling up this structure of empire !   Why did they do it ? Or if they themselves looked no further than their instructions, what was the motive of the authority that gave them their instructions ?   If this was the Company, why did the Company desire to conquer India, and what could they gain by doing so ?   If it was the English Government, what could be its object, and how could it justify such an undertaking to Parliament ?   We may have been at times too warlike, but the principal wars we have waged have borne the appearance at least of being defensive. Naked conquest for its own sake has never had attractions for us.   What then did we propose to ourselves ?

The English Government assuredly has gained nothing through this acquisition, for if it has not hampered their budgets by the expense of conquest, on the other hand it has not lightened them by any tribute.   If we hope to discover the guilty party by the old plan of asking Cui bono ? that is, Who profited by it ? the answer must be, English commerce has profited by it.   We have here a great foreign trade, which may grow to be enormous, and this trade is secured to us so long as we are masters of the Government of India.   Here no doubt is a substantial acquisition, which stands us in good stead now that we find by experience how tenacious of protection foreign Governments are.   May it then be assumed that this trade has been our sole object all along ?

The hypothesis is plausible, and it is made more plausible still when we remark that our Empire began evidently in commerce.   To defend our factories and for no other purpose we took arms in the first instance.   Our first wars in India, as they belong to the same time, so belong evidently to the same class, as our colonial wars with France.   They were produced by the same great cause on which I have insisted so much, the competition of the Western states for the wealth of the regions dis-covered in the fifteenth century.   We had trade-settle-ments in India as we had trade-settlements in America. In both countries we encountered the same rivals, the French.   In both countries English and French traders shook their fists at each other from rival commercial stations.   In America our New England and Virginia stood opposed to their Acadie and Canada; and similarly our Madras, Calcutta and Bombay stood opposed in India to their Pondicherry, Chandernagore and Mahee.

The crisis came in America and India at once between

1740 and 1760, when in two wars divided by a very hollow and imperfect peace these two states struggled for supremacy, and in both quarters England was victorious. From victory over France in India we proceeded without a pause to empire over the Hindus. This fact, combined with the other fact equally striking of the great trade which now exists between England and India, leads very naturally to a theory that our Indian Empire has grown up from first to last out of the spirit of trade. We may imagine that after having established our settlements on the coast and defended these settlements both from the native Powers and from the envy of the French, we then conceived the ambition of extending our commerce further inland ; that perhaps we met with new states, such as Mysore or the Mahratta Confederacy, which at first were unwilling to trade with us, but that in our eager avarice we had recourse to force, let loose our armies upon them, broke down their custom-houses and flooded their territories in turn with our commodities, that in this way we gradually advanced our Indian trade, which at first was insignificant, until it became considerable, and at last, when we had not only intimidated but actually overthrown every great native Government, when there was no longer any Great Mogul or any Sultan of Mysore or any Peishwa of the Mahrattas or any Nawab Vizir of Oude or any Maharajah and Khalsa of the Sikhs, then, all restraints having been removed, our trade became enormous.

But it will be found on closer examination that the facts do not answer to this theory. True it is that our Empire began in trade, and that lately there has been an enormous development of trade. But the course of affairs in history is not necessarily a straight line, so that when any two points in it are determined its whole course is known. The truth is that if the spirit of English trade had been thus irrepressible and bent upon overcoming all the obstacles which lay in its path, it would not have raised wars in India, for the main obstacle was not there. The main obstacle to English trade was not the jealousy of native Princes, but the jealousy of the East India Company itself. Accordingly there has been no correspondence in time between the increase of trade and the advance of conquest.

Our trade on the contrary continued to be insignificant in spite of all our conquests until about 1813, and it began to advance with great rapidity soon after 1830. These dates point to the true cause of progress in trade, and they show that it is wholly independent of progress in conquest, for they are the dates of the successive Acts of Parliament by which the Company was deprived of its monopoly. Thus it appears that, while it was by the East India Company that India was conquered, it was not by the East India Company, but rather by the destruction of the East India Company, that the great trade with India was brought into existence. Our conquests in India were made by an exclusive chartered Company, but our Indian trade did not greatly prosper until that Company ceased practically to exist.

In order to make this clearer, it will be convenient here to give such an outline of the history of the East India Company as may mark the principal stages of its progress and those alone. The East India Company then came into existence in the year 1600, that is, near the end of Queen Elizabeth's reign. In the view we are now taking of the expansion of England it deserves note that this occurrence took place just at that time and at no time either earlier or later. England, we have seen, assumed its modern, that is, its maritime and oceanic, character about the time of the Spanish Armada, since it was then that its first race of naval heroes appeared, and then too that it made its first attempts to colonise America. If this general statement be true, we ought to look in this period also for our first settlements in India. Just in this period we find them, for the creation of the East India Company took place twelve years after the defeat of the Armada.

It was created for trade, and it remained devoted to trade for a hundred and forty-eight years. During this period several important occurrences in its history took place, but none so important as to deserve our attention here. It was in 1748 that the disturbances occurred in the Deccan which forced the Company to undertake on a considerable scale the functions of government and war. Then began its second and memorable period, which is nearly as long as the first; it embraces a hundred and ten years and ends with the abolition of the Company by Act of Parliament in 1858. It is this second period alone with which we are concerned at present. In order to understand the course of development, we must endeavour to subdivide it.

It happens accidentally that there is a certain regularity in the course of events over a great part of this period, which rarely occurs in history and which is very helpful to the memory. The Company being dependent on Parliament for a renewal of its Charter and its affairs having since 1748 taken such a strange turn, it was natural that Parliament should grant the renewal only for a definite term, and at the end of the term should reconsider the condition of the Company and make alterations in its organisation. In this way the Company became subject to a transformation, which was strictly periodic and recurred at absolutely equal intervals. These intervals were of the length of twenty years, beginning with Lord North's Regulating Act in 1773. If then we bear this date in mind, we acquire at the same time four other dates which of necessity are of primary importance in the history of the Company. These are 1793, 1813, 1833 and 1853.

We shall find these five dates quite as important as we might expect, and they form a very convenient framework for the history of the Company. The first is one of the most important of all. If 1748 marks the beginning of the movement which led to the creation of British India, 1773 may be said to mark the creation itself of British India. In that year began the line of Governors-General, though for a long time they had not the title of Governor-General of India but only of Bengal; then too was founded the Supreme Court of Calcutta. The enormous danger which attended the new state of our Indian affairs was at the same time met, and the root of corruption cut through, by the abolition of the power in the Company's affairs of the share-holders or so-called Proprietors.

The next renewal in 1793 is less important, though the debates which then took place are interesting now for the picture they present of the phase of Anglo-Indian life when it was *brahminised*, when the attempt was made to keep India as a kind of inviolate paradise, into which no European and especially no missionary should be suffered to penetrate. But the date 1793 is itself as important as any other, being the date not merely of a renewal of the Charter, but also of the famous Permanent Settlement of Bengal, one of the most memorable acts of legislation in the history of the world.

It was at the next renewal in 1813 that the aged

Warren Hastings, then in his eightieth year, came from his retirement to give evidence before the House of Commons. This date marks the moment when the monopoly begins to crumble away, when the brahminical period comes to an end, and England prepares to pour the civilisation, Christianity, and science of the West into India.

In 1833 the monopoly disappears, and the Company may perhaps be said practically to have ceased to exist. Henceforward it is little more than a convenient organisation, convenient because of the tradition it represents and the experience which it guards, by means of which India is governed from England. At this time too the systematic legislative labours of our Indian Government begin.

Finally 1853 is the date of the introduction of the system of appointment by competition. That old question which had convulsed England in 1783 and which statesmen had been afraid to touch since, the question who should have the patronage of India or how it should be dispensed without shaking the constitution of England, was in this way solved.

But here we are reminded that history cannot for a very long time proceed in this regular manner, so convenient to our memories. The convulsion of 1857 put a final end to this periodicity, and 1873, the centenary of the Regulating Act, is no great Indian date.

It appears from this outline that 1813 is the year when the monopoly was first seriously curtailed and 1833 the year when it was destroyed. Now Macculloch when he speaks of the utter insignificance of our old trade with India has before him the statistics up to the year 1811, and the statistics which show so vast an increase in the

modern trade refer to the years after 1813, and especially
to those after 1833. In other words, so long as India was
in the hands of those whose object was trade, the trade
remained insignificant; the trade became great and at last
enormous, when India began to be governed for itself and
trade-considerations to be disregarded. This might seem
a paradox, did we not remember that in dismissing trade-
considerations we also destroyed a monopoly. But there
is nothing wonderful in the fact that an exclusive
Company, even when its first object is trade, carries on
trade languidly, nothing wonderful in a vast trade springing up as soon as the shackles of monopoly were removed.

On the other hand we do not find that the increase of
trade corresponds at all to the augmentation of our territorial possessions in India.

There have been four great rulers in India to whom
the German title of Mehrer des Reichs or Increaser of the
Empire might be given. These are Lord Clive, the
founder, Lord Wellesley, Lord Hastings and Lord Dalhousie.
Roughly it may be said that the first established us along
the Eastern Coast from Calcutta to Madras; the second
and third overthrew the Mahratta power and established
us as lords of the middle of the country and of the Western
side of the peninsula, and the fourth, besides consolidating
these conquests, gave us the northwest and carried our
frontier to the Indus. There were considerable intervals
between these conquests, and accordingly they fall into
separate groups. Thus there was a period of conquest
between 1748 and 1765, which we may label with the
name of Clive, a second period beginning in 1798, which
may be said to have lasted, though with a long pause, till
about 1820; this period may bear the names of Wellesley
and Lord Hastings; and a third period of war between

1839 and 1850, but of this the first part was unfortunate, and only the second part led to conquests, of which it fell to Lord Dalhousie to reap the harvest.

Now there was no correspondence whatever in time between these territorial advances and the advance of trade. Thus we remarked how insignificant the trade of India still was in 1811, and yet this was shortly after the vast annexations of Lord Wellesley. On the other hand trade took a great leap about 1830, and this is one of the peaceful intervals of the history. About the time of the mutiny annexation almost ceased, and yet the quarter of a century in which no conquests have been made has been a period of the most rapid growth in trade.

And thus the assertion which is often made and which seems to be suggested by a rapid survey of the history, the assertion namely that the Empire is the mere result of a reckless pursuit of trade, proves to be as untrue as the other assertion sometimes made, that it is the result of a reckless spirit of military aggression.

Our first step to empire was very plainly taken with a view simply of defending our factories. The Madras Presidency grew out of an effort, which in the first instance was quite necessary, to protect Fort St George and Fort St David from the French. The Bengal Presidency grew in a similar way out of the evident necessity of protecting Fort William and punishing the Mussulman Nawab of Bengal, Surajah Dowlah, for his atrocity of the Black Hole.

So far then the causation is clear. In the period which immediately followed, the revolutionary and corrupt period of British India, it is undeniable that we were hurried on by mere rapacity. The violent proceedings of Warren Hastings at Benares, in Oude, and Rohilcund were of the nature of money-speculations. If the later history of British India had been of the same kind, our Empire might fairly be said to be similar to the Empire of the Spanish in Hispaniola and Peru, and to have sprung entirely out of the reckless pursuit of gain.

But a change took place with the advent of Lord Cornwallis in 1785. Partly by the example of his high character, partly by a judicious reform, which consisted in making the salaries of the servants of the Company considerable enough to remove the excuse for corruption, he purged the service of its immorality. From that time it has been morally respectable. Now among the consequences of this change we might expect, if gain were the principal inducement to conquest, to see the aggressions of the Company cease. For not only had its agents from this time a character to lose, but it was also impossible for it to engage in purely wicked enterprises of conquest, since under the double government introduced by Pitt in 1784 it would have had to make the English Ministry its accomplice. Now the English Ministry may be supposed capable of crimes of ambition, but hardly of corrupt connivance at the sordid crimes of a trading-company.

The truth is that from the time of Pitt's India Bill the supreme management of Indian affairs passed out of the hands of the Company. Thenceforward therefore an enterprise begun for purposes of trade fell under the management of men who had no concern with trade. Thenceforward two English statesmen divided between themselves the decision of the leading Indian questions, the President of the Board of Control and the Governor-General, and as long as the Company lasted, the leading position belonged rather to the Governor-General than to the President of the Board. Now it was under this system that the

conquest of India for the most part was made, and it is
certain that in this period the spirit of trade did not
preside over our Indian affairs.

With the appearance of Lord Wellesley as Governor-
General in 1798 a new era begins in Indian policy. He
first laid down the theory of intervention and annexation.
His theory was afterwards adopted by Lord Hastings, who,
by the way, before he became Governor-General had opposed
it. Later again it was adopted with a kind of fanaticism
by the last of the Governors-General who ruled in the
time of the Company, Lord Dalhousie.

Now this is the theory which led to the conquest of
India. I have not left myself space in this lecture to
examine it. I can only say that it does not aim at
increase of trade, and that accordingly, instead of being
favoured, it was usually opposed by the Company. The
Company resisted Lord Wellesley and censured Lord
Hastings; if they were strangely compliant in dealing
with Lord Dalhousie, it is to be remarked that in his time
the directors had practically ceased to represent a trading
Company. The theory was often applied in a most high-
handed manner. Lord Dalhousie in particular stands out
in history as a ruler of the type of Frederick the Great,
and did deeds which are almost as difficult to justify as the
seizure of Silesia or the Partition of Poland. But these
acts, if crimes, are crimes of the same order as those of
Frederick, crimes of ambition and of an ambition not by
any means purely selfish. Neither he nor any of the
great Governors-General since Warren Hastings can be
suspected for a moment of sordid rapacity, and thus we
see that our Indian Empire, though it began in trade and
has a great trade for one of its results, yet was not really
planned by tradesmen or for purposes of trade.

LECTURE VII.

INTERNAL AND EXTERNAL DANGERS.

FOR estimating the stability of an Empire there are certain plain tests which the political student ought to have at his fingers' ends. Of these some are applied to its internal organisation, and some to its external conditions, just as an insurance company in estimating the value of a life will take the opinion of the medical officer, who will feel the candidate's pulse and listen to his heart, but they will also inquire how and where the candidate lives, and whether his pursuits or habits expose him to any peculiar risks from without. Now I have partly applied the internal test. The internal test of the vitality of a state consists in ascertaining whether or no the Government rests upon a solid basis. For in every state besides the two things which are obvious to all, viz., the Government and the governed, there is a third thing, which is overlooked by most of us and yet is usually not difficult to distinguish, I mean the power outside the Government which holds the Government up. This power may be slight or it may be substantial, and according to its solidity, or rather according to the ratio of its strength to that of the powers which tend to overthrow the Government, is that Government's chance of duration. Now I made some inquiry into the strength of the supports upon which the Government in India rests, but rather with a view of explaining how it stands now than whether it is likely to last a long time. Let us reconsider then with this other object the conclusions at which we arrived.

We found that the Government did not rest, as in England, upon the consent of the people or of some native constituency, which has created the Government by a constitutional process. The Government is in every respect, race, religion, habits, foreign to the people. There is only one body of persons of which we can positively affirm that without its support the Government could not stand; this is the army. Of this army one part is English, and might be trusted to stand by the Government in all circumstances, but it is less than a third part of the whole. The other two-thirds are bound to us by nothing but their pay and the feeling of honour which impels a good soldier to be true to his flag. This is our visible support. Is there beyond it any moral support which, though invisible, may be reckoned upon as substantial? Here is a question which affords room for much difference of opinion. We are naturally inclined to presume that the benefits we have done the country by terminating the chronic anarchy which a century ago was tearing it in pieces, and by introducing so many evident improvements, must have convinced all classes that our Government ought to be supported. But such a presumption is very rash. The notion of a public good, of a common weal, to which all private interests ought to be subordinate, is one which we have no right to assume to be current in such a population as that of India. It seems indeed to presuppose precisely what we have found to be wanting, that is, a moral unity or nationality in India. This being absent, we ought to presume that, instead of considering what benefits our rule may confer upon the country in general, each class or interest inquires how it separately is affected by our ascendancy, the Mussulman how his religion, the Brahmin how his ancient social supremacy, the native prince how his dignity, is affected by it. The great benefit which we have conferred upon the country at large in putting down general plunder and the omnipotence of a mercenary soldiery, is enjoyed perhaps mainly by a class which, though the most numerous, yet has little influence and a short memory, that class so characteristic of India, the small cultivators whose thoughts are absolutely wrapt up in the difficult problem of existing, whose utmost ambition extends only to keeping body and soul together. Those who used to be plundered, tortured, massacred in the chronic wars, ought no doubt to bless us; but the plunderers, the murderers are not likely to do so; and these, it may be, form the more influential class. It is certain in fact that all those who under the old rule of the Moguls used to be influential in India, those who used to monopolise official posts, those who belong to the race which used to rule and represent the religion which used to dominate, all those therefore whose opinion of us might be expected to be politically important, have suffered by our ascendancy; and that all our philanthropic attempts to raise the native races have had the effect of depressing *them*, and that to such an extent that vast numbers of them have been reduced to the greatest distress. The subject has been discussed in Dr Hunter's book on the Mussulmans of India. In these circumstances it would be very

18—2

rash to assume that any gratitude, which may have been aroused here and there by our administration, can be more than sufficient to counterbalance the discontent which we have excited among those whom we have ousted from authority and influence.

It remains then that our power rests on an army, and on an army of which two-thirds are in relation to us mere mercenaries. This may seem a slight support, especially for so vast an authority, but we are to consider on the other hand what is the force of opposition which has to be overcome. And we find a population which by habit and long tradition is absolutely passive, which has been dragonnaded by foreign military Governments, until the very conception of resistance has been lost. We find also a population which has no sort of unity, in which nationalities lie in layers, one under another, and languages wholly unlike each other are brought together by composite dialects caused by fusion. In other words it is a population which for the present is wholly incapable of any common action. As I said, if it had a spark of that corporate life which distinguishes a nation, it could not be held in such a grasp as we lay upon it. But there is no immediate prospect of such a corporate life springing up in it. In the meanwhile our Government seems in ordinary times sufficiently supported. It is considerably stronger in many respects than it was at the time of the mutiny. The proportion of English to native troops in the army is larger, and many precautions suggested by the mutiny itself have been taken. A mutiny might happen again, but so long as it is a mere mutiny there seems no reason why it should be fatal to our power. The native troops want native leadership, and so long as they find no effective support in the people, so long as their own

objects continue to be, as they were in the last mutiny,
wholly unpatriotic and selfish, so long as they can be
disbanded and replaced by another native army, the
position looked at purely from within seems tolerably
secure. But this statement at the same time brings to
light certain dangers. In the first place, what is said of
the passive habits of the native population applies only
to the Hindus. The Mussulmans have in great part
different habits and different traditions. They do not
look back upon centuries of submission, but upon a period
not so long past when they were a ruling race. Secondly
we are to remember that, much as unity may be wanting,
one kind of unity, that of religion, is not wanting. There
is the powerful and active unity of Islam ; there is the
less active but still real unity of Brahminism. In Dr
Hunter's book on the Indian Mussulmans there is a
chapter entitled 'the chronic conspiracy within our
territory', in which is described the religious agitation
which, under the influence of Wahabite preachers, constantly rouses against our Government (according to
Dr Hunter, but others deny this) just that part of the
population which has the proudest memories, and therefore the keenest sense of indignation against the race
that has superseded them. Brahminism, though a
tenacious, is a much less inspiring religion. Still we all
remember the greased cartridges. The mutiny of 1857,
though mainly military, yet had a religious beginning.
It shows us what we might expect if the vast Hindu
population came to believe that their religion was attacked.
And we are to bear in mind that the Hindu religion is
not, like the Mohammedan, outside the region which
science claims as its own. We have always declared that
we held sacred the principle of religious toleration, and on

that understanding we are obeyed; but what if the Hindu should come to regard the teaching of European science as being of itself an attack on his religion?

Great religious movements then seem less improbable than a nationality-movement. On the other hand the religious forces, if they are livelier, neutralise each other more directly. Islam and Hinduism confront each other, the one stronger in faith, the other in numbers, and create a sort of equilibrium. Is it conceivable that we may some day find our Christianity a reconciling element between ourselves and these contending religions? We are to remember that, as Islam is the crudest expression of Semitic religion, Brahminism on the other hand is an expression of Aryan thought. Now among the religions of the world Christianity stands out as a product of the fusion of Semitic with Aryan ideas. It may be said that India and Europe in respect of religion have both the same elements, but that in India the elements have not blended, while in Europe they have united in Christianity. Judaism and classical Paganism were in Europe at the beginning of our era what Mohammedanism and Brahminism are now in India; but in India the elements have remained separate, and have only made occasional efforts to unite, as in the Sikh religion and in the religion of Akber. In Europe a great fusion took place by means of the Christian Church, which fusion has throughout modern history been growing more and more complete.

Such then is the appearance which our Empire wears, when it is looked at by itself and with reference only to the internal forces which play upon it in India. But in order to form any estimate of its chance of stability it is equally important to consider what influences affect it from without.

Few countries known to history have been so isolated as India. Between Nearchus, the Admiral of Alexander, and Vasco da Gama no European commander navigated the Indian Ocean, but the Arabs appear to have made naval descents on Sind as early as the time of the Caliph Omar. With this exception the only traceable foreign relation of India, except towards the North, has been with Java, and here the influence went forth from India, for we find in the Kawi language of Java the strongest traces both linguistic and literary of Hindu influence. What the sea is to the peninsula, that to the plain of the Ganges is the enormous barrier of the Himalaya. It has the effect of making India practically rather an island than a peninsula. On this side too Indian influence has gone forth into Central Asia, for it is to the north and the east that Buddhism went forth to make its extensive conquests. But on this side too there have been no political relations, no wars or invasions of which we have any authentic knowledge, except at a single point.

We can easily imagine therefore that the isolation of India was for thousands of years complete, and indeed the natives told Alexander the Great, when he appeared among them, that they had never been invaded before.

But this isolation came to an end at last, because after all India is not an island. It has one vulnerable point. There is one point at which the mountain barrier can be penetrated. It can be invaded from Persia or from Central Asia through Afghanistan. Accordingly the whole history of the foreign relations of India up to the time of Vasco da Gama centres in Afghanistan. We may reckon perhaps eight great invasions by this route.

The first is the most memorable of all, but no history of it remains. The Aryan race must have entered by this route, or perhaps we may say that the Aryan race must have come into existence here. The Afghans themselves are Aryan by language, and the correspondence in certain matters between the Zendavesta of Persia and the Vedas of India leads us to place the original Aryan home of the Sanscrit-speaking race somewhere on the frontier of India and Persia.

The next invasion was that of Alexander the Great, famous enough in history, for it first threw open the door of India to the Western world. But it had no permanent consequences, since the Graeco-Bactrian kingdom, which for a time maintained a footing in India, came to an end in the second century before Christ.

The third wants a history almost as much as the first. It is the so-called Scythian invasion, or series of invasions, of the first centuries after Christ. All-important as it is to students of Sanscrit literature, it need not detain us here.

Then comes the invasion of Mahmoud of Ghazni (A. D. 1001). This is one of the most important, because it is at once the end both of the isolation and of the independence of India and also what may be called the practical discovery of India for the rest of the world. Mahmoud is to India, as it were, Columbus and Cortez in one. Since his time foreign domination has never been interrupted, and the way to India through the Khyber Pass has been a beaten road trodden by many adventurers. In several respects too Mahmoud is a precursor of the Great Moguls. He is by birth a Turk, he has a petty throne in Afghanistan, and he is irresistibly impelled to the conquest of India by his Mussulman faith and by the near neighbourhood of the shrines of idolatry. In all these points he resembles Baber.

The fifth great invasion was that of Tamerlane in 1398.

It was purely destructive, but has an importance of its own, which however we shall understand better when we are in a condition to compare it with the seventh and eighth invasions.

Then comes the invasion of Baber in 1524 and the establishment of the Mogul Empire. What Mahmoud had begun he and his successors carried out with more continuousness. Their empire was similar to the Mussulman Empires which had preceded it, but firmer and more consolidated.

The seventh and eighth are desolating incursions like that of Tamerlane. The one was undertaken by Nadir Shah, the tyrant who seized the throne of Persia on the fall of the Sofi dynasty; it took place in 1739, when the Mogul Empire was already in full decline. The other took place in 1760; the author of it was Ahmed Shah Abdali, head of an Empire of Duranis, whose headquarters were in Afghanistan.

Such are the principal invasions which India has suffered. A review of them shows that, though India has but this one point at which she is vulnerable by land, yet at this point she is very vulnerable indeed. For a long time indeed it seems that the way to invade her was not discovered, but at least from the time of Mahmoud of Ghuzni she has become peculiarly liable to invasion, and her history has been completely determined by it. For she has shown extremely little power of resistance. The history of India up to and outside of the English conquest may be thus briefly summed up. It consists in the first place of two great Mussulman conquests and of a great Hindu reaction against the Mussulman power, which took shape in the Mahratta confederacy; the two conquests were both made from Afghanistan; in the

second place, of the destruction of the two great Mohammedan Powers in succession and the decisive humiliation of the Mahratta Power; this was acomplished by
three other invasions from Afghanistan. That you may
understand how this is so I will ask you first to examine
the fall of the Mogul Empire, that is, the second of the
great Mussulman Powers. The ultimate cause of its fall
was perhaps the unwise attempt of Aurungzebe to extend
it over the Deccan; accordingly its decline began visibly at
Aurungzebe's death. But the decisive blow which was
mortal to it, which converted it from a sick man to a
dying man, was the devastating invasion of Nadir Shah,
who came down through Afghanistan in 1739. He sacked
Delhi, and so completely plundered the treasury that the
Mogul Government was never able to raise its head again.
In precisely the same way the Mahratta Power, just at the
moment when it seemed on the point of uniting all India,
was broken by the descent of Ahmed Shah Abdali from
Afghanistan and by the fatal battle of Paniput (in which
200,000 men are said to have fallen) in the year 1761,
that is, when the English were already making themselves
masters of Bengal. And it appears to me that, as these
two invasions were fatal to the Moguls and the Mahrattas,
so the earlier invasion of Tamerlane at the end of the
fourteenth century crushed the earlier Mussulman Power,
which just before under Mohammed Toghlak had reached
its greatest extension.

But now, as Mahmoud of Ghazni threw open India
to invasion from the north, Vasco da Gama opened it
to maritime invasion from Europe. This was, though it
did not seem so at the time, the greater achievement
of the two. For Mahmoud only established a connexion
between India and the Mussulman world of Western and

Central Asia, but Vasco da Gama for the first time since Alexander the Great connected it with Europe, and this time it was Europe christianised and civilised. This could not be remarked at the time because, while Mahmoud came as a mighty conqueror, Vasco da Gama was but a humble navigator. His discovery for a very long time led to no political results. There followed a century which I called the Spanish-Portuguese age of colonial history. Almost throughout the sixteenth century the whole newly-discovered oceanic world was in the hands of two nations, and the Asiatic half of it almost exclusively in the hands of the Portuguese. But in the last years of that century the Dutch succeeded in taking their place. As to the English, when the seventeenth century opened, they were still but timid interlopers encroaching a little in India upon the monopoly of the Dutch.

I explained above how at the end of the seventeenth century England and France had begun to take in the colonial world the position which had belonged in the sixteenth century to Spain and Portugal, and how the whole eighteenth century is filled with the struggle of these two nations for supremacy in it. In 1748 this struggle breaks out violently in India, and it has already become clear to Dupleix that the struggle is political, not merely commercial, and that the prize is nothing less than an Indian Empire. Here then is a momentous turning point in the history of Indian foreign relations. Hitherto she had been connected with the outer world only through Afghanistan; henceforth she is to be connected with it also by the sea.

This new connexion, once established, for a time eclipses the old, especially in the eyes of the English conquerors themselves. As I have said before, the enemy

whom the English for a long time continued to dread
most in India was their earliest enemy, France. Invasions
from Afghanistan had not indeed ceased. Nadir Shah's
invasion took place only nine years before that year 1748,
from which we date the rise of the British Empire. The
invasion of Ahmed Shah Abdali took place thirteen
years later. But these occurrences did not much attract
the attention of the English. For we are to bear in mind
that, though they had begun to conquer, they did not yet
dream how far their conquests would carry them.
Because they were now firmly planted as territorial rulers
in the neighbourhood of Fort St George and Fort William,
they did not as a matter of course think themselves
responsible for all India, or study comprehensively the
relations of the country considered as a whole to the outer
world. The affairs of Afghanistan or the Punjab seemed
almost as much beyond their horizon as those of the
Turkish Empire.

But towards the end of the eighteenth century a
change took place in the view of the English. Hitherto
they had looked most anxiously towards Madras and the
Deccan. Their main fear was lest the French might
make some new alliance with one of the native princes of
the South, might help him with arms and officers or with
a fleet, while he descended upon Madras. This was what
actually took place in that war with France which grew
out of the American Revolution, and never perhaps were
we so hard pressed in India. Hyder Ali descended upon
the Carnatic to the gates of Madras, and from the sea the
greatest of all French sailors, the Bailli de Suffren,
co-operated with him. But fifteen years later the whole
face of our foreign relations in India was changed by
Bonaparte's Egyptian expedition. French policy here

took a new direction. It did not indeed break off from its old connexions in the Deccan. Tippoo was expected to be as useful to the Directory as his father Hyder had been to Louis XVI. But at the same time Bonaparte's occupation of Egypt and his campaign in Syria, movements which were avowedly aimed at England, seemed to show that he had conceived the design of attacking our power in India from the north. Then for the first time we remembered Nadir Shah and Ahmed Shah Abdali; then for the first time we began to look anxiously, as we have so often looked since, towards the Khyber Pass, towards Zemaun Shah, who at the end of the eighteenth century sat in the seat of Ahmed Shah at Cabul, and towards the Court of Persia.

This then is the second great phase of the foreign policy of our Indian Empire. It is marked by the celebrated mission of Malcolm (afterward Sir John) to the Persian Court in 1800. Never before had we had occasion to study what I may call the balance of Asia, or to inquire *quid Tiridaten terreat*, what thoughts agitate the mind of the Persian king. But observe it is not the secret influence of Russia that is feared, but that of France. I said before that perhaps the Duke of Wellington considered himself to be fighting the French at Assaye, not less than that at Waterloo. In like manner you will find that Malcolm in his Persian negotiations has Napoleon and the power of France, not at all that of Russia, in his mind.

But in this second phase, though we have begun to look towards Afghanistan, we have not ceased to be afraid, as in the first phase, of French influence in the South. The life of this same Sir John Malcolm illustrates this. He was selected for the Persian mission on account of the

distinction he had won just before in the war against
Tippoo Sultan of Mysore. Now this is a war against
the French almost as truly as that earlier war in which
Clive first distinguished himself. Tippoo himself was
understood to be hand-and-glove with the Directory:
Bonaparte is his ally, as Suffren had been his father's.
The French called him *Citoyen Tipou*. And what is the
Nizam doing ? It was with the Government of the
Nizam at Hyderabad that the French had had their
earliest connexion half a century before. They knew
even better than the English how to conquer India,
and that the secret lay in training sepoys and putting
them under European leadership. We find that now in
1798 there is in the Hyderabad country a force of 14,000
men, who are disciplined and commanded by French
officers. A certain Raymond is in command of them, and
we read in Kaye's Life of Malcolm that 'assignments
of territory had been made by the Nizam for the pay of
these troops. Foundries were established under competent
European superintendence. Guns were cast. Muskets
were manufactured. Admirably equipped and disciplined,
Raymond's levies went out to battle with the colours
of Revolutionary France floating above them and the cap
of liberty engraved on their buttons.' Now so long as
our nominal ally the Nizam supported such a force and
Tippoo was avowedly in concert with France, our position
in the Deccan was not so materially changed from what
it had been when our Indian quarrel with France first
began. It was still possible that the tables might be
turned on the English in 1798 by Raymond's force, as they
had been turned on the French before by Clive at Arcot.
At this juncture the young Malcolm was sent to Hyderabad,
and he succeeded in disbanding this French force, or, as
he himself calls it, 'expelling this nest of democrats.'

Thus we have two phases of the foreign policy of British India. At first it has but one enemy outside India, namely France, and it expects the attack of this enemy only in one quarter, namely, the Deccan. In the second phase it has still the same enemy, who works in the same way, but his power has become far wider. He has formed, or is supposed to have formed, relations with other Asiatic Powers outside India. These Powers are the Afghans and the Persians, and after the Treaty of Tilsit in 1807 there is added to these another Power, European indeed but beginning already to overhang Asia, a Power which is now named for the first time in the history of British India, Russia.

This second phase is brought to an end by the fall of Napoleon. With him fell completely, though it would be rash to say finally, the influence of France upon India. Her exclusion was secured by the capture of the Mauritius in 1810 and by the retention of the island at the general peace.

There followed a pause in our foreign affairs. Our Empire had no important foreign relations for about twenty years. And then began a new phase. Another European Power takes the place of France as our rival in Asia. This Power is Russia.

In the whole history of Greater Britain from its commencement at the end of Elizabeth's reign we may perhaps distinguish three great periods. There is first the seventeenth century, in which it rises gradually from a humble position to preeminence among colonial Empires. There is next that duel with France both in America and Asia, of which I have said so much. This occupies the eighteenth century. But this too passed, and we have entered upon a third phase, which according to the fashion of historical development, began to form itself long before the second phase was over. In this third phase the English world-empire has two gigantic neighbours in the West and in the East. In the West she has the United States and in the East Russia for a neighbour.

These are the two States which I have cited as examples of the modern tendency towards enormous political aggregations, such as would have been impossible but for the modern inventions which diminish the difficulties caused by time and space. Both are continuous land-powers. Between them, equally vast but not continuous, with the ocean flowing through it in every direction, lies, like a world-Venice, with the sea for streets, Greater Britain.

This third phase may in a sense be said to have begun with the American Revolution, but it is more just to consider it as dating only from about the thirties of the present century. For the great destiny that was reserved for the United States did not become manifest till long after its independence was established. That great emigration from Europe which is the cause of its rapid progress, did not begin till after the peace of 1815, and in the twenties again its importance in the world was vastly increased by the South American Revolution and the establishment of republican government in Spanish America, an event which placed the United States in a lofty position of primacy on the American Continent. Now it was about the same time that the great extension of Russia in the East took place. The moment when we began to feel keenly the rivalry of Russia in the East is very plainly marked on the history of British India. It was in 1830 that Russia in her progress touched the Jaxartes, and soon after she reduced Persia to a condition

which we might take to be one of practical dependence.
When therefore in 1834 and again in 1837 Mohammed
Shah of Persia led an army into Afghanistan, we believed
we saw the hand of Russia, as thirty years before we had
seen the hand of Napoleon when any movement took
place in the same region.   At this moment begins a new
and stormy period in our Indian history, which may be
said to extend to the mutiny, that is, over twenty years.
This period witnessed a series of wars, in the course of
which we conquered the whole north-west, annexed the
Punjab, Sind and Oude, and at last aroused a disquiet in
the minds of our Hindu subjects which issued in the
mutiny.   These disturbances seem traceable in the main
to the alarm caused by Russia.   For it was this alarm
which led to the disastrous expedition into Afghanistan,
and it was in the effort to restore our damaged reputation
that the conquest of Sind was made, and it seems likely
also that if these disturbances in the north-west had not
thus been commenced, the Sikh wars might never have
happened.

Lord Auckland, we are now very sure, did not take
the right way in 1838 to meet the danger he foresaw.
Perhaps he exaggerated the danger; perhaps even now,
after forty years more have passed and the advance of
Russia in Central Asia during that time has been beyond
all anticipation, we still exaggerate the danger.   But the
historical sketch of the foreign relations of India which
I have given in this lecture shows that there exists a
prima facie case for alarm, which cannot but produce a
prodigious effect.   That case rests upon the simple fact
that our three predecessors in the Empire of India, the
Mahrattas in 1761, the Moguls in 1738, the older
Mussulman Empire in 1398, all alike received a mortal

blow from a Power which suddenly invaded India through Afghanistan, and that, on two other occasions quite distinct from these, invaders from Afghanistan, viz. Mahmoud of Ghazni and Baber, have founded Empires in India.

I call this a *prima facie* case for alarm. It is nothing more. Such reasonings *per enumerationem simplicem* can establish only that there is ground for instituting an examination, though unfortunately when history is brought to bear at all upon politics, which happens but rarely, it is commonly done in this random way. We cannot argue from the Moguls and Nadir Shah to the English and Russia. It would be easy perhaps to show that the Mogul Empire never had a solidity at all approaching that of the English Empire, and we might point out also that when Nadir Shah came to Delhi the Empire had already been in manifest decay for thirty years. With respect to Russia on the other hand it would be easy to show that it is a Power wholly different in kind from those Powers, generally more or less Tartar, which have invaded India, a Power certainly far greater and more solid than most of them, but still so different that we cannot assume it to be equally capable of invasion and conquest at a prodigious distance. In short, history proves nothing more than that the way to India lies through Afghanistan. Whether a Power such as Russia can successfully attack by this route a Power such as British India, is a question upon which historical precedents throw no light whatever. It can be answered only by analysing and estimating the military resources, both moral and material, of the two Powers.

But it may be asked, How is it possible to question Russia's power or her will to make distant conquests? Has she not conquered in the North the whole breadth of

Asia and in the centre has she not penetrated to Samarcand and Khokand? What Power ever equalled her in successful aggression? But we must pronounce no man happy, Solon said, till we have seen his end. Can such a career continue indefinitely, when Russia shall have been thoroughly Europeanised at home? As soon as her political awakening is complete, must not a transformation of her foreign policy take place?

On the other hand it may be said, Who can question the ability of England to contend with Russia? But as I have argued, England is very distinct from British India. Russia may be rich enough to conquer vast regions at a distance of thousands of miles, but England is not. British India must in the main defend herself; that is, she can have English troops, but she must pay for them.

We must ask then, What is the inherent strength of British India? And thus its stability depends upon its being strong enough to withstand those internal dangers I spoke of complicated with the external danger from Afghanistan. We were able to put down the mutiny, and perhaps we could defeat a Russian army of invasion. But what if a mutiny and a Russian invasion came together? What if our native army, in some fit of disaffection or in some vague hope of profiting by a change, should prefer the Russian service to the English? This is the danger which since about 1830 has been foreseen. The Government can hold its own within and also without. But it has little strength to spare, and must guard itself anxiously against any coalition between its domestic and its foreign enemies.

Other combinations may be imagined which would be extremely dangerous. Thus it is sometimes argued that sooner or later we must lose India because sooner or later some war in Europe will force us to withdraw our English troops. It is true that without those troops we cannot keep India, and yet some great sudden attack upon ourselves, such as an invasion of England, might compel us to send for them. It is however also true that such a danger is not at present to be foreseen, for what enemy could invade us but France? Now sixty-eight years have passed since we last fought the French; our old hostility to France has become a matter of ancient history; and the aggressive power of France has much declined.

But the subject is too large for the space I am able to give to it, and I must ask you to be content with this imperfect outline.

LECTURE VIII.

WE have now dwelt for a long time on that extraordinary expansion which has had the effect that, considered as a state, England has left Europe altogether behind it and become a world-state, while, considered purely as a nation, that is, as speaking a certain language, she has furnished out two world-states, which vie with each other in vigour, influence and rapidity of growth. We have inquired into the causes, traced the process, and considered some of the results of this expansion. It remains then in this closing lecture to gather up the impressions we have received into a general conclusion.

There are two schools of opinion among us with respect to our Empire, of which schools the one may be called the bombastic and the other the pessimistic. The one is lost in wonder and ecstasy at its immense dimensions, and at the energy and heroism which presumably have gone to the making of it; this school therefore advocates the maintenance of it as a point of honour or sentiment. The other is in the opposite extreme, regards it as founded in aggression and rapacity, as useless and burdensome, a kind of excrescence upon England, as depriving us of the advantages of our insularity and exposing us to wars and quarrels in every part of the globe; this school therefore advocates a policy which may lead at the earliest possible opportunity to the abandonment of it. Let us consider then how our studies, now that they are concluded, have led us to regard these two opposite opinions.

We have been led to take a much more sober view of the Empire than would satisfy the bombastic school. At the outset we are not much impressed with its vast extent, because we know no reason in the nature of things why a state should be any the better for being large, and because throughout the greater part of history very large states have usually been states of a low type. Nor again can we imagine why it should be our duty to maintain our Empire for an indefinite time simply out of respect for the heroism of those who won it for us, or because the abandonment of it might seem to betray a want of spirit. All political unions exist for the good of their members, and should be just as large, and no larger, as they can be without ceasing to be beneficial. It would seem to us insane that if the connexion with the colonies or with India hampered both parties, if it did harm rather than good, England should resolve to maintain it to her own detriment and to that of her dependencies. We find too a confusion of ideas hidden under much of the bombastic language of this school, for they seem to conceive of the dependencies of England as of so much property belonging to her, as if the Queen were like some Sesostris or Solomon of the ancient world, to whom 'Tarshish and the isles brought presents, Arabia and Sheba offered gifts,' whereas the connexion is really not of this kind at all, and England is not, directly at least, any the richer for it. And further we have ventured to doubt that the vastness of this Empire necessarily proves some invincible heroism or supernatural genius for government in our nation. Undoubtedly some facts may be adduced

to show natural aptitude for colonisation and a faculty of
leadership in our race. A good number of Englishmen
may be cited who have exerted an almost magical
ascendancy over the minds of the native races of India,
and in Canada again, where the English settlers have
competed directly with the French, they have shown a
marked superiority in enterprise and energy. But though
there is much to admire in the history of Greater Britain,
yet the preeminence of England in the New World has
certainly not been won by sheer natural superiority. In
the heroic age of maritime discovery we did not greatly
shine. We did not show the genius of the Portuguese, and
we did not produce a Columbus or a Magelhaen. When
I examined the causes which enabled us after two centuries
to surpass other nations in colonisation, I found that we
had a broader basis and a securer position at home than
Portugal and Holland, and that we were less involved in
great European enterprises than France and Spain. In like
manner when I inquired how we could conquer, and that
with little trouble, the vast country of India, I found that
after all we did it by means mainly of Indian troops, to
whom we imparted a skill which was not so much English
as European, that the French showed us the way, and that
the condition of the country was such as to render it
peculiarly open to conquest.

Thus I admitted very much of what is urged by the
pessimists against the bombastic school. I endeavoured
to judge the Empire by its own intrinsic merits and to see
it as it is, not concealing the inconveniences which may
attend such a vast expansion or the dangers to which it
may expose us, nor finding any compensation for these in
the notion that there is something intrinsically glorious in
an Empire 'upon which the sun never sets,' or, to use
another equally brilliant expression, an Empire 'whose

morning drum-beat, following the sun and keeping company with the hours, encircles the globe with an unbroken chain of martial airs.' But though there is little that is glorious in most of the great Empires mentioned in history, since they have usually been created by force and have remained at a low level of political life, we observed that Greater Britain is not in the ordinary sense an Empire at all. Looking at the colonial part of it alone, we see a natural growth, a mere normal extension of the English race into other lands, which for the most part were so thinly peopled that our settlers took possession of them without conquest. If there is nothing highly glorious in such an expansion, there is at the same time nothing forced or unnatural about it. It creates not properly an Empire, but only a very large state. So far as the expansion itself is concerned, no one does or can regard it but with pleasure. For a nation to have an outlet for its superfluous population is one of the greatest blessings. Population unfortunately does not adapt itself to space: on the contrary the larger it is the larger is its yearly increment. Now that Great Britain is already full it becomes fuller with increased speed; it gains a million every three years. Probably emigration ought to proceed at a far greater rate than it does, and assuredly the greatest evils would arise if it were checked. But should there be an expansion of the State as well as of the nation? 'No,' say the pessimists, 'or only till the colony is grown-up and ready for independence.' When a metaphor comes to be regarded as an argument, what an irresistible argument it always seems! I have suggested that in the modern world distance has very much lost its effect, and that there are signs of a time when states will be vaster than they have hitherto been. In ancient times emigrants from Greece to Sicily took up their independence

at once, and in those parts there were almost as many
states as cities. In the eighteenth century Burke thought
a federation quite impossible across the Atlantic Ocean.
In such times the metaphor of the grown-up son might
well harden into a convincing demonstration. But since
Burke's time the Atlantic Ocean has shrunk till it seems
scarcely broader than the sea between Greece and Sicily.
Why then do we not drop the metaphor? I have urged
that we are unconsciously influenced by a historic parallel
which when examined turns out to be inapplicable. As
indeed it is true generally that one urgent reason why
politicians should study history is that they may guard
themselves against the false historical analogies which
continually mislead those who do not study history!
These views are founded on the American Revolution, and
yet the American Revolution arose out of circumstances
and out of a condition of the world which has long since
passed away. England was then an agricultural country
by no means thickly peopled; America was full of religious
refugees animated by ideas which in England had lately
passed out of fashion; there was scarcely any flux and
reflux of population between the two countries, and the
ocean divided them with a gulf which seemed as unbridge-
able as that moral gulf which separates an Englishman
from a Frenchman. Even then the separation was not
effected without a great wrench. It is true that both
countries have prospered since, nevertheless they have had
a second war and may have a third, and it is wholly
an illusion to suppose that their prosperity has been caused
or promoted by their separation. At any rate all the
conditions of the world are altered now. The great causes
of division, oceans and religious disabilities, have ceased to
operate. Vast uniting forces have begun to work, trade
and emigration. Meanwhile the natural ties which unite

Englishmen resume their influence as soon as the counter-
acting pressure is removed, I mean the ties of nationality,
language and religion. The mother-country having once
for all ceased to be a step-mother, and to make unjust
claims and impose annoying restrictions, and since she
wants her colonies as an outlet both for population and
trade, and since on the other hand the colonies must feel
that there is risk, not to say also intellectual impoverish-
ment, in independence, since finally intercourse is ever
increasing and no alienating force is at work to coun-
teract it, but the discords created by the old system pass
more and more into oblivion, it seems possible that our
colonial Empire so-called may more and more deserve to
be called Greater Britain, and that the tie may become
stronger and stronger. Then the seas which divide us
might be forgotten, and that ancient preconception, which
leads us always to think of ourselves as belonging to
a single island, might be rooted out of our minds. If
in this way we moved sensibly nearer in our thoughts and
feelings to the colonies, and accustomed ourselves to think
of emigrants as not in any way lost to England by settling
in the colonies, the result might be, first that emigration on
a vast scale might become our remedy for pauperism, and
secondly that some organisation might gradually be arrived
at which might make the whole force of the Empire
available in time of war.

In taking this view I have borne in mind the
example of the United States. It is curious that the
pessimists among ourselves should generally have been
admirers of the United States, and yet there we have the
most striking example of confident and successful expansion. Those colonies which, when they parted from
us, did but fringe the Atlantic sea-board and had but
lately begun to push their settlements into the valley of

the Ohio, how steadily, how boundlessly, and with what steadfast self-reliance have they advanced since! They have covered with their States or Territories, first the mighty Mississippi valley, next the Rocky Mountains, and lastly the Pacific coast. They have made no difficulty of absorbing all this territory; it has not shaken their political system. And yet they have never said, as among us even those who are not pessimists say of the colonies, that if they wish to secede, of course they can do so. On the contrary they have firmly denied this right, and to maintain the unity of their vast state have sacrificed blood and treasure in unexampled profusion. They firmly refused to allow their Union to be broken up, or to listen to the argument that a state is none the better for being very large.

Perhaps we are hardly alive to the vast results which are flowing in politics from modern mechanism. Throughout the greater part of human history the process of state-building has been governed by strict conditions of space. For a long time no high organisation was possible except in very small states. In antiquity the good states were usually cities, and Rome herself when she became an Empire was obliged to adopt a lower organisation. In medieval Europe, states sprang up which were on a larger scale than those of antiquity, but for a long time these too were lower organisms and looked up to Athens and Rome with reverence as to the homes of political greatness. But through the invention of the representative system these states have risen to a higher level. We now see states with vivid political consciousness on territories of two hundred thousand square miles and in populations of thirty millions. A further advance is now being made. The federal system has been added to the representative system, and at the same time steam and

electricity have been introduced. From these improvements has resulted the possibility of highly organised
states on a yet larger scale. Thus Russia in Europe has
already a population of near eighty millions on a territory
of more than two millions of square miles, and the
United States will have by the end of the century a population as large upon a territory of four millions of square
miles. We cannot, it is true, yet speak of Russia as
having a high type of organisation; she has her trials
and her transformation to come; but the Union has shown
herself able to combine free institutions in the fullest
degree with boundless expansion.

Now if it offends us to hear our Empire described in
the language of Oriental bombast, we need not conclude
that the Empire itself is in fault, for it is open to us to
think that it has been wrongly classified. Instead of
comparing it to that which it resembles in no degree,
some Turkish or Persian congeries of nations forced
together by a conquering horde, let us compare it to the
United States, and we shall see at once that, so far from
being of an obsolete type, it is precisely the sort of union
which the conditions of the time most naturally call into
existence.

Lastly let us observe that the question, whether large
states or small states are best, is not one which can be
answered or ought to be discussed absolutely. We often
hear abstract panegyrics upon the happiness of small
states. But observe that a small state among small
states is one thing and a small state among large states
quite another. Nothing is more delightful than to read
of the bright days of Athens and Florence, but those
bright days lasted only so long as the states with which
Athens and Florence had to do were states on a similar
scale of magnitude. Both states sank at once as soon as

large country-states of consolidated strength grew up in their neighbourhood. The lustre of Athens grew pale as soon as Macedonia rose, and Charles V. speedily brought to an end the great days of Florence. Now if it be true that a larger type of state than any hitherto known is springing up in the world, is not this a serious consideration for those states which rise only to the old level of magnitude? Russia already presses some-what heavily on Central Europe; what will she do when with her vast territory and population she equals Germany in intelligence and organisation, when all her railways are made, her people educated, and her government settled on a solid basis?—and let us remember that if we allow her half a century to make so much progress her population will at the end of that time be not eighty but nearly a hundred and sixty millions. At that time which many here present may live to see, Russia and the United States will surpass in power the states now called great as much as the great country-states of the sixteenth century surpassed Florence. Is not this a serious con-sideration, and is it not especially so for a state like England, which has at the present moment the choice in its hands between two courses of action, the one of which may set it in that future age on a level with the greatest of these great states of the future, while the other will reduce it to the level of a purely European Power looking back, as Spain does now, to the great days when she pretended to be a world-state.

But what I have been saying does not apply to India. If England and her colonies taken together make, properly speaking, not an Empire but only a very large state, this is because the population is English throughout and the institutions are of the same kind. In India the population is wholly foreign and the

institutions wholly unlike our own. India is really an
Empire and an Oriental Empire. It is in relation to India
especially that the language of the bombastic school
offends us, and that we are struck by the misconception
which is betrayed in their highflown imagery borrowed
from the ancient world. And here we cannot, on looking
more closely into the phenomenon, reconcile ourselves to it
by discovering that, though it has not the romantic greatness attributed to it, yet it has a solid value and utility
to us which is of another kind altogether.

Gradually and in recent times a great trade between
India and England has sprung up, but even this, as I
pointed out, was hardly contemplated by those who had
the principal share in founding the Indian Empire. And
it is difficult to see what other great advantages we reap
from it, so that we ask ourselves in some perplexity, what
made us take the trouble of acquiring it. Historically the
answer is, that in our great colonial struggle with France
we were led into wars which left us in possession of
territories in the neighbourhood of Calcutta and Madras,
that we then proceeded to organise our government of them,
that we successfully purged away the corruption which had
sprung up in the first period of conquest, and created an
administration that was pure and under the direct control
of the Government at home; but that afterwards there
arose a line of Governors-General who on high grounds of
statesmanship were favourable to annexation. The policy
now adopted was not sordid, but it may have been
ambitious and unscrupulous. If we are to think, as Mr
Torrens[1] imagines, that Pitt and Lord Wellesley in secret
deliberation determined to replace the American colonies
by an Eastern Empire, such an idea, according to the view
taken in these lectures, belongs to an unsound and

[1] *The Marquis Wellesley*, by W. M. Torrens, M.P. Vol. I. p. 128.

chimerical system of politics. But ostensibly the policy
was justified by arguments chiefly of a philanthropic
kind, and they were arguments of such strength that it
was difficult to resist them.   It was not to be denied that
a most deplorable anarchy reigned in India. Here and there
a tyranny arose which had some degree of stability, though it
was almost always a military government of the lowest type.
But over the greater part of India there prevailed a system
which it would be appropriate to call, not government of a
low type, but robbery of a high type.   Occasionally in
Europe, as in some Highland clans or among the Western
buccaneers or those ancient pirates of the Mediterranean
whom Pompey was commissioned to suppress, robber-bands
have had almost the magnitude and organisation of states,
but they never have reached the scale of the robber-states
of India.   The Mahrattas levied their *chout*, a sort of
blackmail, all over India, and at a later time the Pindarrees
surpassed the Mahrattas in cruelty.   Now this anarchy
arose directly out of the decline of the authority of the
Great Mogul.   It was possible of course for the English to
wash their hands of all this, to defend their own territories,
and let the chaos welter as it would outside their frontier.
But to Governors-General on the spot such a course might
easily seem not just but simply cruel.   Aggrandisement
might present itself in the light of a simple duty, when it
seemed that by extending our Empire the reign of robbery
and murder might be brought to an end in a moment and
that of law commence[1].   Accordingly Lord Wellesley laid
it down that there had always been a paramount Power in
India, that such a paramount Power was necessary to the

[1] 'It is a proud phrase to use, but it is a true one, that we have
bestowed blessings upon millions....The ploughman is again in every
quarter turning up a soil which had for many seasons never been stirred
except by the hoofs of predatory cavalry.' Lord Hastings, February, 1819.

country, and that it became the duty of the Company, now that the power of the Mogul had come to an end, to save India by assuming his function.

And thus we founded our Empire, partly it may be out of an empty ambition of conquest and partly out of a philanthropic desire to put an end to enormous evils But, whatever our motives might be, we incurred vast responsibilities, which were compensated by no advantages. We have now acquired a great Indian trade, but even this we purchase at the expense of a perpetual dread of Russia and of all movements in the Mussulman world and of all changes in Egypt. Thus a review of the history of British India leaves on the mind an impression quite different from that which our Colonial Empire produces. The latter has grown up naturally, out of the operation of the plainest causes; the former seems to have sprung from a romantic adventure; it is highly interesting, striking and curious, but difficult to understand or to form an opinion about. We may hope that it will lead to good, but hitherto we have not ourselves reaped directly much good from it.

I have shown you however that, though it may be called an Oriental Empire, it is much less dangerous to us than that description might seem to imply. It is not an Empire attached to England in the same way as the Roman Empire was attached to Rome; it will not drag us down, or infect us at home with Oriental notions or methods of Government. Nor is it an Empire which costs us money or hampers our finances. It is self-supporting, and is held at arm's length in such a way that our destiny is not very closely entangled with its own.

Next I have led you to consider what may be the effect of our Indian Empire upon India itself. We perhaps have not gained much from it; but has India gained? On this question I have desired to speak with great diffidence. I have asserted confidently only thus much, that no greater experiment has ever been tried on the globe, and that the effects of it will be comparable to the effect of the Roman Empire upon the nations of Europe, nay probably they will be much greater. This means no doubt that vast benefits will be done to India, but it does not necessarily mean that great mischiefs may not also be done. Nay, if you ask on which side the balance will incline, and whether, if we succeed in bringing India into the full current of European civilisation, we shall not evidently be rendering her the greatest possible service, I should only answer, 'I hope so; I trust so.' In the academic study of these vast questions we should take care to avoid the optimistic commonplaces of the newspaper. Our Western civilisation is perhaps not absolutely the glorious thing we like to imagine it. Those who watch India most impartially see that a vast transformation goes on there, but sometimes it produces a painful impression upon them; they see much destroyed, bad things and good things together; sometimes they doubt whether they see many good things called into existence. But they see one enormous improvement, under which we may fairly hope that all other improvements are potentially included, they see anarchy and plunder brought to an end and something like the *immensa majestas Romanae pacis* established among two hundred and fifty millions of human beings.

Another thing almost all observers see, and that is that the experiment must go forward, and that we cannot leave it unfinished if we would. For here too the great uniting forces of the age are at work, England and India are drawn every year for good or for evil more closely together. Not indeed that disuniting forces might not easily spring up, not that our rule itself may not possibly be calling out forces which may ultimately tend to disruption, nor yet that the Empire is altogether free from the danger of a sudden catastrophe. But for the present we are driven both by necessity and duty to a closer union. Already we should ourselves suffer greatly from disruption, and the longer the union lasts the more important it will become to us. Meanwhile the same is true in an infinitely greater degree of India itself. The transformation we are making there may cause us some misgivings, but though we may be led conceivably to wish that it had never been begun, nothing could ever convince us that it ought to be broken off in the middle.

Altogether I hope that our long course of meditation upon the expansion of England may have led you to feel that there is something fantastic in all those notions of abandoning the colonies or abandoning India, which are so freely broached among us. Have we really so much power over the march of events as we suppose? Can we cancel the growth of centuries for a whim, or because, when we throw a hasty glance at it, it does not suit our fancies? The lapse of time and the force of life, 'which working strongly binds,' limit our freedom more than we know, and even when we are not conscious of it at all. It is true that we in England have never accustomed our imaginations to the thought of Greater Britain. Our politicians, our historians still think of England not of Greater Britain as their country; they still think only that England *has* colonies, and they allow themselves to talk as if she could easily whistle them off, and become again with perfect comfort to herself the old solitary island of Queen Elizabeth's time, 'in a great pool a swan's nest.' But the fancy is but a chimera produced by inattention, one of those monsters, for such monsters there are, which are created not by imagination but by the want of imagination!

But though this is a conclusion to which I am led, it is not the conclusion which I wish to leave most strongly impressed on your minds. What I desire here is not so much to impart to you a just view of practical politics as a just view of the object and method of historical study. My chief aim in these lectures has been to show in what light the more recent history of England ought to be regarded by the student. It seems to me that most of our historians, when they come to these modern periods, lose the clue, betray embarrassment in the choice of topics, and end by producing a story without a moral. I have argued in the first place that history is concerned, not mainly with the interesting things which may have been done by Englishmen or in England, but with England herself considered as a nation and a state. To make this more plain I have narrated nothing, told no thrilling stories, drawn no heroic portraits, I have kept always before you England as a great whole. In her story there is little that is dramatic, for she can scarcely die, and in this period at least has not suffered or been in danger of suffering much. What great changes has she undergone in this period? Considerable political changes no doubt, but none that have been so memorable as those she underwent in the seventeenth century. Then she made one of the greatest political discoveries, and taught all the world how liberty might be adapted to the conditions of a nation-state. On the other hand the modern political

movement, that of Reform or Liberalism, began not in
England but on the Continent, from whence we borrowed
it. The peculiarly English movement, I have urged, in
this period has been an unparalleled expansion. Grasp
this fact, and you have the clue both to the eighteenth and
the nineteenth centuries. The wars with France from
Louis XIV. to Napoleon fall into an intelligible series.
The American Revolution and the conquest of India
cease to seem mere digressions, and take their proper
places in the main line of English history. The growth
of wealth, commerce and manufacture, the fall of the
old colonial system and the gradual growth of a new one,
are all easily included under the same formula. Lastly
this formula binds together the past of England and
her future, and leaves us, when we close the history
of our country, not with minds fatigued and bewildered
as though from reading a story that has been too much
spun out, but enlightened and more deeply interested
than ever, because partly prepared for what is to come
next.

I am often told by those who, like myself, study
the question how history should be taught, Oh, you
must before all things make it interesting! I agree
with them in a certain sense, but I give a different
sense to the word interesting, a sense which after all
is the original and proper one. By interesting they
mean romantic, poetical, surprising; I do not try to
make history interesting in this sense, because I have
found that it cannot be done without adulterating
history and mixing it with falsehood. But the word
interesting does not properly mean romantic. That is
interesting in the proper sense which affects our interests,
which closely concerns us and is deeply important to

us. I have tried to show you that the history of modern England from the beginning of the eighteenth century is interesting in this sense, because it is pregnant with great results which will affect the lives of ourselves and our children and the future greatness of our country. Make history interesting indeed ! I cannot make history more interesting than it is, except by falsifying it. And therefore when I meet a person who does not find history interesting, it does not occur to me to alter history,—I try to alter *him*.

COSIMO CLASSICS

COSIMO is an innovative publisher of books and publications that inspire, inform and engage readers worldwide. Our titles are drawn from a range of subjects including health, business, philosophy, history, science and sacred texts. We specialize in using print-on-demand technology (POD), making it possible to publish books for both general and specialized audiences and to keep books in print indefinitely. With POD technology new titles can reach their audiences faster and more efficiently than with traditional publishing.

> ➢ **Permanent Availability:** Our books & publications never go out-of-print.

> ➢ **Global Availability:** Our books are always available online at popular retailers and can be ordered from your favorite local bookstore.

COSIMO CLASSICS brings to life unique, rare, out-of-print classics representing subjects as diverse as *Alternative Health, Business and Economics, Eastern Philosophy, Personal Growth, Mythology, Philosophy, Sacred Texts, Science, Spirituality* and much more!

COSIMO-on-DEMAND publishes your books, publications and reports. If you are an Author, part of an Organization, or a Benefactor with a publishing project and would like to bring books back into print, publish new books fast and effectively, would like your publications, books, training guides, and conference reports to be made available to your members and wider audiences around the world, we can assist you with your publishing needs.

Visit our website at www.cosimobooks.com to learn more about Cosimo, browse our catalog, take part in surveys or campaigns, and sign-up for our newsletter.

And if you wish please drop us a line at info@cosimobooks.com. We look forward to hearing from you.

Printed in the United States
86473LV00001B/15/A

9 781596 052659